P9-DFY-661

LOST TREASURE

LOST TREASURE

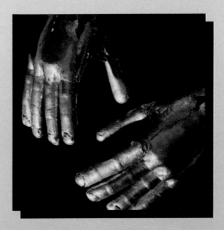

By the Editors of Time-Life Books

TIME-LIFE BOOKS, ALEXANDRIA, VIRGINIA

CONTENTS

ANCIENT TREASURE

Along with the wisdom of the ancients, their gold has long been cherished. The households and tombs of royalty and nobility have yielded the artifacts of their lives; the weapons and toys, utensils, and religious symbols of early civilizations have shed light on ancient customs. But diggers after knowledge have often returned with riches as well—gold and silver and precious gems, cunningly wrought by forgotten masters, no less beautiful for having been buried for centuries. Often the purpose of buried wealth was to ease the passage of its owner from this world into the next: ships and chariots to speed the journey, Egyptian gold or Chinese jade to help prevent the body's corruption, coins to buy off hostile spirits, rich cups and plates, tables, chairs, and thrones for the opulent enjoyment of the afterlife. And always, precious icons to appease the gods and to assure the punishment of those who trespass.

1

The Fabled Wealth of Ur

In summer, the Iraqi plains baked hard under the relentless sun. So English archaeologist Leonard Woolley and his team waited for the hellish heat to pass before taking up picks for their dig. Then, inch by inch, they began excavating the parched earth of Tell Muqaiyar, a collection of ancient mounds in southern Iraq. It took five seasons to sink a pit that stretched forty feet down and four thousand years back in time to the heyday of the city Ur. Storied since biblical times, the great Sumerian metropolis was honored in the Judeo-Christian heritage as the home of Abraham and recorded in Mesopotamian history as the stronghold of Nebuchadrezzar and other formidable kings.

In 1927, Woolley uncovered a cemetery where two thousand of Ur's commoners had been buried with their simple possessions of wood, clay, stone, and copper. After months of inspecting these plebeian graves, Woolley must have felt his heart beat a little faster when his men scraped away the soil covering a handsome golden-shafted spear that stuck straight up in a grave site. There they found the bones of a man whose name, judging by inscriptions on objects buried with him, was Meskalamdug. They also found the first of the magnificent treasures of Ur. Meskalamdug had been

buried in a most extraordinary wig that replicated in gold the curls and crimps and neatly bound chignon of an elaborate coiffure. With the dust of his bones were mixed all manner of gold objects—a dagger, heavy bowls, hundreds of beads, a heap of bracelets and amulets and earrings—and silver things as well.

Meskalamdug's grave goods, though opulent, were outshone by the prodigal marvels in the tombs of Ur's royalty. Kings and queens, Woolley found, were laid to rest in the company of dozens of people who had attended them in life. In death, the servants still followed their masters, perhaps drinking poison once they had arranged themselves in the royal tomb.

In a huge antechamber to the tomb of a queen named Puabi were the neatly aligned remains of ten women bedecked with rich necklaces and headdresses of gold, lapis, and carnelian. Near them lay a lyre sheathed

in gold and topped with the gold head of a bull that boasted a lapis beard and forelock. There was a chariot with gold and silver harness fittings and lions' heads adorning its side panels. Near it lay the remains of grooms and drivers. Groups of long-dead soldiers guarded the entrance to the chamber, whose gleaming profusion of funeral finery was almost as clean and lovely as on the day the tomb was sealed—gold and lapis tubes used like straws for drinking from bowls of gold, exquisite platters and jugs, sets of nest-

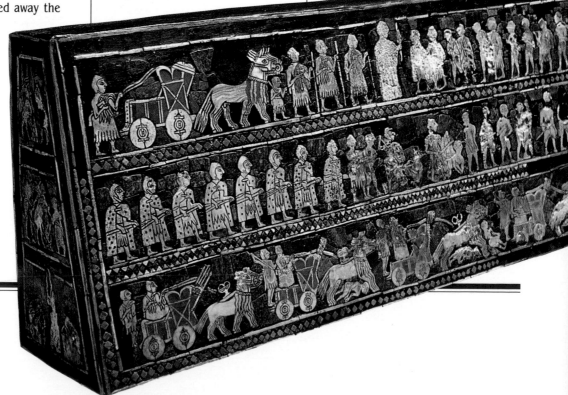

brushed her shoulders. Countless beads of gold, silver, and semiprecious stones lay like a sheet over her body, and pins, amulets, and other ornaments had been arranged nearby.

Unfortunately, the ancient profession of graverobbing was obviously practiced in Ur. Near Puabi's tomb was the tomb of a king who apparently died not long before her and may have been her husband. The robbers had emptied it, leaving only a two-foot-long silver boat complete with oars and an awning to shade its dead passenger. Somehow the thieves overlooked the antechamber crowded with the king's richly appointed entourage. There Woolley found silver spears and golden daggers, headdresses, combs, and earrings.

The value and beauty of the Ur treasure was staggering, yet to Woolley, an eight-foot layer of sediment was in its own right as fascinating a find. It was, he theorized, the deposit of the great flood described in both the Bible's Book of Genesis and the far older Sumerian epic about the hero Gilgamesh. It is a fact that, before it changed its course, the great Euphrates River flowed near Ur. Then as now, the Euphrates often breached its banks, usually in spring when seasonal rains and melting snow from the river's uppermost reaches raised its level. Perhaps, Woolley speculated, circumstances combined one year to produce a flood of devastating and unforgettable proportions that choked Ur with the mythic clay through which he dug on his way to treasure. □

ing tumblers in gold and silver, a winsome male goat standing erect with his forelegs braced against a golden tree, games with boards of precious inlay.

Queen Puabi herself had been laid out in a chamber below with two attendants beside her bier. The weight of forty feet of earth had flattened but not destroyed her headdress, an exquisite confection of gold beech leaves, rings, and six-petaled flowers with lapis centers. In death the queen wore earrings in the shape of half-moons so large that they would have

The Pride of Priam?

In pursuit of a boyhood passion, the middle-aged Heinrich Schliemann excavated his way to a sensational double discovery in 1873. Although the most eminent classicists of his day had denied its very existence, Schliemann found the city of Troy, whose destruction by Greek warriors three millennia ago is recounted in Homer's epic the *Iliad.* And, although treasure had not been his goal, Schliemann happened on an enormous hoard of gold and silver that he declared had belonged to Priam, Troy's king when the city fell.

The search for Troy was sparked by a history book seven-year-old Schliemann received for Christmas in 1829. One of its illustrations showed Troy in flames, and when his father told him that no one knew where the city had stood, the boy resolved to find it one day.

Schliemann's career, whether he planned it that way or not, eventually gave him the freedom and the wherewithal to go looking for Troy. A poor boy, he left school at fourteen and went to work as a grocery clerk. By the age of twenty-five, he had his own grocery import-export business, which made him a millionaire by the time he was thirty-six. He retired from business to steep himself in the Homeric tradition, learning classical Greek so he could read the epic story of the ancient conflict in the poet's own words, not in translation.

Schliemann rejected the prevailing scholarly doctrine that Homer was a mythmaker, not a historian. The events the poet wrote of, according to this position, were ↷

A lyre adorned by a golden, lapis-bearded bull's head *(top left),* a puckish goat grazing on a golden tree *(top right),* and a tableau fashioned of mother-of-pearl and lapis were among the objects entombed in fabled Ur.

9

figments of a great imagination. But the grocery magnate took the *Iliad* as literally as if it had been an eyewitness account. The kidnapping of the beautiful Greek queen Helen by the Trojans was, as far as Schliemann was concerned, a real historical event that precipitated a bloody ten-year-long conflict.

Homer's descriptions of troop movements and geography led Schliemann to focus on Hissarlik, a hill in northwest Turkey, as the likely site of Troy, and there, in 1870, he and his one hundred workers launched their assault.

The great trench the workers dug sank slowly downward through one civilization after another. The layers of ruins were confusing to Schliemann, who had less archaeological expertise than enthusiasm, but he fixed on the layer second from the bottom as the site of Troy. The lowest level was too primitive, predating the practice of metallurgy. According to Homer, metal was wrought into arms and other gear used by Trojan and Greek warriors.

The Turkish summer is too hot for digging, so Schliemann set June 15 as the last workday of the 1873 season. On the morning of the fourteenth, he and his workers were excavating what Schliemann thought were the ruins of King Priam's palace when he spotted a large copper article—and, lying behind it, something that looked like gold. To forestall theft, Schliemann suggested his workers take their morning break. As soon as they left, he fell to digging frenetically, despite, he later reported, the fear that the great fortification wall he was digging beneath would fall and crush him. "The sight of so many objects," he said, "made me foolhardy, and I never thought of any danger."

The hoard formed a rectangular mass, as if it had been packed in a wooden chest long since decayed. There was a gold cup shaped like a ship, huge earrings, and an exquisite gold diadem. It consisted of a circular chain from which were hung five dozen more chains, each decorated with glittering leaves and little idols—sixteen thousand tiny pieces altogether. A silver vase, still neatly upright after centuries in the earth, had been filled with gold items—buttons, studs, and necklace beads in the shape of rings, prisms, leaves, and cubes.

Schliemann's wife, Sophia, stood at his side, and as he handed her one fabulous object after another, she placed them on her shawl. In all, some 8,750 small objects were spirited away from the site wrapped in Sophia's shawl. The couple quickly made arrangements to leave Turkey, fearing that officials would confiscate the treasure.

To Schliemann, the treasure's value was archaeological, not monetary. And, of course, it was a more fabulous fulfillment of his lifelong fantasy than he could possibly have hoped for. When his wife complied with his wish that she try on the diadem, long, heavy earrings, and a necklace of many strands, he reportedly breathed,

"Darling, this is the most beautiful moment of our lives. You are Helen of Troy reborn."

Although Schliemann delighted in publicly twitting the scholars who had scoffed at him, he privately entertained doubts that the spot where he had found the treasure was indeed Troy; the ruins seemed neither large enough nor grand enough to correspond to Homer's description. In fact, archaeologists now believe that Homer's Troy was several layers above the site where Schliemann found "Priam's treasure." Without realizing it, he might have dug through the fabled city he sought. The hoard appears to date to 2200 BC, some one thousand years before the Trojan War. But the great amateur, most scholars now agree,

accomplished what he set out to do: He found the site of Troy.

The story of Schliemann has a sad coda. As befitted his unselfish interest in the treasure, he donated it to an ethnographic museum in Berlin. During World War II, the treasure was divided into several parts and taken to what authorities hoped would be secure places, including the Prussian State Bank, an air-raid shelter at the Berlin Zoo, and two castles in other parts of Germany. The bank and the zoo were destroyed by bombs, and one castle was plundered at the end of the war. Although it has been rumored that "Priam's treasure" was taken to Russia at the end of the war and remains there, it is more likely that the exquisite collection was melted down into bullion. □

Precious Idols

When Moses returned from Mount Sinai carrying stone tablets graven with the Ten Commandments, he was furious to find some religious rebels among his people feasting before an altar that bore a glittering calf of gold. Moses smashed the idol to a powder and made the would-be pagans drink it down with water.

Calf idols of precious metal were worshiped some three thousand years ago not only by renegade Israelites but by some of their Near Eastern neighbors as well. Not until 1990, however, was such an idol actually found, in the rubble of a temple in Israel. An archaeological worker peeked into a football-size pottery container she had found among the ruins and saw a pretty little statue. Dig director Lawrence Stager of Harvard realized at first glance that it was a bull calf. Some five inches long and complete except for a horn, the calf had legs, head, and genitals of silver and a body of bronze that ancient priests probably burnished to a golden gleam.

Although its sculptor used some base metal rather than the pure gold of the notorious biblical idol, the little calf is eyed with envy. Precious enough by virtue of its antiquity and its silver content, the relic is made more valuable still by its beauty and the prestige of being the first one of its kind ever to come to light. □

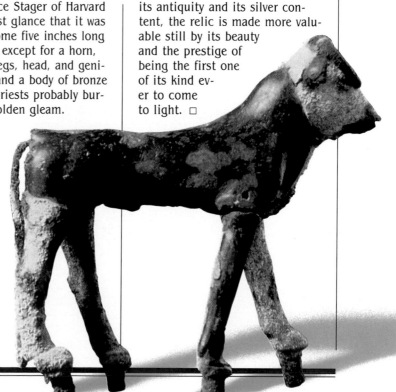

The Treasure of Tut's Tomb

On November 6, 1922, Egyptologist Howard Carter fired off a telegram to his wealthy patron Lord Carnarvon at Carnarvon's home in England: AT LAST HAVE MADE WONDERFUL DISCOVERY IN VALLEY STOP A MAGNIFICENT TOMB WITH SEALS INTACT STOP RECOVERED SAME FOR YOUR ARRIVAL CONGRATULATIONS.

What Carter did not state, but Carnarvon understood, was the name inscribed on the entrance to the tomb: Tutankhamen. Since 1919, Carter, with Carnarvon's moral and financial support, had been digging doggedly in the Valley of the Kings, the burial place of many of ancient Egypt's pharaohs. Already, Carter had added two feathers to his archaeological cap—the tombs of a princess and a pharaoh—although graverobbers had gotten there long before him and had emptied both. But all along, Carter's and Carnarvon's primary quarry was the shadowy Tutankhamen, who died around 1350 BC at the age of nineteen, too young to have won a place among the great pharaohs. In fact, Tutankhamen was remembered chiefly for being the son-in-law of the great beauty Queen Nefertiti.

Carter had had little to go on, but a few inscriptions, statues, and stone bas-relief portraits of the young king had convinced him that Tutankhamen's tomb lay somewhere in the Valley of the Kings. His instincts had brought him to the very entrance of the tomb, but Carter kept his word and waited for Carnarvon to arrive before removing its stone seal. The two men entered a corridor that led to a second door sealed with stones. Carter chipped and scraped away enough stone to let him shine his flashlight into the pitch-black chamber and, with a candle, test the escaping air for noxious fumes.

"At first I could see nothing, the hot air from the chamber causing the flame to flicker," Howard Carter reported later. "But as my eyes grew accustomed to the light, details of the room emerged slowly from the mist: strange animals, statues, and gold—everywhere the glint of gold."

Although graverobbers had entered the tomb before Carter and Carnarvon, they had not picked it clean. Tutankhamen's tomb was a

Supplies for the afterlife fill a chamber *(left)* near the crypt housing Tutankhamen's sarcophagus *(above)*.

repository of things priceless and precious beyond all expectations. Now, seven decades later, it remains the measure by which all other treasure hoards are judged.

The antechamber Carter and Carnarvon first peered into was piled with hundreds of objects bearing the pharaoh's name. Graverobbers had dumped out the contents of boxes and chests and disturbed the ritualistic order in which Tutankhamen's possessions were probably arranged. Although the pillagers may have made off with a king's ransom in treasure, they left behind jewels scattered on the floor, an ebony chair inlaid with ivory, fly whisks decorated with lapis lazuli and turquoise, and four dismantled gilded chariots. Perhaps the pillagers cut short their stay when they read the inscription on one wall that warned, "Death will slay with his wings whoever disturbs the peace of the pharaoh."

The most fabulous treasure of the antechamber was a throne, a perfectly intact miracle of gold and silver, semiprecious stones, and glass, resting on carved lion's paws. Inlaid on the throne's back was an intricately detailed scene of Ankhesenamen, Tutankhamen's queen, helping him with his toilet. Both wore towering crowns and wide collars of precious metal and semiprecious stones that completely covered their shoulders. Above them shone a sun of gold, and gold lions' heads flanked the front edge of the throne's seat.

Other pieces of furniture in the antechamber had animal motifs: A gilded wood couch ended in the carved shapes of cow heads with graceful, lyre-shaped horns. Because of the extremely dry climate in the Valley of the Kings, wood, silk, linen, and other materials that would have turned to dust in a more humid environment came through three thousand years of burial in excellent condition.

Wonderful as the things found in the antechamber were, they paled beside what Carter found in the adjacent burial chamber. It was almost totally filled by an immense box—a shrine of gilded wood inlaid with lapis lazuli. Nesting within, like a set of Chinese boxes, were three more shrines covered with gold leaf.

They contained a variety of small objects, such as two beautiful staffs, one of silver and one of gold, bearing portraits of the king. There were also weapons, vessels and lamps of alabaster, and a silver trumpet decorated with the images of Egyptian gods. The fourth shrine was quite different— a beautiful sarcophagus of rose and yellow stone with winged goddesses of the dead at each corner. Inside the sarcophagus was a gilded wood coffin carved in the form of Osiris, god of the dead. Fitting snugly within the coffin was another gilded Osiris, adorned with a broad garland of olive leaves, willow leaves, and blue lotus flowers, bone-dry but still intact.

The last sarcophagus Carter came upon was an unbelievably splendid sight—Tutankhamen in solid gold. Inside was the mummified body of the pharaoh himself, with 143 jewels scattered over it. A helmetlike mask of gold and lapis lazuli bearing Tutankhamen's features covered the head and ex- ◊

tended down over the shoulders.

Two more chambers glittered with treasure—a pectoral in the shape of a boat carrying the rising sun, rings, scarabs of gold and semiprecious stones, wide gold bracelets set with medallions and amulets, mirrors and perfume flasks of silver and gold, and ivory bowls and fans set with ostrich feathers. Coffer after coffer bulged with a dizzying array of precious objects, the likes of which the world had never before seen.

Carter worked slowly through one chamber at a time, studying, cataloging, restoring. It took six years for him to complete his work. But Lord Carnarvon lived to relish only a few brief months of the triumph his money had made possible. During the night of April 5, 1923, before Tutankhamen's mummy had been discovered, he died in Cairo of pneumonia. The superstitious wondered whether he had been punished, as the antechamber's inscription threatened, for invading the tomb. Two odd events that took place within minutes of Lord Carnarvon's death were noted by his son: For no apparent reason, all the lights in Cairo went out. And thousands of miles away in England, a dog that was greatly attached to Lord Carnarvon let out a howl and died.

Not long afterward, two archaeologists who had come to the Valley of the Kings to assist Carter died suddenly, and the legend of a long-dead but vengeful and death-dealing pharaoh sprang to life. The curse, if curse it was, skipped over Howard Carter, who should have been the prime target. He lived for many more years, dying at his home near London in 1939 at the ripe age of sixty-six. □

The Golden Hill

In 1978, many spectators watched a team of archaeologists recovering an incredible golden treasure from Tillya Tepe, a mound surrounded by Afghanistan's Bactrian plains. Among the onlookers was a melancholy farmer who had tilled the fields next to the mound. His wife was furious with him for not having found the treasure himself. With just a few handfuls of Tillya Tepe's sumptuous hoard, their days of poverty would have been over.

One clue the farmer overlooked was the mound's very name, which means, in the Dari dialect of Persian, "golden hill." From six graves in the golden hill's interior, archaeologists ultimately removed twenty thousand gold ornaments, statues, and vessels.

Only members of the noble class that ruled Bactria two thousand years ago could have taken such riches with them to the afterlife. One woman was buried with a crown cut from sheets of beaten gold. A wide band that had circled her head had five slots, into which fit five lotuslike plants abloom with golden flowers. Like glittering fruit, dozens upon dozens of disks trembled on slender stems of gold wire. Its clever design would have allowed the crown's owner to disassemble it into a compact flat package. Besides being festooned with jewelry, the dead had worn clothing to which hundreds of small baubles had been sewn like so much golden confetti.

The work of the archaeologists was cut short when civil war broke out in Afghanistan in 1979. More than a decade later, there was no word on the fate of the Bactrian treasure. No one could say whether it made its way into the hands of the Afghan government or into the purses of warriors or pillagers or, perhaps, into the pockets of impoverished farmers. □

The Mysterious Treasure

Uncertainties abound in the tale of the Oxus treasure. It is named for the central Asian river on whose banks—according to a report that is at best secondhand—it was dug up. In fact, no one knows exactly where or when the treasure was found, nor by whom. To compound the mystery, the route that took it to its present repository, the British Museum, is a murky one.

Comparisons with treasures unearthed methodically by archaeologists suggest that, except for its coins, the treasure's other 180-odd objects were made during the Persian Achaeminid empire, which lasted from the sixth century BC until late in the fourth century BC. It is far from clear whether the collection was put together by a single person or a family or whether it resulted from an ad hoc collaboration that took place over many years, even centuries, in many places, from Mesopotamia to Bukhara to Rawalpindi to London.

The first Englishman known to encounter the treasure was F. C. Burton, a British Army captain

stationed in a remote corner of Afghanistan. One evening in May of 1880, he was summoned to rescue three merchants who had been kidnapped while en route from Kabul to Peshawar, India, with wares of gold and silver. When Burton and his men reached the cave where the victims were being held, the kidnappers had been brawling over the merchants' precious booty. Burton forced the bandits to hand over the dozens of ornaments and statuettes and vessels that he saw scattered about the cave.

According to merchant Wazi ad-Din's deposition, the person who sold him and his partners the treasure in Kabul said that most of the objects had come from the site of Khandian, an ancient city whose ruins were exposed during the ⟳

Garlanded with an ingenious collapsible gold crown *(detail above)* and festooned with gold ornaments, the body of a wealthy woman was unearthed in one of six 2,000-year-old graves in Afghanistan.

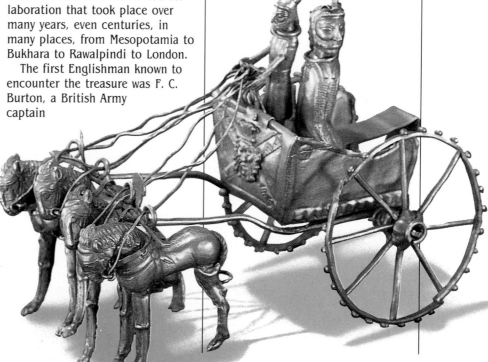

dry season, when the waters of the Oxus fell. The seller also claimed that a small idol and a gold anklet had been traced to the days of Alexander the Great.

After selling their rescuer a handsome gold armlet, the merchants resumed their journey. The Oxus treasure disappeared from official British view for a time. Then, a British general and dabbler in archaeology named Alexander Cunningham turned up with some—but not all—of the hoard. Antiquarians are not sure how he got it, or where, or exactly when. The treasure's history, it seems, grew even more muddled during its stay in India. Some pieces of it had been sold off, and, Cunningham speculated, many of its 1,500 coins had originated somewhere other than the Oxus. It seemed likely that the coins had been

thrown in by the dealer in India for reasons having more to do with commerce than with historical appropriateness. Valuable in their own right, coins can sometimes pinpoint the time that a treasure was first amassed, but the Oxus coins were too much of a hodgepodge to be useful.

Nevertheless, Cunningham had his hands on a trove of marvelous objects. One was a statuette of a nobleman riding in a miniature golden chariot whose driver holds the cunningly wrought reins of a team of four gold horses. Each steed is distinct, with its own arch of the neck or position of the hoofs. Other little statues included a silver image of a stern-faced Persian emperor and a winged gold ibex with beautifully detailed wings, face, hoofs, and horns. There were also many buttons and

big gold spangles meant to be attached to clothing. The Greek historian Herodotus may have had such objects in mind when he wrote that the Persian army "glittered all over with gold."

It is possible only to hazard an educated guess as to the treasure's origins. Cunningham, with little or no evidence, suggested a noble family of the ancient Asian kingdom of Bactria amassed the trove sometime before 200 BC. Another guess is that the treasure began when a soldier gathered unusually sumptuous spoils of war as Alexander the Great's army moved through Persia around 335 BC.

The Oxus treasure remained in General Cunningham's possession until 1897, when it was purchased and bequeathed to the British Museum by the generous Sir Augustus Wollaston Franks. □

Jewels of the Dead

Twice the great palace of Nimrud, stronghold of Assyrian kings from 900 to 600 BC, had been excavated extensively by archaeologists. But during a third major dig, in the spring of 1989, Iraqi archaeologist Muzahim Mahmoud Hussein spied, beneath centuries of dirt in an inner room of the palace, a tomb housing a stone sarcophagus. When Hussein pried up its lid and aimed a light inside, a golden reflection bounced back to his eyes.

Fabulous jewelry was draped across a dusty skeleton and heaped up around it, and more points of light glimmered from individual gold rosettes that had been scattered over the body. In all, almost four hundred exquisite orna-

ments—some crafted from gold alone, others encrusted with lapis lazuli, turquoise, malachite, and tiger's-eye—had been consigned to the grave with the body of a young princess. Three months later, the lucky Hussein struck gold again in a nearby sarcophagus housing the bones of a queen.

Among twentieth-century finds, the Nimrud treasure is deemed by many second only to that of Egypt's King Tut. The Assyrian antiquities number more than a thousand pieces that contain a total of 126 pounds of gold. The pieces are dazzlingly crafted and extravagant to boot—matching bracelets adorned with pairs of intricately detailed lions' heads,

earrings of clustered bells that would have sounded sweetly as the wearer moved, heavy wrist cuffs and anklets six inches wide, and a stunning crown formed of dozens and dozens of rosettes, each an inch and a half in diameter.

Evidently, the ladies who once adorned themselves in the jewels appreciated how precious their ornaments were. There is a curse on the princess's tomb. "If anyone lays his hands on my tomb, or opens my grave, or steals my jewelry, I pray to the gods of the nether world that his soul shall roam in the scorching sun after death," the imprecation reads. "Let the ghost of insomnia take hold of him for ever and ever." □

Although the Assyrian city of Nimrud had been combed for treasure for more than a century, fresh excavations of the palace walls *(background)* in 1989 revealed a rich trove of delicately worked gold, such as this necklace, whose twenty-eight tear-drop pendants are joined to a loop clasped by inter-twined animal heads.

King Solomon's Mines

The biblical King Solomon had so much gold, it is said, that the walls of the temple he built in Jerusalem three thousand years ago were covered with sheets of it and were hung with five hundred gold shields. The royal table was set exclusively with plates and cups and utensils made of the precious metal, and Solomon's ivory throne was decorated with still more gold. Yet this extravagance accounted for only a tiny portion of the gold that poured out of King Solomon's mines in a place called Ophir—by modern estimates, about thirty-one metric tons in all.

But the Bible's geography is frustratingly vague. Despite the many references to Ophir, the Bible never specifies where it was or even how far it was from the city of Jerusalem. Nor is it clear whether Ophir was a single large mine or a whole region rich in gold. Because of the ancient ambiguities, treasure hunters have looked for Ophir—and claimed to have found it—all over the map.

As early as the sixteenth century, Portuguese traders in East Africa reported seeing the ruins of an ancient city that local Muslims said had supplied King Solomon with his gold. But Europeans largely ignored Great Zimbabwe, as the site is called. Then in 1862 a romantic missionary named Merensky published an account of his voyage up what he called the Golden River. The journey ended at collapsed stone walls that lay in the "gold fields of Solomon." Merensky did not find gold there, but thirty years later other explorers unearthed a modest amount—enough to keep the dream of an African Ophir alive. In 1929, however, archaeologists deflated the dream by estimating that Great Zimbabwe had flourished around 1450 BC: It was much too young to have a Solomonic connection.

Science may have stricken Great Zimbabwe from the list of possibilities, but it has strengthened the case for another site, the Mahd adh Dhahab mine (above) in Saudi Arabia. Its name, which means "cradle of gold," seems well deserved. American mining engineer Karl S. Twitchell, at the request of the Saudi king, inspected the ancient mine in 1932. Twitchell found so many traces of gold in the tailings, or rock waste, that he speculated that Ophir and Mahd adh Dhahab could be one and the same. In 1976, a U.S. Geological Survey team seconded his theory. The team also noted that the mine was near a trade route more than four thousand years old that could have been the highway for gold on its way to the Israelite king. □

Coffin of the Conqueror

The sarcophagus was made of beaten gold in the shape of a man. It lay atop a wagon that bore it from Babylon to Egypt—the final journey of a young king who had once swept in conquest across the entire known world. Entombed in the gold was the embalmed body of thirty-two-year-old Alexander the Great, king of Greece, king of Asia, and pharaoh of Egypt.

Splendid as it was, the coffin was modest, considering the man. Alexander had come out of Greece like a juggernaut, rolling from the Himalayas to Sicily. Only twenty-five when he succeeded his father, Philip of Macedon, as monarch of Greece in 337 BC, Alexander had become the ruler of a million square miles and a man of great wealth. His subjugation of Persia alone netted treasure so vast that the numbers of mules and camels needed to carry it off looked like a swarming column of army ants.

It seems likely that a lavish portion of Greek plunder would have gone into Alexander's tomb, since the Macedonian custom was to equip the noble dead with weapons, cups, pitchers, plates, and other essentials crafted in gold and silver for the afterlife. But this is only guesswork. For hundreds of years after Alexander died, notables such as the Roman emperor Augustus made pilgrimages to the hero's tomb in Alexandria, but its precise location was forgotten long ago and has never been found.

The elaborate tomb that Alexander is said to have built for his father, Philip, has also vanished from human memory. But in 1977, Greek archaeologist Manolis Andronikos ecstatically reported discovering in northern Greece the treasure-laden tombs of Macedonian royalty who lived in Philip's time. Some of the most sumptuous objects came from a tomb in which a king was buried—possibly Philip himself, although that is a point of controversy among archaeologists.

Whoever the king was, his bones lay on a cushion of gold-embroidered royal purple silk inside a small casket. A breathtaking gold wreath of oak leaves and acorns rested atop the bones. The casket itself was made of twenty-four pounds of pure gold. A raised star, the symbol of Macedonian kings, adorned its lid, and a tracery of rosettes, lotus blossoms, tendrils, flowers, and leaves ornamented its sides.

More wonders were revealed when Andronikos opened an adjacent tomb, apparently the burial site of the queen. Leaning against a wall was a gold bow-and-arrow case and a large gold plaque showing in relief elaborate scenes of civilians fleeing as soldiers stormed a city. Andronikos opened a magnificent gold casket to find, atop the bones it held, a diadem he has called the most exquisite ornament known from the ancient world. Wrought in gold were leaves quivering at the ends of slender stems and blossoms from which perfect little bees gathered pollen—the kind of object that drives the perpetual search for treasure. □

An intricate crown of gold oak leaves and acorns *(above)* adorned the remains of a Macedonian king, interred with lanterns and domestic utensils *(left)* in a 2,300-year-old tomb in Vergina, Greece.

Carefully fitted suits of jade sewn with gold thread were intended to preserve the bodies of China's Prince Liu Sheng *(left)* and his princess, Tou Wan *(below)*.

Immortal Jade

When the Chinese prince Liu Sheng and his princess, Tou Wan, died more than two thousand years ago, their labyrinthine tomb, as large as a palace and carved in a cliff's solid rock, was furnished with everything that the couple would need in the next world. Their bodies were completely encased in garb that had the power, their mourners believed, to guarantee physical immortality.

In 1968, archaeologists entering the tomb were thrilled to find, in unsullied splendor, the royal couple's opulent funerary clothes—jackets, leggings, masks, helmets, shoes, and gloves—all made of shimmering, wafer-thin rectangles of jade, sewn together with gold wire. Ancient texts mention such attire, but none had ever before been found. The two substances of the burial suits supposedly reinforced one another's potency: Jade was thought to prevent the decay of the human body, and gold was a symbol of physical incorruptibility.

The fabulous suits together contained no fewer than 4,654 pieces of polished jade and three pounds of gold. The finest craftspeople in the kingdom must have taken years to carve the jade and to pierce each piece with four tiny, precisely placed holes through which the wires were run.

Possessing, even in death, such priceless garb did win the prince and princess immortality of a kind. It was not physical, however. When the archaeologists opened the tomb, the outfits of jade that once covered the bodies were empty except for a little dust. □

Mongol Hoards

Many years before his death, the fearsome Mongol conqueror Genghis Khan, after the custom of his people, chose his own grave site. It was in the shelter of a lone tree near the base of Mount Burqan Qaldun in Mongolia's wild Khingan range. During a campaign against the Chinese, the great Khan suffered a fatal fall from his horse, and in August of 1227 the mourning Mongol army abandoned the conflict to take their leader home.

After months of pomp and ceremony, Genghis Khan was finally buried in an elaborate coffin. Into the grave with him went a royal treasure—the crowns of each of the seventy-eight rulers he had subjugated in forays to places as distant as Russia, Persia, and India. In addition to the crowns, a lion, a horse, a Bible copied by a European monk, and a jade tiger as large as life are said to have been buried alongside the great Khan. And, although the historical records do not mention it, there may have been much more in the way of the rich plunder that came with conquest.

In a seeming paradox, after so grand a funeral, the Mongols did their best to obliterate the memory of the grave site. There was neither a marker nor a burial mound, and horsemen rode back-and-forth to erase signs of digging. The so-called forest men of the Uriangut clan were appointed to nurture the offspring of the old tree beside the grave, and eventually it was swallowed up in a trackless forest. Perhaps the Mongols thought to protect their leader's grave from non-Mongol eyes.

The elaborate camouflage was not the only barrier to finding Genghis Khan's grave. Over time, the old names for peaks in the Khingan range fell out of use, so no one knows which one was called Burqan Qaldun in the days of the Mongol empire. Moreover, one ancient record states that the grave was on a southern slope, and another places it on the west.

But the chance, however slight, for gaining wealth and fame still draws optimists to the hunt. They follow in the tracks of a British expedition mounted in 1890 and a Russian one mounted in 1927.

A combination of linguistic and ethnographic detective work and state-of-the-art cartography may yet flush Genghis Khan out of his mountain fastness. American geologist Lindsey Maness has proposed that a painstaking study of the oldest Mongol histories, not in translation but in the original Arabic and Uigur, may turn up fresh clues. There is also the prospect that a satellite could produce an image of the grave site. The various remote sensing devices that have been used for mapping earth's surface are amazingly sensitive, and Maness believes that they can pick up disturbances in vegetation and topography on an otherwise untouched mountainside. With a minimum of fuss, searchers could then head unerringly for the fabled needle in the haystack.

But finding Genghis Khan, Maness speculates, may not in itself guarantee finding the great Khan's treasure. The geologist theorizes that the bulk of the buried wealth lies in the graves of three of the Mongol chief's descendants: Mangu, Ögödei, and Kublai Khan. Still, the patriarch's grave may point the way. If Lindsey Maness is correct, the three descendants of the great Khan are buried nearby. □

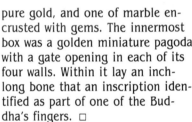

The inch-long finger bone at left, a relic of the Buddha, was hidden within seven nested boxes, the innermost of which is the tiny golden pagoda below.

The Pagoda's Precious Secrets

Already weakened by the passage of centuries, a thirteen-story pagoda at China's ancient Famen Buddhist monastery collapsed into a pile of bricks during heavy summer rains in 1981. Six years later, archaeologists laying plans to rebuild the pagoda discovered beneath the rubble a perfectly preserved marble crypt built in the seventh century.

As astonishing as the crypt itself were the exquisite religious relics secreted in its many chambers. The crypt's rooms were crowded with dozens of objects made of jade, marble, fine porcelain, and glass—along with a priceless assembly of 121 gold and silver pieces. Among them were an alms bowl of solid gold and a silver one in the shape of a lotus flower, as well as sumptuous incense burners, spoons, cups, a grinder and a sifter for preparing tea, staffs, lamps, tongs, dishes, and statues of buddhas. An extraordinary realism marked many of the pieces, including a turtle-shaped box with faithfully rendered shell, head, and feet.

A niche in the last of the crypt's series of chambers held the most precious of the monks' treasures— a set of seven nesting, elaborately decorated caskets. Three of the caskets were of silver, three of pure gold, and one of marble encrusted with gems. The innermost box was a golden miniature pagoda with a gate opening in each of its four walls. Within it lay an inch-long bone that an inscription identified as part of one of the Buddha's fingers. □

Treasures of the Table

In the winter of 1942, a man tilling his employer's field near the English village of Mildenhall turned up thirty-four old pieces of gray metal tableware with his plow. The man dutifully turned over his find to the landowner, who for some reason let four years pass before officially reporting the discovery. Perhaps he was simply too unimaginative to wonder whether the dishes had an unusual value or history; he might also have been unaware of his legal obligation to report unearthing any object from British soil that might be made of gold or silver.

Whatever the cause of his delay, it cost the landowner dearly. At the government's behest, experts in metalwork examined the tableware and declared that the plowman had turned up a trove of Roman silver. It had been hidden around AD 400, they surmised, when barbarians were harrying southern England and Rome was losing its grip on the island. A well-to-do citizen, like many of his contemporaries, had probably buried his silver in the vain hope of retrieving it when peaceful times returned.

This must have been bitter news to the landowner, since the Crown lays claim to such treasure. A prompt report

A wild-haired sea god, fantastical creatures, and nymphs disport themselves across fourth-century Roman silver dinnerware unearthed in Mildenhall.

would have obliged the government to pay the landowner about a half-million pounds, the estimated worth of the Mildenhall find. But because he had dawdled, the fellow earned just a token payment.

Most of the goblets, bowls, plates, spoons, and ladles of the Mildenhall treasure were made during the fourth century AD in ateliers located in Rome or Gaul. A handful of items date from the second century and may have been family heirlooms.

The undisputed masterpiece of the collection is an embossed dish two feet in diameter celebrating Oceanus, a pagan sea god. His face, in the center of the dish, sports a beard of seaweed and is ringed by cavorting nymphs and mythical sea creatures. Beyond them, a dozen revelers drink and dance wildly as the lascivious god Pan plays his pipes.

Banquet guests must have felt more than a little envy when they were served from a dish that mixed sheer luxury and great artistry in such perfect measure. □

Bier Garden

To a succession of farmers in Hochdorf, Germany, the mound rising twenty-five feet amid their fields was a nuisance. All too often, their plows ran into great stones lying below the hill's surface. But archaeologists who heard of the rocky collisions thought a farmer's obstacle might be a scientist's bonanza: The hillock, they theorized, was really a tumulus—a burial mound covering the huge stone tomb of an ancient Celtic noble. A greater depth of soil had probably overlain its roof, but centuries of water and wind had stripped so much away that some of the stones had come within range of plowshares.

It took very little digging for Stuttgart archaeologist Jörg Biel to uncover the ruins of a stone structure in the late 1970s. And what lay beneath the stones was the discovery of a lifetime. Untouched by 2,500 years of weather and undetected by graverobbers were the bones and the most precious possessions of a prince. Laid out on a bronze bier supported by eight bronze pallbearers, the man wore around his neck the sure sign of Celtic royalty—a gold necklace in the shape of a ring. A wide gold band circled one arm and a gold belt girded his waist. Brooches of gold fastened his silk-embroidered clothes, and other pieces of jewelry had been scattered over his body. His dagger and

even his shoes were embellished with gold. To sustain him in the other world, a hundred-gallon bronze cauldron rimmed with reclining lions had been filled at his death with mead. Close by was a golden bowl as fit for a prince in death as in life. □

A foot-long bronze dagger decorated with gold armed the body of a Celtic prince who was opulently interred in Hochdorf, Germany. Delicate gold latticework—here displayed over glass forms—graced the prince's shoes, which deteriorated long ago.

Mrs. Pretty's Barrow

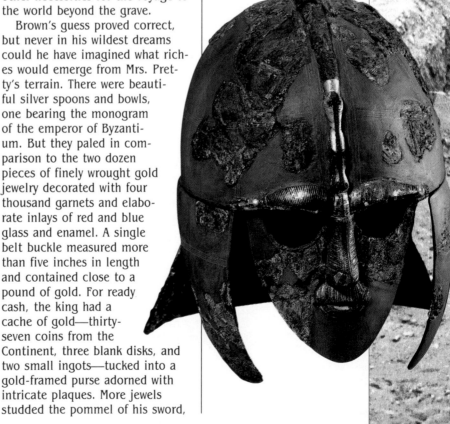

On August 14, 1939, a jury assembled in East Anglia to determine the owner of the most fabulous treasure ever unearthed in England—the gem-studded royal accouterments, solid gold jewelry, and other precious possessions of an Anglo-Saxon king. The crux of the matter was whether the find met the legal definition of a trove—valuables that had been either lost or hidden by someone intending to retrieve them later. If it were a trove and no heir came forward—one seemed unlikely, since the king's identity was uncertain and he had died some 1,300 years earlier—possession would pass to the Crown. If the verdict went against the Crown, the owner of the property where the treasure was found—a Mrs. Edith May Pretty of Sutton Hoo—would become an extremely wealthy person.

As it happened, Mrs. Pretty's drawing-room window afforded a view of several ancient barrows—long, low man-made mounds of earth. Curious to learn what they might conceal—old rumors spoke of buried treasure—Mrs. Pretty decided in 1938 to hire an archaeologist to carry out an excavation. Basil Brown's first year of digging turned up potsherds, bronze and iron implements, and other Anglo-Saxon items of scientific interest but little or no monetary value. Brown also found, however, plenty of evidence that treasure hunters had been at work before him.

In the spring of 1939, Brown attacked the largest of the mounds, which measured some one hundred feet long and nine feet high. One day an assistant showed the archaeologist a few pieces of corroded iron, which Brown identified as a type of nail the Anglo-Saxons had used in their ships. He guessed that the mound concealed a ship that had been transported from a nearby river to serve as the burial site of a great heathen leader. Several such burial ships discovered in England, Brown knew, contained remnants of clothing, food, and other necessities for the voyage to the world beyond the grave.

Brown's guess proved correct, but never in his wildest dreams could he have imagined what riches would emerge from Mrs. Pretty's terrain. There were beautiful silver spoons and bowls, one bearing the monogram of the emperor of Byzantium. But they paled in comparison to the two dozen pieces of finely wrought gold jewelry decorated with four thousand garnets and elaborate inlays of red and blue glass and enamel. A single belt buckle measured more than five inches in length and contained close to a pound of gold. For ready cash, the king had a cache of gold—thirty-seven coins from the Continent, three blank disks, and two small ingots—tucked into a gold-framed purse adorned with intricate plaques. More jewels studded the pommel of his sword,

Its timbers long since rotted, a 1,300-year-old Saxon burial ship excavated in Sutton Hoo, England, left a tantalizing impression in the ground *(right)* and yielded priceless artifacts, including the iron helmet below and an intricate gold buckle *(above)*.

and his helmet sported a crest of silver and was embellished with gilded boars' heads, garnet-eyed dragons, and incised figures of warriors and battle scenes.

But the identity of the king who decked himself out so splendidly remained a mystery. The dates the coins bore suggested that he may have been Raedwald, a powerful ruler who died in 624 or 625. A still-greater mystery was whether his body had actually been interred along with his possessions. No bones were found, but the soil covering the burial ship was so acid that it could have destroyed them. For the same reason, the dig yielded only fragments of wood, cloth, ivory, and other such fragile substances. Only gems and noble metals survived the centuries of burial, their beauty intact.

After hearing the evidence, the jury concluded that the Sutton Hoo treasure had been neither lost nor buried with the hope of retrieval; instead, it had been consigned to the earth in a public ceremony for the king's use and pleasure in the afterlife. They awarded the treasure to Mrs. Pretty, who, with astonishing magnanimity, promptly donated every one of the precious objects to the British Museum and refused to accept any recompense for her generosity. □

Boars, snakes, and inlays of garnet and glass grace a gold clasp unearthed at Sutton Hoo. Its halves are joined with a chained pin.

The Thetford Trove

Arthur and Greta Brooks had spent an unrewarding afternoon prospecting with a metal detector, and the construction site at Thetford, East Anglia, was their last stop. Twilight was falling, so when a five-minute sweep of the bulldozed earth drew a blank, the Brookses called it a day. As they headed toward their car, however, the metal detector emitted a signal, and Arthur Brooks paused to scrape away a few inches of soil.

"I stood above him," Greta Brooks later recalled, "and suddenly we saw a shiny thing, and a little black box, and as we pulled them out we saw there were other things round them in wet sand. There were spikes sticking up."

A quick bit of digging revealed that the spikes were the handles of spoons lodged vertically in the sand. And there were dozens of shiny things—necklaces, beads, bracelets, a buckle, rings, and pendants, many of them set with stones. In the growing darkness, the Brookses checked the area again with the metal detector and, satisfied that they had found everything, took the hoard home.

For the Brookses, the dream of every metal-detecting enthusiast had come true. They had found thirty-three silver spoons and strainers and forty-three pieces of gold jewelry that looked almost as fresh

and unworn as the wares in a jeweler's window. The couple knew that the objects were very old and extraordinarily valuable. They also knew that British law required a prompt report of such finds. Nevertheless, they squirreled theirs away in a safe-deposit box without a word to the authorities.

During the winter of 1980, rumors began circulating that a cache of Roman valuables had been dug up in Thetford. The Brookses maintained their silence, but a government archaeologist playing detective finally tracked them down. In May, more than six months after their momentous discovery, the Brookses handed over the treasure to officials.

Experts valued the hoard at £262,000, or about $528,000, speculating that a frightened jeweler had buried his unsold stock during a time of unrest in the late fourth century. Somehow, his things were hidden along with ritual silver belonging to a Roman temple; the spoons bore the name of Faunus, a god worshiped by pagan farmers and shepherds.

It was not unalloyed greed that kept the Brookses from doing the right thing. As the finder, Arthur feared he might be prosecuted as a trespasser. He also worried that the government might award the landowner a payment equaling the value of the hoard, while he and his wife would get nothing.

In this case, honesty would have been more profitable. A timely declaration would have brought the Brookses full recompense, but because of the delay the government cut the payment by two-thirds. And only Greta Brooks benefited; Arthur died a month and a half after relinquishing the treasure. □

The Well-Traveled Cup

In 1837, a pretty gold cup scarcely three inches tall was added to the British Crown's vast hoard of plate. Workers at the royal estate of Rillaton in Cornwall had been digging stones out of an old burial mound for a construction project when their shovels uncovered a vaulted grave containing a skeleton and a small number of grave goods. The workers handed the goods over to an estate official, who duly sent them to London to their proper owner, William IV.

The king may never have seen his precious new acquisition, for he died shortly after it arrived. His successor, Queen Victoria, had other things to worry about, and the little Rillaton cup might as well have been buried again. It sat unnoticed in the royal collection for a decade or more.

Sometime in the 1850s, the queen's husband, Albert, took a fancy to the cup and carried it down to the family's retreat on the Isle of Wight, where he had set up a private museum for his children. There the artifact stayed until 1867, when it was exhibited at the Royal Archaeological Institute. That same year, a scholarly report containing an engraving of the cup noted that it had probably been fashioned around 1500 BC from a single sheet of gold. It was a rare piece—the author knew of no other cup made entirely of concentric corrugations.

After the exhibition, the cup vanished once again. But it had not been totally forgotten. In 1936, shortly after the death of her husband, George V, Queen Mary

was approached by her royal librarian. Curious about the cup's where-abouts, he showed her the old engraving in hopes of gleaning clues. It looked familiar to the queen, and she soon confirmed that she had located the missing cup. She told the librarian that shortly after George's coronation in 1910, the two of them had been looking over the royal plate for items to use in their new residence when the king's eyes fastened on a curious cup. Until his death, he kept it on his dressing table at Buckingham Palace. It was almost certainly the only Bronze Age cup in England that served as a container for collar stays.

A dressing table—even a king's dressing table—was not, in Queen Mary's opinion, the proper place for such a priceless thing. Her newly crowned son, Edward VIII, was now the owner of the cup and of the rest of the royal plate as well. After hearing the cup's history, he assented when his mother suggested lending it permanently to the British Museum. The vanishing act of the Rillaton cup had, it seemed, finally come to an end. □

The Curate's Cache

It is a fact that Bérenger Saunière, curate of the little French town of Rennes-le-Château, became enormously wealthy in 1892. But theories have been more plentiful than facts about the source of his riches and how they fell into his hands.

Before the priest's fortunes changed so startlingly, he had lived simply in the dusty little backwater south of Carcassonne for seven years. The townspeople apparently liked their priest and shrugged off his worldly ways. A lively and outgoing man, he liked to hunt and to fish and to spend long hours in the company of his favorite young parishioner, Marie Denarnaud. But he also saw to his priestly duties, and around 1888, he energetically tackled a project that other curates had shirked for decades—the renovation of Rennes's sorely neglected eight-hundred-year-old church.

One day a mason handed over to Father Saunière several wooden cylinders that he had found in a hollow column when he lifted the altar stone off the four columns supporting it. Even older than the church, the columns were survivors of the Dark Ages, when Rennes, then named Aereda, had been ruled by barbarian Visigoth kings.

From each cylinder Saunière extracted an old document written on parchment. Two were tedious genealogies, but the other two were written in unreadable, garbled Latin. With his bishop's blessing, the priest traveled to Paris to get a scholar's help in translating them.

Soon after his return from Paris, Saunière was off on another trip, then another and another, to destinations he did not disclose. During this time, the postmaster noticed that Marie Denarnaud was receiving money orders from several European countries.

It soon became apparent that the priest and his *petite amie* had money to burn. To inquisitive villagers and churchmen he said only that he had come into an inheritance. He built himself a splendid house surrounded by an elaborate garden where, with Marie as his hostess, he entertained lavishly.

Saunière's bishop, and perhaps other people too, did not buy the inheritance story. If anyone paused to think about them, the unusual gifts Saunière gave to fellow priests must have raised suspicions. One cleric received a very old, exquisitely wrought chalice, and another a precious collection of coins minted in the sixth and seventh centuries.

Whether anyone linked these rare objects with an old Rennes tradition of hidden treasure during Saunière's lifetime is uncertain, and he remained closemouthed to his death in 1917. But every villager knew the story of Ignace Paris, a local shepherd who came home one day in 1645, pockets bulging with gold coins. He claimed he had been searching for a lost sheep when he stumbled into a ◊

skeleton-filled cave that housed coffers overflowing with treasure. Paris declined to show the villagers the cave, so they declared him a liar and hanged him as a thief.

Several years before her death, Denarnaud confided to her close friend Noel Corbu a tale that seemed to exonerate poor Ignace Paris and to reveal how Saunière had become so rich. The two puzzling old parchments from the altar had encoded all the information needed to locate a fabulous ancient treasure, she said. The clues are said to have included references to a seventeenth-century painting by Nicolas Poussin that depicted landmarks in the Rennes area. Closely examining a copy of the painting and following the deciphered directions, she and the priest measured off lines originating at the altar. At the point where the lines ended, the pair dug down—and into the same vault that the shepherd had found.

To avoid detection, Saunière sold the coins and jewels and precious plate in many different cities over a long period of time. Denarnaud claimed that the trove, which had already yielded millions of

dollars, was still not exhausted. She assured Corbu that she would tell him how to find the treasure, but she died in 1953 without keeping her promise.

Despite their excavations, Corbu and other treasure hunters have come up empty-handed, so where the treasure came from and how it came to be hidden in Rennes-le-Château can only be imagined. One theory is that the treasure once belonged to the Visigoth kings who ruled the region in the fifth century and built Aereda. When they sacked Rome, the barbarians carried off enormously rich booty. When the ultimately triumphant Franks made war on them in the

sixth century, the Visigoths may have hidden their treasure in Aereda, never to retrieve it.

An opposing theory holds that the trove belonged to the Frankish kings who supplanted the Visigoths. A third possibility is that during a peasant uprising in 1250, Blanche, the queen mother of France, hid the royal jewels and gold near Rennes as she and her family fled to safety in Spain.

Unless and until someone finds the elusive cave and whatever remains of the treasure, determining its origin seems impossible. But if Marie Denarnaud told Noel Corbu the truth, Rennes-le-Château remains rich in ancient treasure. □

The Rewards of Ditchdigging

On a summer day in 1985, Ivan Dimitrov was digging a ditch in the back garden of his house in Rogozen, Bulgaria, when his shovel struck metal. Picking up what looked like a cheap aluminum plate, Dimitrov tossed it out of the way and resumed his digging. To his surprise, he turned up more and more things—not just plates, but bowls and jugs and cups. Call-

ing his wife to see his find, Dimitrov dug until he had uncovered sixty-five items that had been jumbled together in a shallow pit a scant twenty inches deep.

Dimitrov and his wife marveled at the beauty that a good washing of the artifacts revealed, but they were at a loss to say where the collection had come from or how it had found its way into their gar-

den. Perhaps reluctant to let the village gossips in on their secret— but certain that they should report the find—the Dimitrovs bypassed local authorities and notified the mayor of a neighboring city. The mayor, in turn, called in archaeological professionals.

The experts' pronouncement was stunning: Dimitrov had found treasure that had been wrought of pure silver when the fabled kings of Thrace ruled northwestern Bulgaria two and a half millennia ago. Some ancient disaster or treachery had apparently driven a noble family to hide its valuables in hopes of retrieving them later.

On the hunch that the last guardian of the fabulous collection might have buried it in two lots for better safekeeping, the archaeologists began exploring the ground around Dimitrov's original dig. Within days, they uncovered the second cache. It was larger than the first, containing one hundred silver vessels, some of them enriched with a thin coat of gold.

The Rogozen treasure was among the most spectacular Thracian silver ever found. Often sculpted in high relief, ravishing goddesses and griffins, heroes and winged horses, palm branches and acorns, fish, birds, bulls, a menag-erie of wild animals, and an array of geometric motifs crowded the graceful forms of the vessels.

There were no fewer than 108 phialae, a rare type of shallow drinking cup. Their richly embellished interiors would have come into view slowly as the level of the wine they held fell, sip by sip. One of the most beautiful phialae measured some six inches across and had a central medallion surrounded by astonishingly realistic bulls' heads with bulging eyes, flared nostrils, and even tufts of hair in tactile relief. Another had a sunburst pattern as intricate as that of a cathedral's rose window.

In the *Iliad,* Homer describes a Thracian silver cup given to Priam, king of Troy. The vessels unearthed by Ivan Dimitrov—now called "the goldsmith" by his fellow villagers—would have been no less fitting tributes for the great rulers of the ancient world. As for Dimitrov, his tribute came in the payment of an undisclosed sum of money from the Bulgarian government. □

A 2,500-year-old Thracian silver pitcher decorated with dancing man-beasts is part of two troves raised from a backyard in Bulgaria.

Alaric's Tomb

A 1,500-year-old legend of buried barbarian booty still impels treasure hunters to comb the countryside around the little city of Cosenza in southern Italy. According to tradition, Roman spoils of empire building were wrenched away in AD 410 when King Alaric and his Visigoth horde sacked Cosenza. Their next target was North Africa, but the young king fell ill and died en route.

A translation of sixth-century historian Jordanes's Latin text states that Alaric was buried near Cosenza, along with his favorite horse and an unspecified portion of Visigoth treasure. To foil would-be graverobbers, the Visigoths chose a most unusual burial site— the bed of the Busento River. They directed prisoners they had captured to build a dike to divert the river temporarily. Then, in the exposed riverbed, the captives dug a huge trench for Alaric and his possessions. After restoring the river to its normal course, the prisoners were killed so that the exact location of the grave would remain a secret. Beneath the waters, legend had it, a staggering 25 tons of gold and 150 tons of silver lay buried with the dead king.

Over the years, the hunt around Cosenza has proceeded like an unruly dart game; each fortune hunter has picked his or her own target, but none has scored a bull's-eye. For some, the search has been just a passing fancy, but for a Calabrian veterinarian named Vincenzo Astorino it has been an obsession for decades. He favors a seventeenth-century monk's version of the legend to Jordanes's. In his *Almanacco Perpetuo,* Brother ◊

The likeness of Alaric, the fifth-century Visigoth king who died in Italy after his armies sacked Rome, gazes balefully from an eighteenth-century engraving.

Rutilio Benincasa, like Jordanes, reports that King Alaric died in Cosenza. The monk states, however, that Alaric was buried not in the Busento River but beside it, in the church of San Pancrazio. With the help of a Calabrian woodcutter, Astorino discovered the ruins of the church. It seemed a piece of good luck that the large pasta factory on whose grounds the ruins were located belonged to a friend of his. With the friend's support, Astorino was about to begin excavations in 1967 when the government halted the project because he was an amateur and might damage the site.

More recently, a geologist has fixed on an enormous, apparently man-made conical mound near Cosenza as a link to Alaric. Vincenzo Rizzo believes the hill is a tumulus—a burial mound traditional among ancient Germanic peoples. He is not convinced Alaric is buried there. It may be only a cenotaph, or memorial, to the king. He notes that locals call the site *Grifone*—Italian for "griffin," the mythological creature said to guard a king's tomb. Moreover, Golden Horse Peak looms nearby—a possible allusion, Rizzo believes, to the splendid trappings of Alaric's horse.

An ancient misspelling and a modern misunderstanding, Rizzo believes, have combined to generate the false notion of a riverbed burial. When Jordanes wrote "Busentinus," he may have had in mind not a river but a nearby town called, in his day, Bisuntinus (now known as Bisignano).

Treasure fever continues to inflame Cosenza from time to time when yet another site is proposed. So strong is the lure of Alaric's treasure that it overpowers the centuries of contradictions and ambiguities. □

Kingly Greed, Knightly Gold

Despite their vaunted riches, kings of old were often short of ready cash. Thus when his daughter's marriage to Edward II of England approached, Philip the Fair of France did not have enough money for a proper dowry. Like every other temporarily embarrassed European medieval potentate, Philip knew he could count on the Knights Templars for a loan. A loan, however, would have entailed repayment, a burden that the king clearly did not relish. And thereby hangs a tale.

For years, the order of knights had been the bankers to kingdoms all over Europe. Yet their position as financiers was accidental. French knights had founded the organization in 1118 to protect pilgrims in the Holy Land from Muslim attack during the Crusades.

Each member took vows of poverty and chastity, but donations to the order of land, money, jewels, and other riches made it wealthy. Renowned for their honesty and fierce defense of fellow Christians, the knights were often asked to transport bullion and other valuables between Europe and the Holy Land.

Jerusalem was the headquarters of the order. When the Muslims drove the Christians out of the Holy Land in 1187, the knights reestablished themselves in France. Benefactors such as Alfonso I of Aragon, who bequeathed them his entire kingdom, had made the Knights Templars vastly rich, and they had grown still richer by buying the estates of impoverished

lords. Vows of poverty aside, the knights' temple in Paris had strongrooms reputed to hold a fortune in gold, silver, and gems.

Their wealth, financial clout, and independence—the Knights Templars owed allegiance to no one except the pope—made King Philip the Fair increasingly greedy on the one hand and nervous on the other. And his ambivalence spelled bad news for the knights. Friday, October 13, 1307, was especially unlucky for the order. On that day, King Philip decreed the arrest of every member of the Knights Templars in France.

It was certainly King Philip's goal to confiscate the treasure in the temple and everything else of the order's property that he could get his hands on. According to

many historians, he did just that.

But another story, perhaps apocryphal, asserts that Philip was thwarted by Pope Clement V, who alerted the Templars' grand master, Jacques de Molay, to the king's plot. Before the fateful Friday, the gold, silver, and jewels were taken out of Paris in three wagons covered over with hay. The destination was Normandy, where Templar ships were ready to spirit the treasure out of the country. Partway to the coast, though, the Templars decided to hide the treasure. Since then, speculation has centered on a triangle formed by the towns of Sees, Gisors, and L'Aigle; but in all the centuries that have passed, no proof of Templar treasure has ever surfaced.

In a variant tale of the treasure's

disappearance, de Molay is said to have sent his nephew, Count Guichard de Beaujeu, to the temple, armed with directions for finding the treasure. The capitals of two pillars there, according to the grand master, pivoted outward to reveal hollow interiors overflowing with riches. Beaujeu removed everything, including the crown of the kings of Jerusalem, a candelabrum from King Solomon's fabled treasure, and gold statues of four evangelists, which allegedly once graced the Holy Sepulcher.

As to the treasure's next repository, the story suggests two possibilities: the island of Cyprus and the Beaujeu château in France. However, not a single jewel or coin has ever been found to lend the tale substance. ☐

Digging in Derrynaflan

Farmer Michael Webb was not happy with the Irish government. Authorities had offered him only a pittance for the Celtic altar set he had found while prospecting with his metal detector in a ditch near Derrynaflan, a ruined fifth-century church. In court, the government rejected his claim on the 1980 find; he did not own the land, nor did he have permission to excavate it. It was, the state argued, almost a sacrilege for an amateur to disturb the ground so near a national monument such as the church. Still, the government would pay Webb ten thousand pounds, or $14,645, in compensation.

Webb was not willing to give up

the treasure for a song. Experts from several British museums were dazzled by the artistry of the altar set, which was especially valuable because it was complete. Altogether, the bejeweled silver chalice, the large platter with a stand, the ritual wine strainer, and the bronze bowl found at Derrynaflan were estimated to be worth as much as eight million pounds, or $11.7 million.

Webb's dream of being a millionaire seemed about to come true when, in 1986, a higher court declared him the rightful owner and ordered the state to pay him not a measly ten thousand pounds, but five hundred times that much.

Unfortunately for Webb, the state appealed to the Supreme Court

and won. Declaring that the Derrynaflan hoard rightfully belonged to the state, the court awarded Webb twenty-five thousand pounds—not a bad return on his investment of one hundred pounds in a metal detector, but a far cry from the wealth that he had freed piece by piece from the Irish soil. ☐

Smuggled Treasures of the Dead

Virtually every society that buries its dead with their precious possessions has its share of graverobbers. And every now and then, through luck or craft, the thieves succeed beyond their wildest dreams. In January of 1987, Peruvian Ernil Bernal and his brother Chalo tunneled into a crumbling *huaca*, or pyramid, in the village of Sipán and literally struck gold.

After digging through twenty-four feet of the pyramid's concrete-hard adobe, they came to a stone-walled tomb stuffed with enough treasure, they later claimed, to fill twenty-five sacks. Its total worth was incalculable.

The Bernals had not chosen their target randomly. It was common knowledge along the north coast of Peru that such sites could reward a pillager handsomely. The pyramids sheltered multiple tombs of the leaders of the Moche, a prosperous people who flourished there from AD 250 to 750 before abruptly disappearing. For decades, archaeologists had repeatedly suf-

fered the frustration of excavating a Moche grave, only to discover that the local *huaqueros*—graverobbers—had beaten them to it.

Huaqueros had no trouble locating buyers for their finds. Collectors in Peru were handy customers, and enterprising smugglers found ways to evade customs officials and send the goods to Europe and the United States.

The Bernals' find created a sensation among those interested in contraband grave treasure, and the police heard about it within days. But most of the booty had already disappeared into Lima's black market. In a raid on Ernil Bernal's house, authorities confiscated only thirty-three objects. There were two gold peanuts, complete with all the ridges and grooves of the real thing but three times larger; a pair of gilded feline heads with fangs of shell; and a solid gold human head with deep blue lapis eyes.

The police summoned archaeologist Walter Alva, director of Peru's Brüning Archaeological Museum,

to Sipán—standard practice in the case of looted tombs. What he thought would be nothing more than a salvage operation led him to a tomb that may be the richest ever excavated in the Western Hemisphere. After four months of painstaking work, he found the entrance of a tomb that the pillagers had missed. It lay, in fact, just a few feet past the point where the graverobbers had stopped digging. Inside, the "Lord of Sipán," as Alva dubbed the tomb's principal occupant, had been laid out in a shower of gold and silver and copper and lapis. He wore an enormous headdress, bracelets, earrings, and several massive necklaces. Moreover, fabulous ceremonial objects had been interred with him, among them an intricately decorated gold rattle. Mixed with the remains of the entourage buried with the man were ornaments more modest than his, but still stunning in their artistry and value.

Under Peruvian law, any pre-Columbian object unearthed from the country's soil belongs to the nation as part of its heritage. But the sums commanded by the exquisite Moche treasure were high enough to tempt more than one person to defy the law. One buyer reportedly offered $100,000 for one small figurine of gold.

A California antiquities dealer named David Swetnam was lured by the promised profits of the Bernal cache. With the help of an American collector living in Lima, Swetnam bought up Sipán gold worth a half-million dollars. Fearful that the goods would be intercepted by U.S. customs officials, he shipped them to England. A friend there was about to send a crate of household items to the United States, and he agreed when Swetnam asked if he could include some of his own things.

Swetnam's scheme collapsed when the crate was unpacked in California and his friend, eying the gold pieces, realized that he could be prosecuted as an accomplice to smuggling. He alerted customs officials, and Swetnam was sent to jail for six months.

As things turned out, the jail time may have been well spent. When the Peruvian government sued in a U.S. court for the return of the 1,400 pieces that customs had seized from Swetnam, it lost. The judge ruled that Peru had failed to prove that the pieces were stolen. In spite of the fact that he had been convicted for smuggling the Sipán treasure in the first place, Swetnam regained possession of almost all of it.

Only nine of the confiscated pieces were returned to Peru, along with one hundred or so objects that Swetnam had sold to collectors before the customs agents arrived. These customers, among them an American Nobel laureate in physics, surrendered their expensive purchases for the most pragmatic of reasons—to avoid prosecution. □

Funereal Bones and Baubles

When the Spanish conquistadors scoured Mexico for gold in the sixteenth century, they overlooked an extraordinary hoard in Monte Albán, an ancient city perched above a lush valley in what is now the state of Oaxaca. There, a number of nobles of the Mixtec tribe had been buried amidst a king's ransom in gold, silver, pearls, turquoise, and jade.

When the nobles' cavernous tomb was opened during an archaeological dig in 1932, the first man to enter gasped aloud at what his flashlight picked out in the gloom. A mosaic of pearls, gold beads, and small flat pieces of turquoise shimmered on the floor, and gold and silver gleamed among the human bones that were piled high in the tomb's center. The archaeologists carefully picked out of the grisly heap bells and loose beads and ornaments of all sorts. From one arm bone alone they removed six gold bracelets and four silver ones. There were elaborate necklaces, many containing hundreds of beads, as well as opulent accouterments for warriors of high rank. One noble fighter had worn a diadem composed of a wide gold band and a large plume of beaten gold—a splendid variation on the red leather bands and eagle feathers worn by ordinary warriors. Another piece of warrior's equipment was an exquisite gold breastplate in the shape of a man's head and torso. Its owner wore a helmet shaped like a jaguar and crested

with finely detailed gold feathers.

Besides the profusion of silver and gold, the tomb was overflowing with ornaments and vessels of jet, rock crystal, jade, and amber—a lapidary tour de force. In addition to these priceless Mixtec grave goods, the tomb held evidence that the Mixtec nobles were not its first occupants.

Oddly enough, the tomb had been inhabited earlier by the Mixtec's traditional enemy, the Zapotec. It contained large stones carved with Zapotec hieroglyphics, and archaeologists dug up a few of the civilization's clay urns. Apparently, the Mixtec captured Monte Albán from their enemy and, unbothered by scruples or superstition, threw out the tomb's Zapotec contents, bones and all, to make way for their own dead. Whether they found Zapotec treasure equal to what they themselves placed in the tomb is a mystery. □

The dazzling gold breastplate of a Mixtec noble was cast in a number of pieces that were then soldered together.

Deadly Aztec Gold

The conquistador Hernán Cortés must have believed that he had found at last the New World's El Dorado: Before him stood Montezuma, emperor of the Aztecs, heaping up magnificent treasures of gold and silver, all tribute to Cortés's Spanish king. The emperor apologized that he had no more to give to Cortés and his captains, but the Spaniards were well pleased. In fact, they could hardly wait to fall upon the glittering piles and divide them up. They had in their hands a treasure so enormous that history has seldom seen its equal. Yet antiquarians have been able to identify with reasonable certainty only one piece that was once part of Montezuma's hoard—a thin, slightly curved gold bar about ten inches long, two inches wide, and almost half an inch thick. It is presently on display in Mexico's National Museum of Anthropology.

A construction worker discovered the bar in 1981 at a spot once covered by the lake, long since filled in, that surrounded Montezuma's capital of Tenochtitlán like a great moat. There, on a causeway that once spanned the lake, many Spaniards lost both their treasure and their lives during the night of June 30, 1520. In the four and a half centuries since then, an untold number of treasure hunters have searched the area that is now Mexico City, the metropolis that stands on the ruins of Tenochtitlán. But not one of them is known to have found the least scrap of gold or silver.

Had they found any, it would probably have been disappointingly utilitarian. The objects in the emperor's hoard are said to have been extraordinarily beautiful, but the Spaniards were interested not in aesthetics but in cold, hard bullion. At their command, goldsmiths melted down the treasure into compact, easily portable forms, such as the gold bar the construction worker found.

Despite Montezuma's peaceful acceptance of the foreigners, bloody conflict erupted in Tenochtitlán after the white men perfidiously put him under arrest. Deciding to take their spoils and abandon the city while they still could, the Spaniards waited for cover of night to make their way across the causeway connecting the island city to the mainland. Foot soldiers and officers alike stuffed their pockets and shirt fronts and rucksacks with gold and silver, tucked more under their helmets, and slung chains around their necks. The precious weight they carried slowed the army's progress, and three canals cut across the causeway slowed it still more. The plan had been to carry a single portable bridge to be placed in turn over each of the canals. But the weight of men and horses wedged the span so tightly between the walls of the first canal that no amount of tugging and prying could free it.

Like a gathering storm, a few arrows fell on the Spaniards stopping at the edge of the second canal. The lethal rain fell harder as the lake filled with canoes carrying bowmen summoned by Aztec sentinels who had spotted the fleeing Spaniards. Some of the invaders tried to swim for safety but were dragged down by their heavy booty.

So many bodies of the slain and the drowned piled up in the canals that they themselves became a bridge to safety for the remnants of the Spanish army. What came to be called the Night of Sorrow was followed by a dreadful retreat toward the Gulf of Mexico, where Cortés's ships waited. Many never made it, falling dead along the way of wounds or hunger.

The disastrous night scattered the treasure in a thousand directions. The triumphant Aztecs doubtless retrieved much of it from the dead who crowded the lake. Whatever they missed, though, may still lie buried in the ancient muck. Between Tenochtitlán and the Gulf Coast, some soldiers probably emptied their pockets of a fortune in gold that had become, literally, an unbearable burden. If lucky passersby did not pick every golden grain from every dead Spaniard's pocket or scoop up all of the rich spoils so despairingly cast off, fragments of an emperor's treasure may still trace the retreat like a fairy-tale trail of crumbs. □

SUNKEN TREASURE

Sunken ships and lost treasure are linked in legend, and with reason. The perilous trade routes of the Indies and the New World were strewn with the ships of traders and kings. Weather, shipboard hardships, treacherous crews, war, and piracy accounted for many shipwrecks. The seas claimed a large share of the gold, silver, gems, and other prizes that European merchants sought in the mysterious lands across the ocean. The stories of these sunken treasures are voluminous and rich. But, like fine fabrics, they are filmy and soft. Truth and fiction are their warp and weft, with fact and conjecture furnishing both texture and glitter. About one matter there is no question, however: There is treasure at the bottom of the sea, and for all that has been raised, still more beckons.

2

The Sinking of the *San José*

By the early eighteenth century, harrying rival fleets throughout the West Indies had become national policy among British naval vessels. So it was that Admiral Charles Wager sailed out from Jamaica one spring morning in 1708 aboard the seventy-gun HMS *Expedition*, accompanied by the warships *Kingston, Portland,* and *Vulture,* in search of Spanish plunder. Wager headed for the waters off present-day Colombia, where lay the century-old routes of the Spanish bullion trade—and where a new *flota*, or convoy, was preparing for the passage to Spain.

In Spain's colonial heyday, this was an annual affair, with untold tons of gold and silver from mines in Central and South America making their way to the coastal towns of Portobelo and Cartagena for shipment to the mother country. But the Spanish War of Succession had interrupted the once-heavy galleon traffic. Thus the seventeen-ship armada that commanded Wager's attention carried the first shipment of New World riches to be sent home in six years. The much-delayed load was especially large.

The king's treasure—his mandated 20 percent of all homebound riches—had been divided among four heavily armed warships: The flagship, or *capitana*, was named the *San José*; the second-in-command, or *almiranta*, was the *San Martín*; the names of the fleet's third galleon, or *gobierno*, and a somewhat smaller vessel called an *urca* are now lost. The other thirteen ships of the flota were lightly armed merchant vessels carrying passengers, private riches, and merchandise.

Near sunrise on Friday, May 28, British lookouts sighted the fluttering pennants of the treasure fleet, and Wager signaled pursuit. In the face of the quicker, better-armed attackers, most of the armada fled toward port, leaving the armed, treasure-laden warships to fight a rearguard action.

Wager ran down and fired on the *San José* and hit her. Acrid smoke billowed and blood flowed aboard the stricken ship; still, the Spaniards fought furiously for an hour, until a British shot exploded the *San José*'s powder magazine. The galleon sank in a thunderous blaze of flame. Wager then broadsided the *San Martín* and left her for disabled.

Wager's expedition dealt a blow to Spain's economy, but England's earnings from the venture were slight. The captured gobierno yielded a mere fourteen silver ingots and thirteen chests of pieces of eight. But the *San Martín* escaped. And the contents of the *San José*—estimated at between 7 million and 30 million pesos—went to the bottom of the sea. There it still rests, off the Colombian coast, perhaps the largest unrecovered treasure in the Western Hemisphere. Submerged with the riches are the bones of 589 seamen who perished that day.

Harking to eyewitness accounts, experts place the galleon's grave site somewhere in the waters off tiny Barú Island, southwest of Cartagena's harbor, possibly in the vicinity of a coral ledge appropriately called the Bancos del Tesoro—the Treasure Banks. □

In an eighteenth-century painting by Samuel Scott, the richly laden *San José* explodes during a battle with English warships off Cartagena.

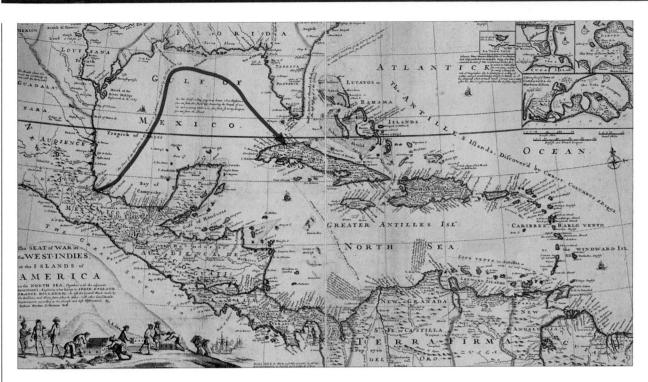

The Unlucky *Juno*

Tempests and contrary currents always made sailing between the New and Old Worlds a chancy affair, but the Spanish frigates *Anfitrite* and *Juno* encountered greater than usual troubles almost immediately on leaving harbor. They sailed from the Mexican port of Veracruz en route to Cádiz, Spain, on January 15, 1802, a day when storms strafed the Gulf of Mexico. Gales tattered the *Anfitrite*'s sails and rigging and yanked a mast from the *Juno*. The ships were forced to put in for repairs at San Juan, Puerto Rico, before daring the Atlantic depths.

While refurbishing was under way, word came that a Spanish troopship would soon arrive in Puerto Rico from Africa. The frigates were to rendezvous with it and transport soldiers, some traveling with wives and children, home to Spain. Although the trip from Africa to Spain via the Caribbean was long and indirect, the route was often used to avoid headwinds and strong currents running south along the African bulge.

On October 1, nearly ten months after leaving Veracruz, the frigates again set sail for Cádiz—this time crammed with one thousand passengers. Once more they encountered vicious storms. A week out, south of Bermuda, the two ships became separated and the *Anfitrite* sailed on. The *Juno*, captained by Don Juan Ignacio Bustillo, strayed northwest, bucking the swells.

Late on the night of October 22, the *Juno* sprang a leak. For the next five days, seamen frantically pumped, bailed, shifted cargo, dumped supplies, and caulked spreading cracks in the hull, striving to buoy the craft. An American schooner, the *Favorite*, had spied distress signals and was trying to escort the foundering *Juno* to shore. But the schooner lost her own mainsail and could only stand by helplessly as the frigate rode ever lower in the water. Shortly after midnight on October 27, the *Juno* sank in high winds.

Carried down with the 425 crew and passengers on board was the ship's primary cargo—ten tons of Mexican silver. Even today, hidden beneath a pile of ballast rock and cannon, the treasure awaits a finder. It lies east of Delaware Bay, near the edge of the Continental Shelf, perhaps in shallow water. □

The Graveyard of the Atlantic

Over the past four centuries, at least 697 ships have come to grief on North Carolina's Outer Banks, the two-hundred-mile ribbon of barrier islands that separates Pamlico Sound from the Atlantic Ocean. Spanish galleons, British frigates, American schooners—all have been snared by the shifting shoals and churning waters of the Banks, leading mariners to dub that stretch of coast the Graveyard of the Atlantic.

The Banks' treachery derives from their unique position, thrusting into the ocean where cold arctic currents collide with the north-flowing subtropical waters of the Gulf Stream. The clash breeds storms, fog, and riotous seas that can toss spume ten stories high.

Battered in an underwater maelstrom, the sands off the Banks constantly rearrange themselves. In heavy weather, the dread Lookout, Frying Pan, and Diamond shoals can waylay even savvy sailors. More than one hundred wrecks lie buried within twenty miles of Cape Hatteras lighthouse. Each testifies to the shoals' wickedness.

The first European explorer to chance the Banks was Giovanni da Verrazano, a Florentine seeking a route to the Orient in 1524. He escaped unscathed. But two years later, in June 1526, a brigantine carrying settlers to the Spanish colony of Chicora on the Cape Fear River was swallowed by the Banks. This tragedy was only the beginning. As the gold trade reached full flood and Spanish captains sought to speed their passage home by riding the Gulf Stream, more and more ships succumbed.

Ironically—perhaps because they had no choice—many who survived wrecks on the Outer Banks settled there, in the thickly vegetated hummocks that lay on the sheltered inland side of the dunes. Among live oaks, wax myrtle, and prickly pear, they built one-room houses and cultivated large gardens. The Bankers, as they were known, made their living fishing and, if the tales are true, did a brisk trade in a pursuit called wrecking. They reputedly lured ships to disaster by a variety of stratagems. Torches carried down the beach at night, for instance, might persuade a passing captain to draw nearer to what he supposed to be a fellow traveler. He would soon find himself aground, his ship stranded and pillaged.

The Bankers' bad reputation stemmed in part from the exploits of miscreants such as Stede Bonnet, Calico Jack Rackham, and Edward Teach, also known as Blackbeard. In the eighteenth century, these colorful scoundrels discovered that the islands made perfect blinds for their piratical forays. However, most Bankers probably engaged in brigandage infrequently—if only because the Banks provided a steady supply of salvage from ships that foundered at the unaided hand of nature.

Today, skeletal hulks and tilting spars litter the beaches and surf line, while countless other wrecks, undocumented and uncharted, haunt the shifting sands. After storms, beachcombers may find pottery shards and bits of glass, worn timbers, brass fittings, and sometimes even coins—small tokens of lost fortunes entombed in the Graveyard of the Atlantic. □

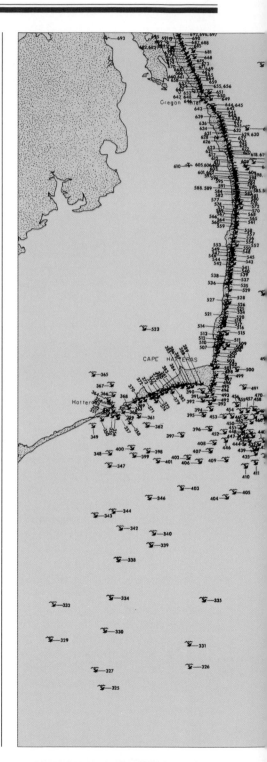

Shipwrecks charted by Duke University's Marine Laboratory thickly line Cape Hatteras on North Carolina's Outer Banks. This map shows the location of 373 of the 697 ships that sank off the Outer Banks between 1526 and 1945.

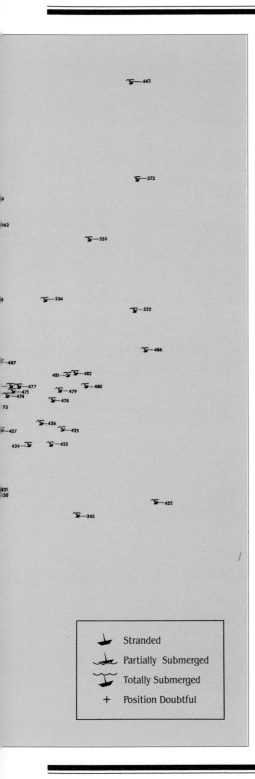

Stranded

Partially Submerged

Totally Submerged

+   Position Doubtful

The Settlers' Revenge

In one hurricane alone, three ships carrying New World gold to Spain sank just off North Carolina's Outer Banks, where at least some of their treasure still lies.

Normally, the New Spain convoys set out only in springtime, well before hurricane season. But in 1750, the *flota* was delayed in Veracruz by illness among the sailors. It was not ready to head north from Havana, the customary last stop before the long voyage to Spain, until August—the start of the hurricane season. Led by the *Nuestra Señora de Guadalupe,* the armada slipped through the Straits of Florida without mishap. But as the days passed, warning signs appeared. The seas began a queasy heaving, and the wind rose ominously. A gale racked the ships, and the convoy was blown far off course into the vicinity of Cape Fear, North Carolina. The hurricane drove the hapless vessels before it, scattering them along three hundred miles of seacoast.

The first to go down was *El Salvador,* a galleon that was smashed in the surf of Topsail Inlet west of Cape Lookout near present-day Beaufort. Four survivors struggled out of the surf, leaving behind a cargo of guns, silver, balsam, cocoa, and cochineal, the insect carcasses used to make scarlet dye. According to a duplicate of the flota's registry that had been placed on another ship for safekeeping, *El Salvador* carried twenty chests of gold and silver coins. But captains and crew routinely smuggled undeclared treasure into Spain, thus avoiding the 20 percent tax—the *quinto*—levied on all New World findings. Shipwreck scholars suspect that *El Salvador* may have been ferrying private treasure worth twice as much as the official tally. Some estimates place the total value of the cargo at almost one billion dollars.

The *Soledad* foundered farther north at Drum Inlet. A few officers and crewmen survived. The ship herself remained above water long enough for an anonymous sloop to scavenge some chests of money, to the chagrin of part owner Don José de Respral Deza. However, nature took more of the don's wealth, for soon the *Soledad* vanished into the sands. There were thirty-two thousand registered pieces of eight aboard, and an undetermined amount of contraband coin as well.

The *Nuestra Señora de Guadalupe,* captained by her part owner, Don Juan Manuel de Bonilla, stumbled into Ocracoke Inlet with one mast remaining and her crew desperately pumping to keep her afloat. Sheltered there, Bonilla at first hoped to mend his wounded ship and continue. The *Guadalupe* soon settled in twenty feet of water, however, and the Spanish crew, with help from local men, began transferring onto shore a cache of jewels, gold, and silver.

For the locals, the memory of Spanish marauders soon outweighed their altruism. Three years earlier, Spaniards had invaded the Outer Banks and, lore has it, killed several settlers, burned homes, and slaughtered livestock. Now, the residents retaliated by absconding with part of the treasure taken from the ship. Whatever remained on board, perhaps including jewelry and silver, still rests in the sands of Ocracoke Inlet. □

The Sacred Mirror of the Inca

Lake Titicaca in Peru, at 12,500 feet the world's highest lake, was the cradle of civilization for the ancient and mysterious Inca. Buried in its muddy depths, some say, is a burnished golden disk, etched with the sacred image of the sun.

In 1553, the conquistador Francisco Pizarro and his Spanish troops captured and killed the Incan leader Atahuallpa and pillaged the Coricancha, or Golden Enclosure, in Cuzco. This complex of buildings guarded a central preserve called the Intipampa—the Square of the Sun. There a sacred golden solar image was placed so that, mirrorlike, it reflected the rays of the rising sun. Wrenched from its place, this holy disk was awarded by Pizarro to his henchman Mancho Serra de Leguicamo.

The story of the sun mirror appears in Spanish chronicles written shortly after Pizarro's conquest of the Inca. The accounts blend fact and legend, romance and reality, so that the truth of the tale of Pizarro's gift is murkier than the mud in which the disk may lie. One version has it that the next evening after receiving the treasure, the imprudent de Leguicamo gambled away a share of his prize in an all-night dice game with a horseman, Pedro de Barca. De Barca, for his part, had fallen in love with the Incan princess Toyllor-Tica and at her behest had set out to win back the disk.

The lovers absconded with the mirror during a break in the game and headed south with fifty Incan priests, the story goes. Spanish pursuers overtook them on the shores of Titicaca just as the disk was being rafted to a small island. In the ensuing melee, the priests, the princess, and her lover were slaughtered and the balsa pontoons that supported the mirror were shattered. The treasure sank.

If the tale of cupidity and intrigue is to be believed, the disk now lies within easy reach of shore; a metal detector, scuba gear, and luck are all that would be needed to restore the sacred disk to the light of the sun. □

The Golden Enclosure, located at the left in this fanciful picture of Cuzco by Theodor DeBry, supposedly housed the legendary Incan sun mirror captured by Francisco Pizarro, painted at left by a sixteenth-century artist.

The Wreck of a Royal *Capitana*

Operating with sketchy knowledge of routes and coastlines, Spanish pilots led many a ship astray, often with disastrous results. On one notable occasion in 1654, an error in navigational judgment cost King Philip IV at least three million pesos' worth of treasure from the mines of the vast Peru viceroyalty, which comprised the present-day states of Peru, Chile, Bolivia, and Ecuador.

On October 18 of that year, a newly built galleon, the pride of the Pacific fleet, hove out of Callao, Peru, captained by Don Francisco de Sossa. The name is now lost, but this ship held the place of honor as the *capitana*, the lead vessel in the convoy ferrying the year's output of silver from the viceroyalty to the southern coast of Panama. From there, the riches were to be hauled overland to Portobelo and sent on to Spain via Cartagena and Havana.

After leaving Callao late in the day trailed by another galleon—the second-in-command, or *almiranta*—and a tender boat, the convoy pursued a north-northwesterly course along the coast. Six days into the trip, the pilot, believing he had cleared the thrusting prong of Punta Santa Elena on the Ecuadorian coast, swung toward the east to make for Panama. He had, however, mistaken his position. About midnight on October 25, a lookout aboard the capitana cried, "Breakers ahead!" Crewmen sprang from their berths to find them-

selves rudderless, their ship caught on the rocks in Chanduy Bay along the northern reach of the Gulf of Guayaquil. The almiranta, warned by shots from its stranded companion, strove to turn back, but it, too, had touched bottom. To avoid further damage, the prudent captain chose to anchor until daylight, when the full scope of the situation could be assessed.

The next morning the almiranta was able to slip into open waters, relatively unharmed. But the capitana's dilemma appeared hopeless. Half the hull had been ripped away, and water had risen five feet in the hold. Hastily, Captain de Sossa instructed his men to cut down several masts and lash them together with rigging so that at least part of the silver in the upper hold could be rafted to shore.

Later that day, de Sossa went back to the galleon and succeeded in rigging a sail on the bowsprit, enabling him to engineer a move off the rocks and into a channel a mile off the beach. Otherwise helpless to assist, the almiranta had gone on to the next port to spread word of the capitana's plight.

Divers flocked to Chanduy Bay from the pearl beds of Panama and from Peru. Under the direction of the tenacious de Sossa, they and the crew spent the next several months retrieving as much of the cargo as possible, at times hacking and burning away the ship's hull to reach the holds. By the end of the year, de Sossa recorded in his log an impressive list of items pulled from the drowned ship, including 390 large silver ingots, 975 boxes of merchandise, 160 boxes of pieces of eight, and 28 boxes of worked silver. All this he dutifully sent on to Portobelo for shipment to Spain.

Roughly half the original cargo was recovered. The rest—with a value of as much as five million dollars—lies in the sands off Ecuador. According to a 1656 report by an Ecuadorian attorney general, the capitana "finally settled in four and one half fathoms near a small bay in the form of a horseshoe" near the fateful Punta Santa Elena. □

The Lost Manila Galleons

The Pacific Ocean was undoubtedly the most arduous and dangerous water that early sailing ships undertook to cross. Yet for 250 years, from 1565 to 1815, galleons of the Manila trade plied the vast gulf between America and Asia, ferrying riches from port to port.

Roomier than the ships that sailed the Caribbean, the unwieldy Pacific vessels each carried from 1,200 to 2,000 tons of cargo. Some two-thirds of the capacity was devoted to treasure and merchandise. From the Americas came silver pesos, iron, wines, and millinery. From the Orient flowed spices, pearls, gold jewelry, ivory, jade, amber, silks, tea, porcelains, and lacquerware.

The center of this trade was the Philippine city of Manila, the Pearl of the Orient. Merchants came to this hub from China, Japan, Thailand, Indonesia, and India, eager for commerce with Acapulco, the major Pacific port of Spain's American colonies.

The richness of commerce between the two cities encouraged smuggling, and smuggling meant overloading the awkward galleons. The result was that dozens of the cumbersome treasure ships, each bearing at least two million dollars' worth of exotic goods, ended up at the bottom of the Pacific. The ships' captains were often responsible for their own demise. Shoving in more and more goods—including considerable contraband—the greedy officers not only overloaded their ships, but also, at times, reduced their stores of food and water.

Most of the lost galleons perished during the eastward crossing. The westward Manila-bound journey took a mere three months, thanks to favorable currents and prevailing winds. But the return to Mexico averaged six months and could take a year—every day marked by battles against opposing currents and contrary winds. If sailors survived the elements, they might die from scurvy or other ailments caused by a lack of drinking water and proper food. Even after pilots found a more favorable course around the Hawaiian Islands and down the American coast late in the sixteenth century, a trip aboard a Manila galleon remained a grim gamble that might end in death.

Most of the vessels lost in the Manila trade vanished without a trace, their whereabouts when they sank probably unknown even to their crews. But unlike Caribbean ships, many of which carried only perishable trade goods, the Manila galleons were always laden with durable precious metals and jewels, scattering the Pacific routes with millions of dollars' worth of exotic treasures from the East. □

The Spanish sailing routes through the Philippine Islands are superimposed on a 1734 sailing chart drawn by the Jesuit cartographer Pedro Murillo Velarde. Manila lies near the ship's figure in the left center of the chart.

Shown here against a background of Asian pearls, a painting by the seventeenth-century Dutch artist Johannes Vingbooms depicts the harbor of Acapulco in Mexico, through which the riches of the Orient were shipped on their way from Manila to Spain.

Greed Kills

One of the Manila galleons that sank from being crammed beyond capacity was the *Santa Maria Madalena.* In 1734, she sailed from Manila so heavily saddled with badly arranged cargo that she capsized just after leaving her mooring. A ship of nearly two thousand tons, she must have carried considerable treasure. Even so, there is no record of any attempts to relieve the *Santa Maria Madalena* of her bounty, despite her accessibility and well-documented position. □

A Treasure Ignored

By the end of the eighteenth century, Spain had lost most of her New World colonies, and the logistics of the Philippines trade changed. Now, ships could transport goods directly from Manila to Spain over a westward route, across the Indian Ocean and around the Cape of Good Hope at the southern tip of Africa. In these less familiar waters, a number of ships faltered.

In 1802, a commercial ship making the trip failed to reach Spain. And, although most of her crew survived to give an accurate account of her location, no attempt was made to retrieve her cargo of gold and silver. The *Ferroleña,* a clumsy cargo vessel of a type called an *urca,* left Manila in early September, heading along the southern coast of China. Less than two weeks later, on the night of the fifteenth, a typhoon battered the *Ferroleña* onto the Cauchi Reefs about one hundred miles north of Hong Kong, smashing it to bits and spilling its treasure onto the shallow rocks.

Twenty-nine crewmen perished, but 150 others swam to shore. Protected from the predations of local thieves by a troop of Chinese soldiers, the survivors were soon picked up by an English ship.

Despite the speedy rescue, the question of what to do about the *Ferroleña's* lost cargo, including 850,000 silver pesos, seems never to have been addressed. Apparently, the urca's entire cargo sits just offshore in the rocky Chinese waters. □

Bobadilla's Nugget

In 1502 on the island of Hispaniola, an Indian girl found a huge gold nugget in a stream. Apparently, it had washed down from the nearby Nuevas mines, a lode thirty miles north of the colonial capital city of Santo Domingo. According to a contemporary account by the friar Bartolomé de Las Casas, the girl presented the nugget—a thirty-five-pound treasure—to her Spanish masters, Francisco de Garay and Miguel Diaz.

The Spaniards "celebrated the discovery by roasting a suckling pig," according to Las Casas. "They carved and ate, all the while imagining a gold platter so fine that kings themselves had not the like of it."

That dream was never realized, however, for Hispaniola's cruel and mercenary governor, Francisco de Bobadilla, soon learned of the find, and he promptly bought the nugget. Shortly thereafter, Bobadilla was recalled to Spain. He set out with the nugget and about 200,000 pesos in gold, taking a place on the *Santa Maria de la Antigua*, flagship of a fleet of thirty-two caravels.

The fleet put to sea in early July, against the advice of Christopher Columbus, who happened to be in port on his final visit to the New World and warned that a hurricane was imminent. Bobadilla, who had arrested Columbus two years earlier on trumped-up charges of disloyalty, disdained the sailor's advice, proving anew two facts well known in their day: Columbus was a canny weatherman, and Bobadilla was an arrogant fool.

Four days later, a hurricane smashed across the Antilles, destroying twenty-seven ships, including the *Santa Maria de la Antigua*. The scourge of Hispaniola died, unlamented, along with five hundred other victims. Together with the rest of Bobadilla's hoard, the nugget, which Las Casas claimed was "as big as the bread loaves they make in Alcalá and Seville," went down in Mona Passage, between present-day Puerto Rico and the Dominican Republic.

The treasure lost with the fleet is valued today at more than $3 million. As if that were not bait enough for generations of treasure bugs, the legend of Bobadilla's riches has become so inflated that the 35-pound nugget that surely existed has grown into a fabled—but illusory—3,300-pound solid gold table, a piece of furniture that, if it were real, would fetch some $15 billion. □

A Treasure Forbidden

In 1656, England and Spain were once more engaged in their on-again, off-again military tug of war for mastery of the seas. Thus in September, as Spanish galleons bearing riches from South America neared their destination port of Cádiz, an English squadron led by Captain Richard Stainer attacked.

The evenly matched sides exchanged volley for volley, each suffering numerous hits. But when the smoke cleared, Stainer had captured two ships and sunk two more, allowing only three to escape. One of the naval prizes yielded a disappointing store of hides and sugar. But the other gave up forty-five tons of gold and silver, packed among dishes, basins, candlesticks, and other homebound Spanish housewares.

The ships that sank carried a similarly bounteous lode, including 1.7 million pieces of eight and the personal effects of the viceroy of Peru, who was returning home with jewels, gold and silver plates, and precious chalices. The Spaniards valued the total loss at nine million pesos.

Virtually every item aboard the lost ships is cataloged in Spain's Archives of the Indies in Seville. The Spanish government has never permitted private salvage of the 1656 fleet or any other wrecks that lie within Spain's territorial waters. So the fleet's bounty lies untouched, even though it rests within a few miles of shore, fully accessible to divers with modern equipment. □

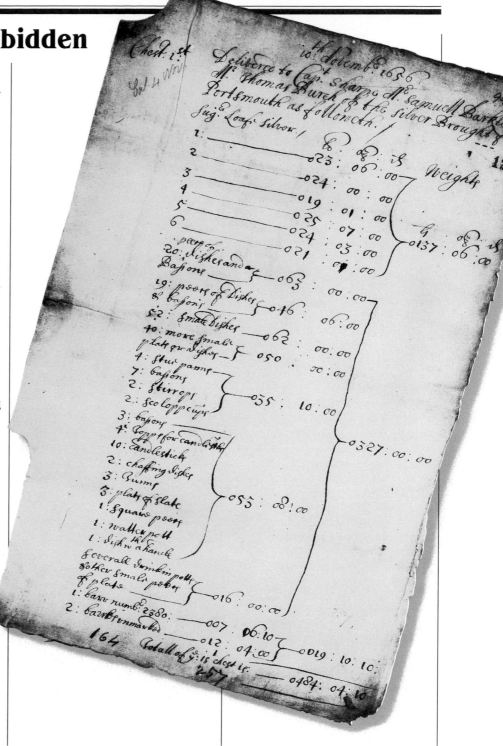

The Pride of the Portuguese

As the Spaniards sailed westward to assert their rule over the Atlantic and the Pacific, their neighbors in Europe, the Portuguese, struck eastward to lay claim to the Indian Ocean and the Asiatic fringe of the Pacific. The Portuguese targets were the Moluccas, or Spice Islands, and the mainland of India, with their tropical foodstuffs, fabrics, gems, and other exotica. Portugal established far-flung military and trading bases in Goa on the west coast of India, in Malacca in Malaya, in Macao in south China, and in the Moluccas, which are now part of Indonesia.

Among the point men for this enterprise was Alfonso de Albuquerque, the second viceroy of India, who rapidly hardened the Portuguese hold over southern India, Malaya, and the Moluccas. In 1512, Albuquerque set sail from Malacca for Goa with a fleet of two worm-eaten galleons and a junk, bringing with him a group of Javanese carpenters and their families. His flagship, the *Flor do Mar*, was stuffed with elaborate woodwork, brocades, great amounts of gold jewelry, precious stones, and gold-plated palanquins that had once carried the king of Malacca. In his travels, Albuquerque had also obtained a gold-inlaid table and life-size statues of animals that had guarded the sepulchers of Malaccan rulers.

Albuquerque's tightly formed flotilla made its way past many of the coast's dangerous shoals, but when a storm struck off the coast of Sumatra, the *Flor do Mar* ran aground in shallows and broke in half. After a harrowing rescue operation that saved the crew but left the Javanese to perish, Albuquerque and the other survivors continued to Goa aboard the second galleon, the *Trindade*. Amid the confusion of events, all but four Portuguese sailors on board the convoy's junk were slaughtered by mutinous Javanese shipmates, who had been impressed into service in the first place.

The *Flor do Mar* is deemed by some modern authorities to be the richest wreck in history. The Malaysian government, in announcing in 1988 that it had located this unparalleled trophy in the Strait of Malacca, put the worth of the cargo at three billion dollars.

Some have attributed the wreck's value to the Malaccan funereal statues, which, according to many accounts, were made of solid gold. But if Albuquerque's fortune is ever pulled dripping from the ocean, there may be many disappointed salvagers: Contemporary documents disclose that the animals were mere iron. □

Gesturing with the authority of his office, Alfonso de Albuquerque, Portugal's second viceroy of India, is depicted in a seventeenth-century painting.

This rendering of the murder of *Batavia* survivors was part of the "Unlucky Voyage," a Dutch periodical's account that was published two decades after the ship sank.

The Ordeal of the *Batavia*

In the early seventeenth century, Dutch merchants decided to claim their share of riches from the new-found East and formed the Dutch United East India Company. The firm concentrated on the trade in pepper and ginger from Sumatra, cinnamon from Ceylon, camphor from Borneo, cloves from the Moluccas, and silks from China, as well as other spices and luxuries.

The doughty Dutch plied the seas from Africa to the South Pacific, unfazed by the hazards of long-distance shipping. The annual loss of roughly one out of ten of their ships was simply a cost of doing business. But the wreck of the *Batavia* was a tragedy beyond any accountant's reckoning.

The 300-ton flagship, carrying twelve chests of silver coins for trade with the islands, led a convoy from Holland in October 1628. On rounding southern Africa, the *Batavia* became separated from the rest of the convoy and struck out alone across the Indian Ocean.

The intention of the captain, Francis Pelsaert, was to sail almost to Australia before turning north to Java. However, before dawn on June 4, 1629, the *Batavia* smashed into the Abrolhos Islands, a dangerous fifty-mile stretch of reefs and barren islets lying forty miles west of Australia's coast.

Of the 300 passengers on board the *Batavia*, 250 people made it to a nearby island with twenty crates of bread and two small casks of drinking water. Captain Pelsaert and a few crewmen then set sail in two small boats to attempt a 2,000-mile journey to Java for help. The barren, unpopulated Australian continent offered no relief. The voyage required a month. Three days after landing in Java, Pelsaert boarded the frigate *Saardam* and headed south to rescue his marooned shipmates.

In the meantime, a troublesome crewman named Jerome Cornelisz roused a band of thugs, drunks, and peasants from among his companions and killed 125 of the remaining passengers. A few of them, including battle-hardened soldiers loyal to the company, escaped to another island, where they repulsed repeated attacks by the murderous hooligans.

When Pelsaert reached the Abrolhos in the *Saardam* on September 16, he executed the mutineers, then began a salvage operation. He raised ten of the twelve chests of silver from the wreck of the *Batavia*, then sailed with the survivors for Java.

The *Batavia* was forgotten until 1963, when an Australian crayfisherman spotted one of her cannon through the pellucid waters while setting out his pots. This brass relic and, later, four more cannon made of bronze, were recovered, together with coins and clay pipes. Also retrieved were some rare navigational instruments, including a brass astrolabe. One expedition discovered the skeletons of Cornelisz's victims, buried in shallow graves on one of the islands.

Still hidden on the seafloor are two more chests full of silver, probably pinned beneath another of the *Batavia*'s cannon. □

Brotherhood of the Coast

Along the wild Coco River, which tumbles out of the mountains to form the border of Honduras and Nicaragua, it is said that a fortunate searcher may find pearls, pieces of eight, diamonds, and gold. The valuables were strewn there in the course of the ruination of a band of seventeenth-century adventurers.

In those days, fortune hunters and scoundrels came from all over Europe seeking wealth in the New World. Those who roamed Central America pillaging, gambling, and fighting were known as *filibusteros*—a word that meant freebooters. Others called them buccaneers, or worse. They called themselves the Brotherhood of the Coast. For many months in 1687, one gang of nearly five hundred freebooters pursued plunder along Central America's Pacific coast. Then, toward the end of the year, the filibusteros headed back across the isthmus toward the Caribbean. They carried some of their booty in packs and trailed a string of horses bearing heavier loads. Ravenau de Lussan, a member of the group who later chronicled its activities, reported that each of its members had 3,780 pesos' worth of gold and precious stones.

After more than three weeks on the march, the tired and hungry freebooters reached the Coco River and decided to chance its rapids in small boats to speed their return to the coast. Drowning and starvation took a heavy toll until, on March 9, 1688, an enfeebled band of survivors drifted into the Caribbean at Cabo Gracias a Dios.

In the face of their jungle hardships, few of the buccaneers had been able to hold onto their treasure. Most had lost sacks of booty in the Coco's turbulent waters. If de Lussan's account can be believed, some $100 million worth of treasure may still gleam among the stones of the river. □

Beset by hostile natives and nature, Ravenau de Lussan and his fellow buccaneers battle the rapids of the Coco River during their flight to the Caribbean in an engraving by Maurice Besson.

The Wounds of the *Chagas*

The Portuguese carrack, able to carry as much as two thousand tons of cargo and seven hundred passengers and crew, was the supertanker of its day. Often heavily fortified, with towering poop decks and many-tiered forecastles, these ungainly floating warehouses afforded maximum protection to enormous cargoes of riches bound for Europe from the Orient.

One such vessel was the twelve-hundred-ton *Las Cinque Chagas,* a dolorous ship right down to her name: *Las cinque chagas* is Portuguese for "the five wounds," a reference to the wounds of the crucified Christ. The *Chagas* sailed for Lisbon from Goa in 1593, overloaded with one thousand passengers and one thousand tons of the most precious cargo to leave an eastern port: rubies, diamonds, pearls, ivory, perfume, drugs, porcelain, carpets, ornaments, silks, spices, coins, and ingots of silver and gold. Even the seamen, it was said, had private stashes of jewels.

After crossing the Indian Ocean, the *Chagas* wintered in Mozambique. Stuffed too full already, she nevertheless took on extra stores of gold and a consignment of slaves. Soon after leaving port, the ship was becalmed. During the lull, an epidemic arose that killed half the souls on board.

This was only the first misfortune to befall the wallowing carrack. Stores had been seriously depleted, and both passengers and crew persuaded the captain to stop in the Azores for fresh supplies. He agreed only reluctantly, however, for the region was thick with English privateers.

The *Chagas* almost made it to safety. But as she neared the islands of Pico and Fayal, three British privateers descended—the *Royal Exchange,* the *Mayflower,* and the *Sampson.* The burdened *Chagas* made a futile run for the nearest safe port, one hundred miles away. The speedier British soon caught up, and by the next morning she was under fire from all three attackers. The shelling lasted for six hours. Thinned by death and sickness to a mere seventy of its original four hundred, the Portuguese crew fought on. *Chagas* sailors rained down missiles from the superior heights of the carrack's bow and stern, fending off boarding parties from both the *Royal Exchange* and the *Mayflower.* The carnage was terrible. Eventually, passengers began leaping into the sea, hoping to fare better there than on the besieged decks, which had been torched by the British.

The battle still raged among the flames when, at noon, the *Chagas* exploded and sank, sending hull and treasure to the bottom. The human devastation, too, was nearly complete: Of the one thousand who had left Goa aboard the ship, thirteen survived.

The last known position of the *Chagas,* taken on the afternoon of June 13, 1594, was eighteen miles south of the channel dividing Pico and Fayal islands. Thirty-nine hours later, she was probably attacked just off Fayal. The seafloor slopes steeply away from the volcanic Azores, so *Las Cinque Chagas* could lie in water as deep as twenty-five hundred feet. Treasure hunters suspect the wreck sits on the brink of a canyon bordering the Fayal reef, but no one has mounted a serious salvage effort, leaving to others an immense collection of East Indian wealth. □

Tragedy and Treasure

In the imagination of the time, the 1782 wreck of *Grosvenor* and the subsequent ordeal of its passengers figured large. A testament to the dangers of the sea, the disaster also embodied primordial fears of being cast up on alien shores—a terror that ran deep in the consciousness of expansionist Europe.

Owned by the East India Company, the *Grosvenor* began its fateful journey in Madras, India. The 729-ton merchantman made a stop in Trincomalee, Ceylon, and was scheduled to call at Cape Town before going on to the Gold Coast of Africa on her way to Britain.

John Coxon, the *Grosvenor's* captain, was well liked but lacking in both vigilance and judgment—shortcomings that would prove fatal to most of his 149 passengers and crew. Coxon's abilities were tested on the night of August 4, as the ship sailed into a mounting storm off the coast of present-day South Africa, 500 miles from Cape Town. Believing that his craft was safely running more than 250 miles from land, the captain retired. He awoke to the alarms of lookouts, who had spied the terrifying apparition of seas breaking on a nearby shore. There was no time for evasion; the sighting was followed almost immediately by a sickening grinding as the ship struck a reef.

Held above the raging seas by the rocks, the ship did not begin taking on water at once, and Coxon hoped that by cutting down the mainmast he could lighten the ship and sail free of the reef. But as the wind grew fiercer, even this desperate tactic failed. Water poured into the battered hull.

Viewing the *Grosvenor's* plight from the shore was a group of natives, who helped sailors secure a thick hawser as a lifeline from ship to shore—a line carried by ⟩

A dramatic engraving shows the *Grosvenor's* survivors trying to make their way to shore *(above, right)* along a hawser stretched from the sinking ship.

crewmen who bravely swam through the roaring surf. It was a vain, desperate effort, however: The punishing surf overpowered all but a few of the two dozen passengers who tried this route to safety. Soon the ship cracked in two. The stern section was flung toward shore, bearing with it most of the women and children. After a fearful ordeal in the waves, they were able to wade to safety. The ship's other end veered seaward and sank.

For most of the 123 survivors, the nightmare in the waves was only the prelude to weeks of torture and eventual death on land—the harsh land of Africa. Coxon led the stunned party into the interior, expecting a difficult but bearable march to some Dutch settlement. He guessed it would take no more than two weeks to reach safety. The captain and the travelers were ignorant of the country and its people, however; they alienated natives who might have helped them, and they were constantly harassed.

Then Coxon divided the exhausted and demoralized band, sending the stronger members forward and leaving the enfeebled stragglers to the mercy of the land. Nearly four months after the wreck, six sailors stumbled into a Dutch settlement three hundred miles east of Cape Town. A search party then found ten more sailors and two passengers alive. The rest of the wreck survivors, 105 including Coxon, were never heard from again.

As the story of the *Grosvenor* and its survivors spread, the purported size and value of the ship's cargo grew apace until, in the feverish minds of believers, the ship had supposedly borne untold riches in jewels, silver, and gold bars, and a gem-encrusted "Peacock Throne" once used by Mogul kings.

In fact, the *Grosvenor* probably carried only a modest consignment of silver, gold, and gemstones belonging to the East India Company and the passengers. Whatever its value, the cargo lies within sight of the coast, its location known exactly. Nevertheless, numerous salvage attempts have failed to recover more than a few cannon and coins. Today, the most visible reminder of the *Grosvenor*'s end is a roadside sign marking the site of the tragedy and alerting travelers to the wealth that might lie in the swirling currents and sands, so tantalizingly close to shore. □

For Whom the Bell Tolls

Tradition is the byword of Lloyd's of London, the famed insurers. Even today, in the age of computerized probabilities and satellite communications, one anachronistic maritime ritual is regularly played out at Lloyd's headquarters on Lime Street. When a great loss occurs or other bad news breaks, the bell of the *Lutine* is struck once. When the news is good, the bell rings twice.

Originally in the service of the French, the thirty-two-gun frigate *Lutine* was captured by the British in 1793. Six years later, while the king of England waged war against the Dutch, the frigate was dispatched to Hamburg with a cargo of coin and bullion worth £1.2 million. The money would secure credit for British merchants from banks on the Continent.

But the mission failed when the ship was overwhelmed in a gale on the night of October 9. Blown far off course onto the sandy shoals near Terschelling, one of five barrier islands at the mouth of the Zuider Zee, the *Lutine* sank. All hands were lost. Lloyd's sent agents to the scene, for its underwriters had issued a policy on the bulk of the cargo. The insurer settled the claim. And, as is customary, the company assumed rights to the wreck. So did Dutch fishermen and adventurers, who made a habit of poking through the remains when the ship was exposed at ebb tide. A few carried away bars of gold and silver, or coins of French, Spanish, or English mint.

But large-scale salvage attempts were hampered by drifting sands.

By the middle of the nineteenth century, the *Lutine*'s skeleton lay beneath twenty feet of silt. Nevertheless, in 1859 the ship's bell, identified by the royal insignia of the Bourbon family, in whose behalf the *Lutine* once sailed, was raised and enshrined in the offices of Lloyd's.

The custom soon began of tolling the bell once when a ship was reported lost, and twice when an overdue ship reached port. The practice has altered somewhat: Today, the bell tolls not only for ships, but to mark events, good or bad, that have unusual importance for Lloyd's or Britain. But in Lloyd's modern steel-and-glass headquarters, the old observance persists; the pealing bell chronicles the fate of ships.

The *Lutine*, too, persists, lying with most of her cargo beneath the changeable sands off the wind-whipped coast of the Netherlands. □

The brass bell of the *Lutine (top of page)* and Frank Mason's painting of the ship on its final voyage both hang in the offices of Lloyd's of London. Company tradition dictates that the ship's bell is rung once to signal bad news, twice to herald good news.

The Admiral Nakhimov

In the two-year-long Russo-Japanese War, the relatively small island nation proved its naval might against the forces of the Great Bear. First, the Japanese wasted the Russian Pacific Fleet. Then they dispatched the ships of the Baltic Fleet that Czar Nicholas II had sent to restore Russian hegemony.

In the spectacular Battle of Tsushima, on May 27 and 28, 1905, the Japanese outmaneuvered and outfired a Russian fleet steaming toward the Sea of Japan from the East China Sea. Although the Russian ships outnumbered Japan's, the encounter was not much of a contest. In an overnight engagement, the Japanese sank seventeen vessels, including six battleships, and captured five others. Among the casualties was the cruiser *Admiral Nakhimov,* which vainly attempted to scoot away early in the battle.

Far from being a cowardly act, the *Nakhimov*'s flight was prudent and obedient. The warship was carrying £50 million worth of British gold sovereigns secured by the czar to refill his depleted war chest. The money had been raised in Europe, then shipped home with Russia's Second Pacific Squadron, of which the *Nakhimov* was a part. When the battle was joined, the cruiser's commander, a Captain

Ruitoff, hoped to save his cargo from capture by slipping away amid the smoke and confusion.

However, the ship suffered two torpedo hits. The crew was rescued by other Russian ships, and the *Nakhimov* was scuttled near the Japanese island of Tsushima on Ruitoff's orders. He later wrote to the czar, "I sank the things which I was bringing to you in fifty fathoms of sea, and they can never be utilized by the enemy."

As is often the case, "never" was an ill-chosen word. In 1980, over Soviet protests, the Japanese declared the *Nakhimov* a spoil of war and granted salvage rights to an eccentric octogenarian shipbuilder named Ryoichi Sasagawa. He estimated that the treasure would be worth $35 billion—a wildly opti-

An unidentified warship steams between falling shells, sinking ships, and lifeboats in a contemporary artist's portrayal of the 1905 Battle of Tsushima. Seventeen Russian ships were sunk, including the treasure-laden Russian cruiser *Admiral Nakhimov.*

mistic guess. Sasagawa's team pulled up mostly junk. Hope of riches arose when ingots thought to be platinum were raised from the deep. The metal proved to be mere dross, however, part of the ship's ballast. The gold remains on the bottom, and the Japanese government persists in claiming as its own any eventual haul. □

Bargain Booty

Some scheme to find rich wrecks. Some scour ancient shipping lanes or pore over archaic documents. Others simply buy their treasure at auction.

In March of 1989, the U.S. Maritime Administration auctioned off 750 boxes filled with three million Saudi Arabian silver riyals and an unspecified amount of silver bullion. The winning bid, submitted by Hugh O'Neill and Brian Shoemaker of Washington, D.C., was a mere $50,010, plus 10 percent of the fortune, to be paid when and if the buyers retrieve it.

Not surprisingly, the bargain booty carries a hidden price tag. It is held fast in the hold of a World War II American freighter, the SS *John Barry*, lying one thousand fathoms below the surface of the Arabian Sea.

The silver was part of a shipment of money and matériel making its way to Russia when the *Barry* was torpedoed by a German submarine on August 28, 1944. □

Corregidor Pesos

General Douglas MacArthur's flight from Corregidor, the tiny Philippine island lodged at the mouth of Manila Bay, marked a low point in the Allies' battle for the Pacific in World War II. As the Philippines prepared for inevitable occupation by Japanese soldiers in the spring of 1942, a small team of men rushed under cover of darkness to prevent a vast store of silver from falling into enemy hands.

For more than three hundred years after Spanish galleons began plying the Eastern trade routes, the Filipino economy had been based on the silver Mexican peso. But when the United States gained ascendancy over the archipelago at the beginning of the twentieth century, the government there gradually shifted to paper currency and stockpiled the silver coins, together with gold from the Philippine treasury. All the wealth was placed in a reinforced concrete bunker on Corregidor.

Shortly after the attack on Pearl Harbor, U.S. Army Major General George F. Moore realized that the treasury on Corregidor was in jeopardy and took steps to move the money elsewhere. Twenty tons of gold and silver were taken to Hawaii aboard the submarine *Trout*. Japan's fleet moved quickly, however, preventing further evacuation of either men or treasury. Moore therefore ordered the Philippine silver to be dumped just south of the island in a one-hundred-foot-

The cave-riddled island of Corregidor *(background)* was photographed from a captured U.S. gun emplacement shortly after the Philippines fell to Japan.

deep section of Manila Bay, stipulating that knowledge of the location be restricted to only a handful of military personnel.

A group of trusted men was ◊

drafted. For nearly a week at the end of April, the men spent night after perilous night risking enemy patrol boats and artillery fire to barge their precious loads to the designated zone. The team removed 2,632 wooden crates from the vaults on Corregidor, each bearing 6,000 silver pesos—15,792,000 pesos in all.

However, the supposedly secret disposal of the cache was well known to the Japanese, and soon after the American surrender on Corregidor, prisoners of war were ordered to dive for the treasure. First, Filipino divers brought up eighteen crates of silver. Many of these men, accustomed to shallower waters, perished from the bends. Next, a team of Americans was mustered and provided with diving equipment that might have permitted the recovery of most of the silver. However, the prisoners sabotaged the search and reduced their haul to slightly more than two million pesos, or about 350 crates.

Following the war, U.S. military divers and private companies pulled nearly 12 million pesos from the bay bottom. They found the coins not only in the circumscribed dumping zone off Corregidor, but also strewn in long trails leading out to the zone, indicating the haste with which the treasure had been dumped.

The tally leaves more than a million pesos—roughly four million dollars—submerged offshore as a reminder of those dark times in American and Filipino history. □

STOLEN TREASURE

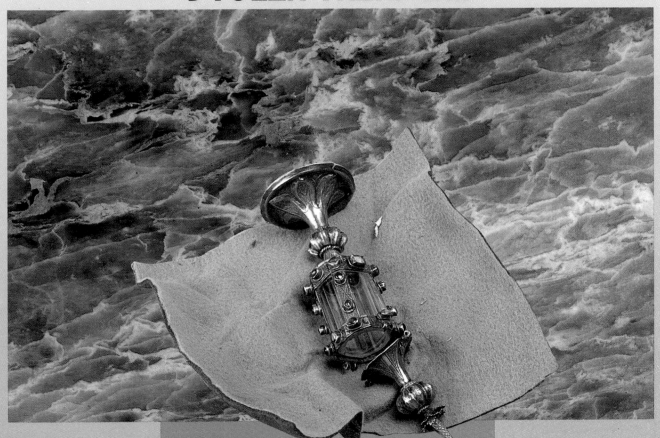

Riches and robbers are blood brothers. Not all fortunes are founded on crime, but great wealth invariably invites iniquity. Spanish treasure attracted swarms of pirates to the Caribbean. The wealth of nations has always lured greedy kings, crooked generals, avaricious politicians, and confidence artists.

The credo by which they operate is simple: Crime pays, and handsomely. However, the beneficiary is not always the perpetrator. History abounds with stories of hanged pirates and jailed generals whose booty wound up in the hands of their enemies or accusers.

Sometimes the loot simply disappears. The earth, the sea, and even, it seems, the air itself swallow up stores of swag and hold them fast.

3

King John and The Wash

Vilified in legend as a despot and a usurper, England's King John was unpopular in his own time, and history has done little to improve his reputation. In fact, however, the monarch who is best remembered for reluctantly signing the Magna Carta—and thus laying the foundation for British democracy—was not completely without redeeming features.

Autocratic and ambitious—but probably no more so than other kings of the time—John helped bring order to English local government by imposing his will on Britain's fractious nobility. But after a lifetime toiling for wealth and military victory, King John of England, monarch from 1199 to 1216, met death with neither in his grasp. Exhausted in body and mind, John died days after losing all of England's royal treasure and

jewels to the waters of a vast, desolate, and boggy tidal flat some seventy-five miles north of London.

From his brother and predecessor, King Richard the Lion-Hearted, John had inherited a bare treasury and the obligation to continue a faltering war against France. To finance the conflict, John instituted ruinous taxes, heavy fines, and other royal extortions customary in the Middle Ages. The financial burdens of his fund-raising efforts so inflamed the aristocracy that the king soon had not only a foreign war on his hands, but a civil war as well. This was settled—after a fashion—at Runnymede on June 19, 1215, when the barons compelled John to sign the Magna Carta, granting increased rights to the nobles. But neither John nor the barons were willing to live up to the

agreement, and within a year the civil war resumed.

The king achieved considerable success in this, his last military campaign, restoring territory and punishing rebels from London to the Scottish border. But although victory was within his grasp, a tragic, unforeseen end to his reign was fast approaching. The monarch had endured seventeen strife-filled years on the throne; the strain had aged him far beyond his forty-nine years. In October of 1216, after weeks of hard fighting and long journeys, John stopped to rest at the town of King's Lynn, where he was overtaken by fatigue and dysentery. Nevertheless, John and his entourage left Lynn two days after their arrival, pressing northwest into Lincolnshire.

As was customary in those turbulent times, the king's court and treasury traveled with him in a large and cumbersome baggage train. As John and his army marched from Lynn, in their path lay The Wash, a wide expanse of muddy marsh soaked by four rivers and flooded twice daily by tides from the North Sea. The shortest route lay across part of this treacherous wasteland, through dangerous quicksand. A safer route over solid ground was substantially longer.

Chronicles disagree on the details of what happened to John and his retinue in The Wash. The king sometimes followed a route different from his baggage. Per-

England's King John courses across the pages of a fourteenth-century Latin manuscript of his laws for the city of London.

haps he went around the bog; perhaps he crossed over it. Perhaps he saw disaster overtake his baggage train; perhaps he only heard of it after it had happened. Perhaps the party strayed from the path in heavy mists and sank in the sucking mud. Perhaps they miscalculated the tides, and men, horses, carts, and cargo were swept away.

Their true fate is not known. What is certain is that the luggage train containing the rich furnishings of John's reign disappeared somewhere in The Wash. The loss was staggering: State records and the royal treasury went down. The regalia and wardrobe of office were lost, along with an inventory of royal heirlooms whose contents seem almost mythical. One chronicler of the time enumerated dozens of gold and silver goblets, England's coronation regalia, plus the regalia that John's grandmother had worn as empress of Germany.

Broken in spirit and body, John died in the palace of the bishop at Newark, on October 18, 1216.

King John's treasure remains lost. Fortune hunters have searched the marshy coastlands without success, and today enthusiasm for the hunt has largely died away. The ancient route has been obscured, and much of the old estuary is buried under as much as twenty feet of silt. Even more daunting than the dirt is the fact that finders would not be keepers; any treasure found would be the property of the British Crown. □

The first map of Great Britain, made in 1250 by Matthew Paris, shows The Wash (boxed area), a great marshy confluence of rivers and sea where King John's treasure vanished on October 12, 1216.

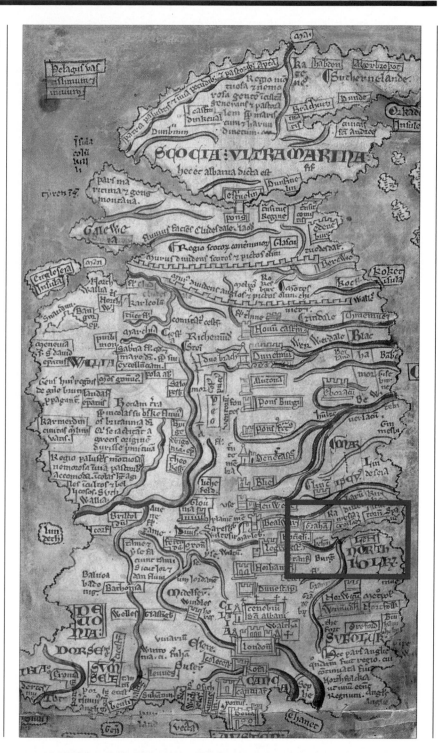

The Queen's Own Pirate

Beloved by a grateful queen and country for defending England against the Spanish Armada, Sir Francis Drake also won fame and fortune by circumnavigating the globe, exploring the New World, and plundering Spanish ships and settlements there.

Drake was renowned for succeeding against the odds, but on at least one occasion he may have succeeded too well. A legend persists that Drake once had to jettison a huge fortune just to keep his ship afloat. Most of the lost fortune—if indeed there was one— still lies off the coast of Ecuador.

In the late sixteenth century, Spain was in her glory. Gold, silver, and other riches extracted from her New World colonies had helped make her the greatest power in the world. Officially, Spain and England were at peace; unofficially, they were rivals for any territory and riches they could seize.

England's Queen Elizabeth I was too canny to directly antagonize King Philip II of Spain. Instead, she sent Drake and other mariners on voyages of exploration whose true purpose was to intercept the flow of Spanish riches. Drake earned the Spanish sobriquet El Dragón—the Sea Serpent—for his depredations on the Spanish Main.

In 1578 and 1579, El Dragón sailed north along South America's Pacific coast in his flagship, the *Golden Hind.* The journey, part of a three-year circumnavigation of the globe, turned into a triumph of plunder. Drake looted Spanish ships and colonial towns with ease, for the defenders did not expect an Englishman where only Spaniards had sailed before.

During his three-year circumnavigation of the globe at the end of the sixteenth century, Sir Francis Drake, depicted in the painting at left, changed the name of his flagship *(above)* from the *Pelican* to the *Golden Hind* in honor of a sponsor, Sir Christopher Hatton, who bore the hind, or female deer, on his coat of arms.

The richest of Drake's conquests was the *Cacafuego*, a Spanish treasure ship overtaken near Ecuador. She was an easy prize; her captain was duped by Drake into mistaking the *Golden Hind* for a Spanish galleon. The *Cacafuego* was bursting with gold, silver, and jewels. It took several days to load the loot onto the *Golden Hind.* When the job was done, Drake's flagship rode dangerously low in the water.

Off Cano Island—now called the Island of Plate—Drake paused to repair his ship and divide the booty. Legend has it that he used a washbowl to ladle out coins to the crew—sixteen bowls apiece. Each man also got a share of the larger jewels and artifacts. Groaning under the weight of so much good fortune, the flagship was barely seaworthy, so still more loot— perhaps as much as forty-five tons of it—was heaved overboard.

Curiously, few efforts have been made to salvage Drake's booty. An English tugboat captain is said to have raised eighteen tons of it from the seafloor during the Depression. If this is true—and if the original reports of the size of the prize were accurate—nearly two-thirds of El Dragón's abandoned fortune still lies waiting where the queen's own pirate dumped it. □

The Thief Turns Constable

Pirate Henry Morgan stained the Spanish Main with blood for five years in the latter half of the seventeenth century, capturing ships, looting settlements, and brutalizing his captives on sea and land. Morgan was called the biggest scoundrel in an age of scoundrels, showing not even the warped loyalty that is said to bind thieves together. In the end, his evildoing stood him in good stead. He died in bed, a prosperous man endowed with honors by his king.

Morgan, like many British scoundrels, made his living in the quasi-legal trade of preying on the Spanish—a vocation winked at by English law, since the depredations weakened the Spanish and brought gold and silver to English coffers. Morgan was one of the most successful buccaneers—although in his most famous exploit he overlooked far more loot than he took, leaving a great hoard that probably remains buried to this day.

In January 1671, Morgan and his men sacked the city of Panama, capital of Spain's American empire. Overlooking the Pacific, the city boasted thousands of handsome cedar buildings, an ornate governor's palace, four richly appointed churches, and a splendid cathedral. Panama was one of Spain's principal depots for the shipment of silver, gold, and gems home from the New World.

Morgan and nearly two thousand cutthroats hacked their way across the isthmus from the Caribbean to attack the city on its unfortified landward side. They captured the prize after a bloody battle during which the city was destroyed by fire. Although Morgan's men found a rich lode of treasure, much of the city's wealth escaped their grasp. As the pirates approached on land, the city's inhabitants crammed two galleons full of their wealth and sent the ships safely to sea. Other treasure remained hidden beneath the city in a mazelike network of tunnels and vaults that could be flooded with seawater. While the pirates were preoccupied with drink and rapine, the entrances to the tunnels were destroyed. Most of this trove still lies buried beneath the site of the old city.

Even so, the pirates led away 175 mules loaded with loot, along with six hundred prisoners to be ransomed or sold into slavery. Morgan meted out niggardly shares to most of his band, then slipped aboard his ship and sailed away to the West Indies with the lion's share of the booty.

Some say the pirate captain buried his spoils, and a cache of gold and silver unearthed in 1733 on an island off Nicaragua has long been said to be part of his haul from Old Panama.

On landing in Jamaica, Morgan was first lionized, then charged with piracy and sent home to England for trial. However, no judge dared convict the popular pirate. In fact, King Charles II knighted him and returned him to Jamaica as deputy governor and a justice of the peace. The thief was made constable.

The old pirate discharged his duties with all the zeal of a convert, earnestly referring to his erstwhile partners in crime as "ravenous vermin." Morgan claimed to "abhor bloodshed" and lamented that he was "so often compelled to punish criminals with death."

Henry Morgan, turncoat pirate, died in his bed in 1688 and was buried with the pomp attending those favored by royalty. At his funeral, all the ships in Jamaica's harbor fired salutes. □

Henry Morgan, dressed in finery appropriate to his later office as deputy governor of Jamaica, was also the ruthless pirate who overlooked great riches when he sacked Panama City in 1671.

Bart Sharp's Dull Discovery

By the end of the seventeenth century, pirates' pickings in the Caribbean were growing slim. English governors were less tolerant of freebooters, Spain defended its territories more effectively, and the more vulnerable towns and seaports encircling the Caribbean had been attacked so often that they had little left to loot.

But there was untapped wealth lying along Pacific shores, a fact brought home most notably by the successful sacking of Panama City by Henry Morgan in 1671 (page 59). The mines, church riches, and other wealth of the Spaniards might not be so well guarded, the pirate entrepreneurs thought, along Pacific coastlines.

Offsetting potential rewards, however, were the difficulties of setting up operations in the Pacific. There was no Panama Canal in those days, so the men faced a jungle trek across the Isthmus of Panama (then called Darien) to get to the Pacific. Once there, they would have to capture ships in which to do their marauding. Finally, they would have only one way to bring their bounty-laden ships back to their Caribbean home base: a twelve-thousand-mile voyage around the southern tip of South America through the barely explored Strait of Magellan.

Nevertheless, in March of 1680, several hundred idle, greedy buccaneers banded together in eight ships with as many captains and sailed for the isthmus. " 'Twas gold was the bait that tempted a pack of merry boys of us," wrote one inspired member.

Leaving their ships on the Caribbean shore, the band set off across the isthmus carrying canoes. They enlisted the patronage of an old Indian named Don Andreas, who styled himself "the Emperor of Darien." The pirates dubbed him "the true Lord of Panama" and declared themselves his servants, hoping to disguise their piracy as a legitimate defense of native claims—a diaphanous veil of protection against future prosecution.

Once on the Pacific coast, the raiders parlayed their fragile canoes into two light Spanish ships, then several warships. One of the warships was the 440-ton *Trinidad.* She would serve them for the rest of the voyage.

The pirates tried and failed to capture the new city of Panama—rebuilt in stone since Morgan's conquest. Raids on other settlements were similarly unsuccessful, for Spanish warships arrived to defend their possessions on land and sea. Leadership flagged, and the force dwindled as men deserted or were killed in battle.

Finally, a competent chief emerged, one Captain Bartholomew Sharp, called by his admirers a "sea artist and valiant commander." Giving up on Panama, Sharp steered the *Trinidad* for the western coast of South America in search of treasure ships coming from Peru. He was the first English captain to visit these waters since Sir Francis Drake had sailed there so profitably one hundred years earlier (page 58).

Although unsuccessful at raiding the well-defended Spanish seacoast towns, Sharp's band—now numbering only seventy-three men—struck pay dirt on July 19, 1681. They captured two Spanish freighters, the *Santa Rosario* and the *San Pedro,* off the coast of what is now Ecuador. The escapade turned out to be the pirates' greatest success—and a fabulous failure.

The ships contained gold, silver, and much-needed provisions. The *Santa Rosario* also yielded "a great book full of sea-charts and maps," detailing all the Spanish sailings in the southern seas. The astute Sharp realized that to King Charles II back home in England, this prize of naval intelligence was worth more than a shipful of gold. It would pay for the pirates' efforts and insure against successful prosecution for piracy.

Less obvious to Sharp and his brethren was a more conventional treasure borne in the *Santa Rosario's* hold—hundreds of silver ingots, which the buccaneers left behind because the metal's dull gray color led them to think the bars were made of some base metal, perhaps tin.

One ingot was retained for bullet making. It was only when this lump was melted down that the raiders realized their mistake—long after the *Santa Rosario* had been set adrift. □

An ornate compass rose points north toward Panama City in a detail from a 1684 likeness of Bart Sharp's captured Spanish charts of the Pacific.

The Wicked Winds of Politics

The name of Captain William Kidd is nearly synonymous with piracy and treasure, even though it is unlikely that much loot remains today to tempt the venturesome salvager. Most of the booty that Kidd is supposed to have buried was probably recovered nearly three centuries ago.

In the early 1690s, after several successful years as a privateer in the West Indies, Kidd was a settled, comfortably rich merchant captain with large New York real estate holdings, his own ship, and a wife and daughters. In 1695, however, this placid life was disrupted by a prominent New Yorker, Colonel Robert Livingston. He de-vised a scheme that would draw Kidd back into privateering and, in the process, make Livingston and his backers very rich. So that the plan could win official sanction, it was presented to the governor of New York and New England, Lord Bellomont, as a device to help rid the seas of pirates.

The backers were the noblest of the noble: Britain's first lord of the Admiralty, the lord keeper of the Great Seal, the secretary of state, the master general of ordnance, and, of course, Lord Bellomont himself. Their offer: a king's commission to prey on French ships and pirates in the Indian Ocean and the Red Sea, and to divide the riches taken from the ships. However, Kidd and his crew were to receive less than half the usual privateer's split. Usually, captain and crew on such ventures would keep 60 percent of their take, with 40 percent going to the backers. On this venture, the crew was allotted 25 percent, and Kidd had to split his meager 15 percent with Livingston. And in the event there was no booty, Kidd would have to help repay the backers. Nevertheless, it was an offer that Kidd could not easily refuse. Livingston and Bellomont made it clear that rejection of the offer would be deemed disloyal to the Crown. Greed and the high titles of the sponsors helped win him over.

In 1696, Kidd sailed from England in a ship called the *Adventure Galley.* After taking on additional crew in Rhode Island and New York, he set out on what became an ill-starred, forty-two-thousand-mile voyage to Mada- ◊

A portrait of Captain William Kidd *(above)* is framed in pieces taken from the timbers of his ship, the *Adventure Galley.* Scraps of velvet, silk, and gold lace in the lower left corner were removed from Kidd's execution clothes.

The arms of the French East India Company adorn a pass William Kidd thought would shield him from prosecution after he pirated the vessel *Quedah Merchant.* The document disappeared before Kidd's trial, only to surface some two hundred years later.

gascar, the Comoros Islands, the Red Sea, the coast of India, and back to the Caribbean.

For more than a year Kidd sailed without taking a prize, his few attempts bringing him into conflict with English ships. The crew grew restive and spoke of mutiny if the captain did not find them a prize, legal or not. One upstart gunner, William Moore, advocated outright piracy to relieve the ship's sorry state. Kidd killed him during an argument. The incident cowed the crew temporarily, but eventually the captain came to fear his men more than he feared the potential displeasure of the king. At last, the *Adventure Galley* fell into piracy, plundering several small ships and selling their cargoes.

When news of Kidd's piracy reached England, Tory politicians seized upon it to attack the four nobles in London who had sponsored him. The captain became a pariah of the high seas, and orders went out to every British port that he and his crew should be arrested on sight.

Kidd's luck turned from bad to worse. As he sailed for home, his crew deserted him, stripped his ship of its guns, and threatened to kill him. Changing ships in Madagascar, Kidd set sail for New York by way of the Caribbean. There he transferred his personal share of booty to yet another ship.

Kidd stopped at Gardiners Island, off the eastern tip of Long Island, long enough to bury chests of gems and gold. Some speculate that he also buried other caches, hoping the day would come when his legal difficulties would be over and he could enjoy his wealth.

On June 10, 1699, nearly three years after he set sail from Eng-

land, Kidd dropped anchor off New York. Two of the ships he had looted carried French passes—documents granting the vessels the protection of the French government—which the captain had confiscated in order to prove that he had captured the ship as a privateer, not a pirate. Kidd was certain that the passes and his friendship with Lord Bellomont would save him from the courts.

The captain was wrong. Bellomont took the passes and had Kidd arrested and sent to England to stand trial for piracy and for the murder of crewman Moore. The defendant insisted he was "the innocentest person of all" and the victim of political chicanery. Nevertheless, the court convicted him of piracy and sentenced him to death by hanging for Moore's murder. The French passes never appeared at the trial, but surfaced 219 years later in the Public Record Office in London.

In a final desperate attempt to save his neck, Kidd promised "goods and treasure to the value of 100,000 pounds" buried in "the Indies" in return for the king's mercy. The offer was refused, and Kidd was hanged on May 23, 1701. King William III had already shared in the captain's booty by way of Bellomont. The duplicitous governor had unearthed the Gardiners Island hoard, but in a display of scruples motivated by fear of prosecution, he sent the treasure to the king.

No one knows whether the treasure promised to the sovereign was real or simply a desperate fiction. Real or not, Kidd's buried riches have fueled the imaginations of treasure hunters from New England to the Caribbean. □

From Privateer to Pirate

On the high seas in the eighteenth century, the line between law and lawlessness was often indistinct. International relations were such that nations, England among them, licensed ship captains as privateers, free to harass and rob the ships of their enemies. Thus, as long as France remained an enemy of England, British privateers could raid French ships with impunity, even relying on the protection of British warships if necessary.

The trouble was, England's enemies sometimes became allies overnight. Worse, months could pass before news of the change reached the privateer. Last night's hero could become this morning's criminal—and never learn of his change of status until his arrest.

The experience of the privateer ship *Charles* illustrates the hazards of the trade. In the summer of 1703, some of Boston's finest citizens sent the *Charles* to prey on French ships off the coast of Newfoundland. She was to wage war on England's foes. That mandate drew so greedy and bloodthirsty a crew that a mutiny erupted before the ship cleared harbor at Marblehead, Massachusetts. The mutineers cast Captain Daniel Plowman overboard and chose Jack Quelch as their new captain. Plowman disappeared; as events unfolded, Quelch perhaps wished he had followed.

Had Quelch sailed north to harass ships of the French, with whom England was at war and stayed at war, successful plundering might have made him a patriot. Instead, he made for the eastern coast of South America and

the richer spoils of Portuguese shipping. By the next spring, he and his men had victimized seventeen Portuguese ships, capturing two hundred pounds of gold dust, more than two hundred silver ingots, and a fine collection of jewels. On the way home, Quelch attacked a Spanish galleon that was stranded on a reef, relieving her of a quantity of silver and gold.

On May 20, 1704, the *Charles* docked at Marblehead. Quelch and his crew swarmed ashore with their loot, leaving the empty ship for her owners to find. But Colonial constables soon arrested Quelch for piracy. England had made peace with Portugal a year earlier,

although the news reached the Colonies only after the *Charles* had sailed. There was also the matter of Captain Plowman's death.

Quelch denied all. He claimed he had been appointed captain by Plowman just before the poor fellow died and had sailed to Brazil on Plowman's orders. Quelch claimed to have taken only the Spanish loot, which he said he was about to report to the ship's sponsors. But Quelch's crew had already spread the word of their newfound Portuguese wealth throughout Marblehead's barrooms. Some of the men boasted of stashing the loot on the Isles of Shoals, a notorious pirate haven off New Hampshire.

Star Island *(upper right in photo),* **one of the Isles of Shoals near Portsmouth, New Hampshire, may be where privateer and pirate Jack Quelch buried treasure from his last voyage.**

In all, twenty-five of the original gang of forty-three *Charles* crewmen were rounded up for trial. An unrepentant Quelch and six companions were sentenced to hang for piracy and for the murder of a Portuguese captain.

Quelch's fortune is said to rest on an island near Cape Ann, Massachusetts. The remainder may still be hidden somewhere in Marblehead or on Star Island in the Isles of Shoals. □

The Strait-Laced Brigand

In spite of romantic tales of buried treasure, there probably are not that many underground hoards. Most pirates squandered their loot on drink and debauchery; they simply did not keep it long enough to bury it.

But Bartholomew "Black Bart" Roberts was different from his fellow buccaneers: He drank tea rather than rum, and his other tastes were equally abstemious. For this reason, experts agree that stories of Bart Roberts's hidden treasure are probably true, and that millions of dollars' worth of gold, silver, and jewelry may be waiting for someone lucky and tenacious enough to locate and exhume it.

While other pirates spent their booty, Bart Roberts focused on accumulating it. He was only a pirate for some four years; he died in 1722 at the age of about forty in a battle with a British naval ship. This black-haired Welshman raided more than four hundred vessels from Africa's Gold Coast to Brazil, from the Caribbean to Newfoundland. Yet authorities searching Roberts's ship, the *Royal Fortune*, after his death found only three hundred pounds' worth of gold dust, a minuscule portion of the treasure that the pirate stole in his time. His ship had been known to sweep that much loot from a single prize.

The great trove of hidden treasure that Roberts is thought to have amassed has eluded fortune hunters for nearly three centuries. Expert opinion places the stash somewhere in the Isles of Idols, uninhabited dots of land seventy-five miles off the coast of Sierra Leone. Surprisingly, there have been no prominent expeditions to the islands.

Some of the spoils of Black Bart's raids did come to light, however, around 1900, when two young men dug up a hoard of gold and jewels presumed to have been deposited by Walter Kennedy, a deserter from Roberts's band.

Kennedy, a one-time pickpocket and burglar, deserted in 1720, taking his share of booty with him. After burying it and making a crude map of its whereabouts, Kennedy made his way to London, where his luck changed: A spurned sweetheart exposed him as a pirate, and he was hanged in 1721.

But Kennedy's map seemed to take on a life of its own, returning to New England in the hands of an unnamed Englishman in 1878. While the fortune hunter sought work to finance his quest, he left his sea chest—with the map enclosed—in the care of Emeline Benner Lewis of Middlesex, Vermont. Twenty years later, when the Englishman still had not returned, Mrs. Lewis and her nephew, George Benner, opened the chest and found the map.

Naturally, a map marking the location of buried treasure attracted Benner's attention. Following its directions, he and a friend dug along Maine's Kennebec River and unearthed a chest containing a quantity of gold coins, a pearl necklace, and a nine-inch cross studded with diamonds. A Boston bank bought the lot for twenty thousand dollars—a substantial sum at the turn of the century.

Benner later repaid the sea's generosity by serving as custodian of Boston's Marine Museum of the Old State House. □

Teetotaling dandy "Black Bart" Roberts, portrayed above by a Dutch artist, was a relentlessly efficient pirate, fully earning the fearsome reputation advertised by the skeleton flag *(top)* that flew from his ship, the *Royal Fortune.*

The Pirate King

In 1811, New Englanders were startled by a peculiar proclamation in the *Boston Gazette*. One Jonathan Lambert of Salem, Massachusetts, announced his absolute possession of Tristan da Cunha, a cluster of five desolate islands in the middle of the South Atlantic. Thenceforth, Lambert proclaimed, the isles would be a kingdom called the Islands of Refreshment. The seat of rule was Lambert's own residence, which he dubbed Reception. He went on to invite "all those who may want refreshments to call at Reception, where they will be speedily supplied with such things as the Islands may produce, at a reasonable price." The invitation was accompanied by a warning that no one interfere with his "sovereign rights."

No ordinary Yankee entrepreneur, this self-anointed merchant emperor was a successful pirate, known for his violent plundering off the coast of South America. Now Lambert had pirated an entire group of islands, and he intended to make Tristan da Cunha a prosperous provisioning station that would sell fresh food and water to the growing number of sailing ships plying the route between the Old World and burgeoning colonies in the New World, Africa, and Asia.

In order to execute their plans, Lambert and fellow pirates had struggled ashore on Tristan da Cunha with the inevitable large iron chest filled with loot—gold coins and jewels. They also brought an assortment of vegetable seeds, fruit and coffee trees, and livestock.

Despite all the capital outlay, the Islands of Refreshment—undermanned and faced with arduous farming conditions—foundered commercially. Undeterred, Lambert hatched yet another grandiose scheme. He would slaughter the islands' abundant elephant seals, selling their oil and skins in Brazil. This plan also failed, and Lambert's men quarreled over wages and what was left of the treasure they had brought ashore. When a shipload of His Majesty's troops arrived to secure the island for Britain in 1816, they found only one survivor of the original party, an Irish-Italian named Tomasso Corrie. He told them that his erstwhile companions, including Lambert, had gone fishing and never returned. Although he had lost his old shipmates, Corrie seemed to enjoy life with the occupying soldiers. His popularity with the troops was partly assured by the ready supply of gold coins that Corrie spent mostly on rum in the outpost's canteen. His gold excited much curiosity, and the soldiers were quick to note that when the pirate left them to replenish his funds, he was never gone long. He intimated that his hoard's hiding place was "between the two waterfalls" and said he would show the spot to the soldier who pleased him most. The promise ensured the fawning attention of the troops, who waited on Corrie's every whim. On the evening of September 27, 1817, when rum had made the old pirate especially voluble, he seemed ready to reveal his secret. But before he could tell the tale, a blood vessel burst in his head. Corrie died in midsentence, the victim of a stroke.

Despite decades of searching, no one has ever found the treasure of Jonathan Lambert. The possibility of discovery was virtually extinguished in 1961, when a volcano erupted on Tristan da Cunha, pouring lava over the slope between the two waterfalls, probably burying the legacy forever. □

The Gulf's Greatest Pirate

Few men ever experienced such a checkered career as Jean Laffite, the blacksmith, broker, pirate, fugitive, and "savior of New Orleans" in the War of 1812. Fewer still have retained the legendary presence of Laffite, whose reputed treasures are said to be buried in nearly every sheltered cove along the Gulf Coast of the United States.

In 1809, Laffite and his brother Pierre owned a respectable blacksmith shop in New Orleans. But they were absentee owners, leaving day-to-day operations to their slaves so the brothers could tend to another business—one more rewarding, if somewhat less respectable, than blacksmithing. They were brokers and agents for the many pirates and smugglers who made their headquarters at nearby Barataria Bay. Described on charts of the day as a "smuggler's retreat," Barataria's coastline was pitted with marshes and deep bayous that provided hideouts galore.

The Baratarians, as they were known, considered themselves privateers rather than pirates. They claimed legitimacy because they held licenses—letters of marque, they were called—issued by the tiny, newly independent Republic of Cartagena (now a port city in Colombia), authorizing them to prey on Spanish shipping.

The handsome, cocky Jean Laffite soon parlayed his agent's influence into leadership of the pirate fleet. His control over the unsavory rabble of mutineers, deserters, and former privateers who gathered along the Louisiana coast made him a powerful man—so powerful that Governor W. C. C. Claiborne of Louisiana offered a five-hundred-dollar reward for the pirate leader's arrest. Laffite countered by offering fifteen thousand dollars for the arrest of Governor Claiborne.

Neither arrest took place, perhaps because Laffite apparently did have principles and loyalties: When the British tried to enlist his help against the Americans in the War of 1812, the pirate boss instead tipped the Americans to British plans. Moreover, he used his fleet to help General Andrew Jackson successfully defend New Orleans in 1815. For this service, President James Madison granted Laffite and all his cronies full pardon for their earlier crimes.

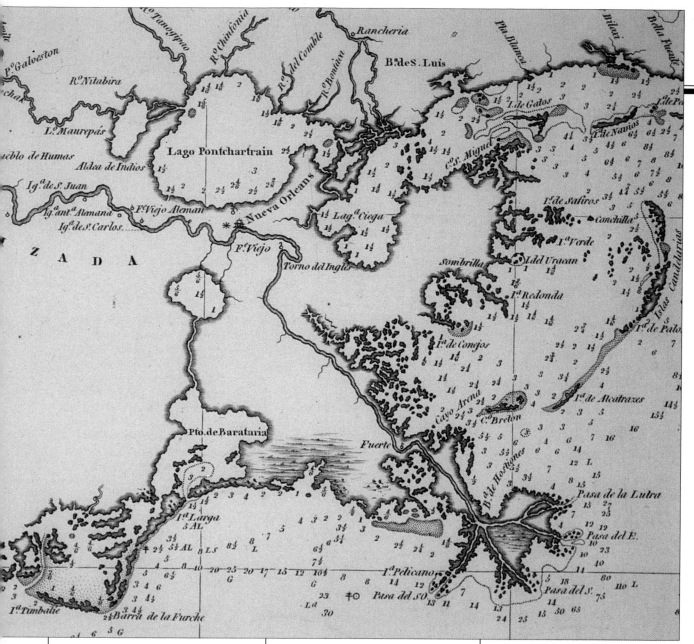

But piracy was too attractive to be abandoned, and Laffite soon founded another smugglers' haven, this one on Galveston Island, off the coast of Texas. Although he had collected letters of marque from Mexico authorizing him to take Spanish ships, Laffite took American merchant ships as well. The operation was broken up in 1820 by the U.S. Navy, and Laffite sailed away into legend.

It is said that when the blacksmith-turned-pirate abandoned Galveston he took with him a personal fortune of ten million dollars. But legends have clung to Galveston Island ever since, alleging that, whatever treasure he carried away, Laffite left behind an equal measure buried in the island's sands. Indeed, the entire Texas Gulf Coast may be considered Laffite country. From

Galveston to Aransas Pass, near Corpus Christi, discoverers of silver and gold have claimed that their finds were parts of Laffite's supposedly limitless fortune. The dashing pirate is said to have strewn golden loot in wrecked or scuttled ships along a thousand miles of Gulf coastline—and his ghost is said to hover protectively about more than one of his underwater vaults. □

Posing heroically in the idealized portrait at left, Jean Laffite led a pirate band called the Baratarians, named for their headquarters in Barataria Bay near New Orleans. The well-protected bay is in the lower center of the 1807 nautical chart of the Louisiana coast (above). **The numbers are depth soundings in fathoms.**

Bitter Billy Bowlegs

William "Billy Bowlegs" Rogers enjoyed piracy so much he had two separate careers of it. First he served with Jean Laffite, chieftain of the pirates who coursed the Louisiana coast south of New Orleans *(page 66)*. When Laffite's outfit was disbanded after the War of 1812, Billy formed his own successful pirate fleet. Throughout his careers, he was married to a Choctaw Indian woman, and they raised their six children on a comfortable Louisiana plantation.

But the pleasures of land could not keep Billy away from the excitement and profit offered by the sea. He set up a pirates' colony on the wild shores of Santa Rosa Sound, near Pensacola on Florida's panhandle, protected from a prying government by swamps, sand bars, and bayous. Even though the United States was cracking down hard on pirates in those days, there was plenty of booty to make the risks worthwhile. Billy had prudently buried at least two generous caches of loot, and it seemed he was doing everything right. But all good things must end.

Lured out of semiretirement by the promise of adventure and even more wealth, Billy embarked on what turned out to be his last cruise—one far more adventurous than he might have wished. Chased by an English warship, Bowlegs was forced to scuttle his treasure-laden schooner in four fathoms of water in Choctawhatchee Bay, not far from his headquarters. He barely escaped to Louisiana.

He soon returned to the site of the debacle—family in tow—to organize a salvage effort with a few survivors from his crew. The effort failed, and the proceeds of their final piracy remained in the sands at the bottom of the bay.

Billy retired. But rather than rest on the laurels—and on the buried proceeds of past escapades—miserly Bowlegs and his family moved into a log cabin, one with a view of the site of his last defeat and his sunken hoard.

There he kept diligent watch. And there, in 1888, at the age of ninety-five, Billy died in bitter penury, protecting his last loot to the end. He never broke his vigil, even to unearth the treasure stashed along Santa Rosa Sound—booty that would have enabled him to pass his last days in comfort. □

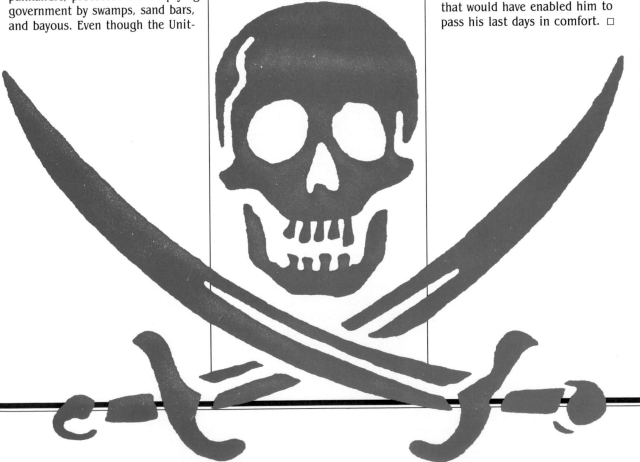

The Irish Crown Jewels

On its face, the disappearance of the Irish Crown Jewels from Dublin Castle in 1907 was a case of brazen theft aided by official ineptitude. Although many details of the loss were well known and unchallenged, no thief was convicted, and the jewels remain at large today.

The Irish Crown Jewels, fashioned of diamonds, emeralds, and rubies, were worn on formal occasions by the lord lieutenant of Ireland—the English monarch's representative—and by the sovereign on state visits.

When no dignitary was wearing them, the jewels were secured in a safe in the offices of the ruling English government in Dublin Castle. The burden of their care fell to Sir Arthur Vicars, Ulster king-of-arms, and three heralds: Francis Shackleton, Peirce Mahoney, and Francis Bennett-Goldney.

On July 3, 1907, Vicars was absorbed in preparations for a visit by King Edward VII when a porter advised him that the cleaning woman had found the outer door of the king-of-arms' office unlocked that morning. Vicars seemed unperturbed by the news. He was similarly unmoved to hear, three days later, that the house-keeper had found his office's strong-room door ajar. Later that day, the safe in which the crown jewels were kept was found unlocked—a circumstance that, at long last, seemed to merit Sir Arthur's attention. He investigated and found that all the state jewels were gone.

The thief or thieves had been careful and unhurried. All of the plundered jewelry cases had been restored to their proper places in the safe, and the tissue paper that had held the jewels was tidily ◊

A 1907 poster *(right)* trumpets a reward for the return of the Irish Crown Jewels shortly after they were stolen from Dublin Castle *(below)*. Among the lost items were the Star and Badge of the Order of St. Patrick, shown in a nineteenth-century painting.

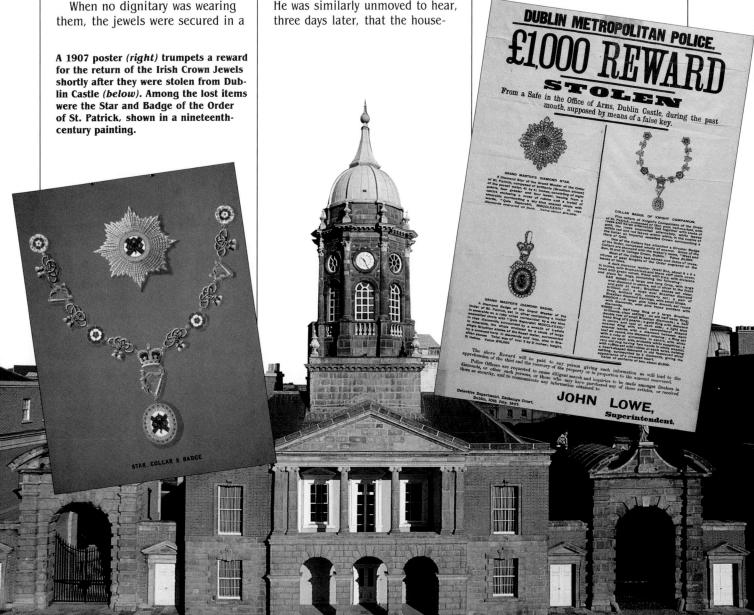

tucked inside. Most curious of all, a small piece of blue ribbon had been neatly excised from the badge of the Order of St. Patrick—an operation requiring a jeweler's screwdriver, considerable skill, and at least ten minutes' time.

Police determined that none of the locks had been picked, and local locksmiths denied making copies of any of the keys—not those to Vicars's office, the strong-room, or the safe. Vicars himself had possession of the only two keys known to open the safe.

For his part, Vicars expressed the thought that the theft was a practical joke and that the jewels might be "returned to my house by parcel post tomorrow morning." The jewels did not appear.

Scotland Yard was called in, and within a month the herald Shackle-ton became the prime suspect. Rumors flew, but no charges were ever filed. Nevertheless, the king decreed that the four men respon-sible for guarding the jewels pay for the theft with their jobs. Vicars refused to leave office and demanded a hearing. A royal commission censured him and or-dered his dismissal.

In 1921, Vicars was murdered and his house set afire by a band of marauders. The victim's bullet-riddled body was tagged with a note: "Spy. Informers beware. IRA never forgets." But the Irish Re-publican Army denied any part in his killing.

The other principals in the case also fared poorly. Francis Shackle-ton served time in prison for swindling an elderly woman. His fellow herald, Peirce Mahoney, died in 1914 under mysterious circum-stances from a gunshot wound. Francis Bennett-Goldney was killed in an automobile accident in 1918.

In 1908, when the crime was only a year old, it was "solved" by the fictional detective Sherlock Holmes, whose creator, Sir Arthur Conan Doyle, was a friend of Arthur Vicars. In "The Adventure of the Bruce-Partington Plans," a tale clearly based on the Irish theft, Holmes neatly accounted for the motive, means, and method of the crime, which he laid at the door of Shackleton's fictional equivalent.

But the real theft remains un-solved. The disappearance of the jewels and violent death of two principal characters have never been explained, and the jewels have never since graced the person of English royalty. □

Brother Twelve's Millions

In 1927, a diminutive Englishman with dark, hypnotic eyes led a group of devoted followers to a spot on Vancouver Island off the west coast of Canada. He claimed that a vision had drawn him there. As his disciples watched, he un-rolled a map corresponding to the site—drawn, he said, while he was in a trance—and declared that this would be their home, a colony to be named the City of Refuge.

The little man called himself Brother Twelve, the designated earthly representative of eleven other Masters of Wisdom who lived on an elevated astral plane. This new home, he said, would bring his followers safely through an im-minent Armageddon, a "period of demolition" from which only they would emerge.

In a period of seven years, Brother Twelve—in reality a former sea captain by the name of Edward Arthur Wilson—amassed an im-mense personal fortune from dona-tions to his cause. Eventually, how-ever, his community collapsed amidst charges of slavery, sadism, black magic, free love, and theft.

Brother Twelve's ministry had begun on a more auspicious note, attracting thousands of sincere seekers of spiritual health. His charismatic presence inspired his audiences, and people flocked to sit at his feet in the City of Ref-uge beneath a giant moss-draped maple known as the Tree of Wis-dom. Hundreds of eager colonists signed over all they had for the privilege of building and living in the haven. Thousands more sent generous donations.

Spiritual guru Brother Twelve, a.k.a.
Edward Arthur Wilson (wearing hat),
confers with a group of his followers
beneath the "Tree of Wisdom" at his
British Columbia colony.

The settlement soon expanded to nearby DeCourcy and Valdes islands, where the disciples cleared the land, plowed fields, and planted crops, toiling for the good of their souls as Brother Twelve lived in luxury.

A prophet of financial doom, Brother Twelve predicted the stock market crash of 1929 and the Great Depression. He had no faith in paper currency and, as banks folded, he converted all donations into gold. Like a housewife canning fruits and vegetables in the kitchen, Brother Twelve poured the coins into one-quart Mason jars, sealing them with hot paraffin. The colony's carpenter made more than forty rope-handled cedar boxes to hold the jars, so that the guru could easily transport his hoard.

Ever mindful of security, Brother Twelve kept his treasure on the move. He would bury it in one place, then remove it to a new location a few days later, hoping to outwit a possible thief.

But the greedy prophet of doom eventually scandalized and alienated his followers. First, he claimed that he and his mistress were the reincarnations of the Egyptian ◊

divinities Osiris and Isis. When his Isis went insane, he took another mistress, a foulmouthed sadist known as Madame Zee, who delighted in whipping the disciples in the name of spiritual discipline. In midnight rituals in the cabin of their sailboat, the *Lady Royal,* the demonic pair attempted to kill their enemies with black magic.

In 1933, appalled by their leader's evil, the faithful revolted, suing Brother Twelve for the return of their money. The guru and his mistress scuttled the *Lady Royal,* destroyed the settlement, and disappeared with the treasure in the colony's tugboat. Brother Twelve reemerged later that year in Switzerland, leaving in British Columbia a legend that refused to die. His own fate remains a mystery, as does the location of his treasure.

Although some historians believe there never was any gold, most modern investigators think some of the gold-filled jars may have been left behind, remaining hidden on the old refuge lands on DeCourcy and Valdes islands. They suggest that Brother Twelve may not have had time to gather his entire hoard, or he forgot where some of the often-moved jars were buried, or he simply could not transport a half-ton of gold.

Over the years, treasure seekers have dug throughout the islands, but none has reported any more success than the elderly caretaker of the property, who discovered a vault that once held Brother Twelve's treasure. Reaching expectantly into the darkness, he withdrew only a curling scrap of tarpaper. Carefully straightening the scroll, the caretaker read Brother Twelve's last angry message: "For Fools and Traitors—Nothing!" □

The Peak of Obsession

Perhaps a Franciscan friar helped a group of impoverished colonists mine gold and hide it. Perhaps an Apache chief named Victorio killed settlers and travelers, stole their gold, and hid it in a cave.

These tales and more, involving a huge hoard of gold supposedly hidden below the slopes of Victorio Peak in southeastern New Mexico, had circulated for years in the nearby town of Hatch. When Milton "Doc" Noss and his wife, Ova, settled there in 1935, they added to the legend.

As Ova later recalled, the couple were hunting deer with friends on Victorio Peak one day in 1937 when Doc was separated from the party. When he returned, he whispered to his wife that he had stumbled on a treasure cave. Later he took her to the spot, and as she waited at the entrance, he disappeared through a narrow opening in the rock. Emerging a couple of hours later, Doc presented Ova with coins, jewels, and a gold ingot. It was, she said, "the happiest moment

Happily anticipating wealth, "Doc" and Ova Noss were photographed in 1939, not long before their fortunes changed with a landslide that blocked Doc's treasure cave.

in our lives. Right then, when he first came up, we knew we had something. We knew it was ours."

In fact, the question of ownership was not that simple. It was illegal in those days to own large amounts of gold or to trade the metal on the open market, and the couple had no way to sell their find. Nevertheless, over the next two years, Doc brought out and reburied more than eighty gold bars. He

guarded his secret jealously: He never even allowed his wife into the cave, nor would he let her see where he buried the ingots. He brought a box of letters to the surface, presumably the property of the original owners. But he burned them lest they reveal the names of other possible claimants to the treasure.

According to the claims the Nosses filed with the New Mexico State Land Office, the treasure lay in a series of interconnected caverns extending more than a half-mile into the mountain. The caves held swords, guns, saddles, and old Wells Fargo chests, as well as thousands of gold ingots.

Watching over the treasure, according to the claims, were dozens of skeletons—perhaps the first people, but not the last, to die in connection with the trove.

Doc's foraging stopped abruptly in 1939. A dynamite blast that he had set off to widen the cave's mouth instead triggered a landslide that sealed it shut. Doc himself was shot to death in 1949 during an argument with a partner over the gold.

After his death, Ova Noss tried futilely to find the ingots that Doc had buried. She lived in a shack on the claim until 1951, when agents of the United States government ran her off. The area was part of

Gunned down in 1949 in a dispute over gold, Doc Noss lies slumped across his truck's bumper a half-hour after a partner shot him. Noss was running for his own pistol at the moment he was shot.

the White Sands Missile Range and was off-limits to civilians.

Ova Noss died in 1979, none the richer for all the gold she had thought of as hers. But her heirs and others, drawn by the legend of Victorio Peak, continue to probe for the riches beneath its flanks. □

An Old Dusty Book

It was as beautiful as it was old—a ninth-century manuscript of the four Gospels, painstakingly hand copied and illuminated by a skilled medieval scribe six centuries before Gutenberg invented movable type. Its binding was jewel-studded gold and silver, a treasure in its own right.

The manuscript came to be called the Quedlinburg Gospels after the town of Quedlinburg in what became, after the end of World War II, East Germany. Precious as it was, the book was but one of several priceless artifacts that lay for many years in the ancient Quedlinburg Lutheran church. Others included three elaborately decorated reliquaries, one of them more than a thousand years old. Supposedly, it was a gift to the church from King Henry I, who ruled that region in the tenth century. The Gospels and other objects, whose value as gold and gems was far outstripped by their historical significance, all became casualties of war, mourned by art lovers everywhere.

During the last days of World War II, officials of the Quedlinburg church removed the treasures and put them into a mine shaft for safekeeping. A short time later, American troops occupying the area were charged with the trove's protection. The Americans had arrived in April of 1945. Soon thereafter, the treasures disappeared.

It was not until forty-five years later that the looted Quedlinburg antiquities showed signs of surfacing. In April of 1990, the art world buzzed with news that the West German government (the two Germanys were still a few months away from reuniting) had reclaimed the illuminated Gospels. The transaction was conducted in Switzerland, where the law conceals the details of secret art sales. The name of the seller, an American, was not disclosed, and the three-million-dollar price—thought to be a fraction of the book's true worth—was coyly described as a "finder's fee."

Speculation was rife: Now that the precious manuscript had turned up, could the rest of the Quedlinburg hoard also be found?

What had been an art-world intrigue became a detective story. The sleuth was a West German lawyer and historian named Willi Korte, an experienced tracker of artworks that had disappeared from Berlin museums during and after World War II. Using his many contacts in the arts, Korte began assembling pieces of information about the Quedlinburg treasure into a fascinating picture.

From an art dealer who had bid for the Gospels, Korte learned that the book had been stored in a bank in the Texas farm town of Whitewright, not far from Dallas—but some five thousand miles from Quedlinburg. Guessing that the rest of the trove might also be there, Korte flew to Texas, presented himself to officials of the First National Bank—the only bank in Whitewright—and asked to see the rest of the Quedlinburg treasures.

"When I walked into the bank, I didn't know who had taken the works, only that they were probably there," said Korte. The look on one bank officer's face told him that "there was something to discuss."

Emerging from the discussion was the implication that the man who took the treasures from the mine shaft in Quedlinburg was Joe Tom Meador, who had studied art in Texas and France. Born in Arkansas and raised in White-

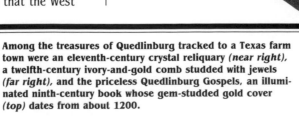

Among the treasures of Quedlinburg tracked to a Texas farm town were an eleventh-century crystal reliquary *(near right)*, a twelfth-century ivory-and-gold comb studded with jewels *(far right)*, and the priceless Quedlinburg Gospels, an illuminated ninth-century book whose gem-studded gold cover *(top)* dates from about 1200.

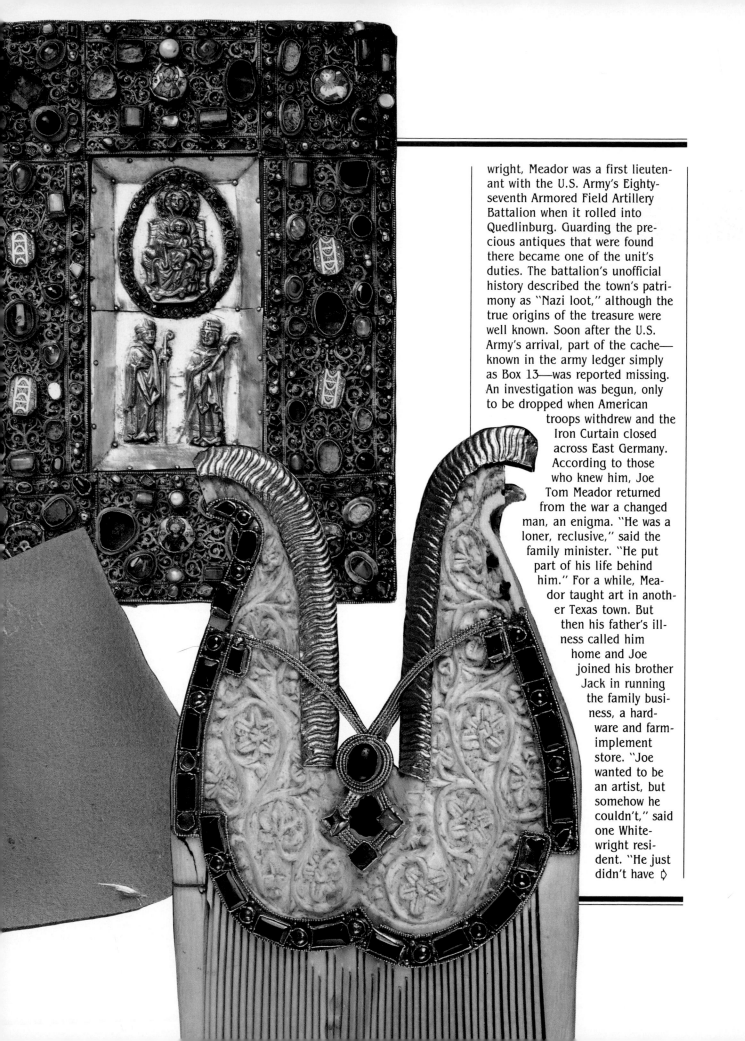

wright, Meador was a first lieutenant with the U.S. Army's Eighty-seventh Armored Field Artillery Battalion when it rolled into Quedlinburg. Guarding the precious antiques that were found there became one of the unit's duties. The battalion's unofficial history described the town's patrimony as "Nazi loot," although the true origins of the treasure were well known. Soon after the U.S. Army's arrival, part of the cache—known in the army ledger simply as Box 13—was reported missing. An investigation was begun, only to be dropped when American troops withdrew and the Iron Curtain closed across East Germany. According to those who knew him, Joe Tom Meador returned from the war a changed man, an enigma. "He was a loner, reclusive," said the family minister. "He put part of his life behind him." For a while, Meador taught art in another Texas town. But then his father's illness called him home and Joe joined his brother Jack in running the family business, a hardware and farm-implement store. "Joe wanted to be an artist, but somehow he couldn't," said one Whitewright resident. "He just didn't have ◊

anything in common with most people here, so he had to turn to other things." Other things included the role of local connoisseur and art aficionado, and, as such, Meador occasionally showed some of his Quedlinburg artifacts to the townspeople. "Everybody in town knew he had this old dusty book," said one resident who had seen the Quedlinburg Gospels. Meador kept the book and several other items in the back room of his store, wrapped in a blanket.

When he displayed his booty, he told people that he had found the objects "in the gutter" and had "liberated" them. But an acquaintance said Meador was tormented by what he had done and wrestled with his conscience over giving the artifacts back.

Joe Meador died in 1980, saddling his heirs with the problem. In his will he left all his property to his brother Jack and his sister Jane Meador Cook. But he made no mention of the stolen treasures from Quedlinburg. Under United States law, no one can gain legal title to stolen property, through inheritance or otherwise. Nevertheless, Jack and Jane took possession of the artifacts, and in the mid-1980s engaged an attorney to seek buyers for the goods, an effort resulting in the sale of the Gospels in 1990.

But once Willi Korte had tracked the hoard to Whitewright, a series of lawsuits, threats of prosecution, and negotiations began, resulting in the return of the treasure to Quedlinburg. Before the hoard departed, however, some of it was displayed publicly in Dallas, near where it had lain in obscurity for nearly half a century. □

Guardians and Thieves

During the Allied occupation of Germany that followed World War II, American military personnel were ordered to guard, preserve, and protect the lives and property of civilians. Nevertheless, some soldiers, like members of conquering armies throughout history, plundered what they had been set to guard. The most notorious of the American wartime thieves were three army officers who made off with a mammoth haul—the jewelry, tableware, and family heirlooms of one of the most prominent old European noble families, the Hohenzollern House of Hesse.

The Hohenzollerns, a family linked to both the British royal house and Kaiser Wilhelm II, lived through most of the war in a house on the grounds of the family castle in Kronberg, near Frankfurt. In 1944, when Allied bombers were devastating German cities, the family decided to protect its ancestral treasures by burying them beneath the castle's cellar floor.

Before hiding their patrimony, the Hohenzollerns took the precaution of making an inventory. It ran to four or five typewritten pages listing diamonds, emeralds, rubies, and pearls; rings, bracelets, necklaces, brooches, and tiaras that had been worn by European royalty on state occasions; three sets of dinnerware, one fashioned of solid gold decorated with gems; and family memorabilia, including a Bible that was autographed by Martin Luther and letters to Britain's Queen Victoria from her daughters.

All were sealed in a lead box within a wooden crate, and the burial hole was sealed by a stonemason and covered with a pile of potatoes. At the same time that the trove was buried, the family also hid 1,600 bottles of rare vintage wines, a precaution that would come to cost them dearly.

In April of 1945, General George S. Patton's Third Army swept into the region. Patton told the Hohen-

zollerns to vacate their house and castle immediately; the castle became a military headquarters and later a rest camp under the command of Women's Army Corps captain Kathleen B. Nash. GIs recuperating from battle consumed 1,800 bottles of everyday wine that had not been concealed and then went snooping for more.

First they discovered the rare wine. Then they eagerly blasted open part of the floor that looked as though it had been tampered with, and they came up with the family treasure. This they turned over to Captain Nash.

The army assured the Hohenzollerns that the treasure would be locked safely in a wing of the castle. But in April of 1946, when Princess Sophie of Hesse wanted to use some jewelry for her upcoming wedding, the cache was nowhere to be found. The family treasure had been stolen. The goods had an estimated material worth at the time of between $1.5 million and $5 million, independent of their historic value.

Army investigators compiled a list of ten suspects, but soon singled out three: Captain Nash and two erstwhile guests at the castle, Colonel James W. Durant and his former assistant, Captain David Watson. By the time of their arrest, Durant and Nash had returned to the United States and married—a fact that indicated complicity and thus helped cast suspicion on them. The trio soon confessed that they had schemed to steal the treasure, sell it off, and start a business with the proceeds.

To make their pile of loot more compact, the thieves had pried jewels from their mountings and mailed them home in shoeboxes, destroying heirlooms in the misguided hope that the loose gems would be easy to sell. Honest dealers would have turned them away, however, for the size and antique cut of the gems betrayed their age and distinguished provenance.

One by one, stolen items were retrieved from their hiding places. Nash had given a set of sixteenth-century gold dinnerware studded with gems to her sister, who, innocent of its value or its history, ◊

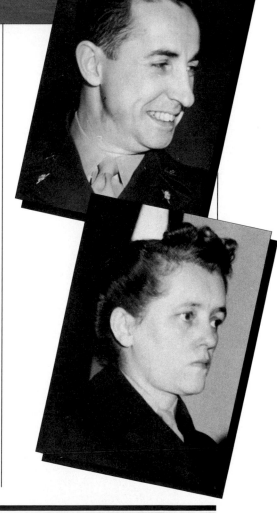

Arrested in the United States, army colonel James W. Durant and his wife, Women's Army Corps captain Kathleen Nash Durant (above), confessed to stealing the Hohenzollern family jewels from Schloss Friedrichshof (top), near Kronberg, Germany.

used it in her kitchen. Colonel Durant, a former government lawyer and decorated war hero, had stored hundreds of loose diamonds and other gems in a cardboard box, which he kept in a ten-cent rental locker in a Chicago train station. Other gems, along with cash, were buried in three pickle jars by a roadside in Virginia, Durant's home state. Watson, still serving in Germany at the time of his arrest, led investigators to rings and tiaras and other jewels. Some of the precious original settings were found in a goldsmith's shop in Belfast, Northern Ireland.

Only a fraction of the treasure—estimated at between one-tenth and one-third—was recovered, leaving a vast quantity of gems and artifacts unaccounted for. All three officers were dishonorably discharged from the army and sent to prison. Durant, as the alleged mastermind, got the longest sentence, fifteen years. Nash was sentenced to five years, and Watson to three. □

Hitler's Hoard

Even as he was destroying the nations of Europe and laying waste to their cultures, Germany's Adolf Hitler was energetically amassing art, including some of the most prized works of Western civilization. Hitler's Nazi hordes were not the first conquerors to plunder the treasures of defeated foes, or even the most successful at rapine; Napoleon may have stolen more art. Nevertheless, the Germans looted on a gargantuan scale, taking literally millions of art objects—drawings, sculptures, prints, tapestries, antique furniture, frescoes, virtually anything that could be moved. Stolen paintings alone numbered in the tens of thousands.

Hitler's program for collecting art was founded on greed and a desire for revenge. As an aspiring art student in Austria, he had been denied admission to Vienna's Academy of Fine Arts. The director advised him to study architecture instead. Stung by the rejection, Hitler scorned formal schooling and went on to eke out a living as a commercial artist. The academy's rejection might be said to have altered the course of history.

Even as Hitler was developing his scheme to subjugate much of the human race, he formulated a master plan to rebuild his hometown of Linz, Austria, as a showplace in the new German empire that he intended to establish. The town's crowning glory would be the greatest art gallery in the world, a rebuke to those who had dismissed his talents.

Hitler began building his per-

German dictator Adolf Hitler (seated) studies a model of Linz, Austria, with architect Hermann Giesler (center) and Hitler's personal servant, Heinz Linge.

sonal art collection soon after he came to power in 1933. Initially, the collection could hardly be described as great: The Führer knew what he liked, but his taste tilted to the sentimental and excessively heroic.

As he began collecting "good Aryan art"— art commensurate with his vision of a blond, heroic German master race—Hitler sought to destroy all other kinds. In 1934, he declared modern art to be "degenerate" and its practitioners "racially and culturally intolerable." The Nazi regime forced the dismissal of all Jewish or politically liberal art professors and museum directors. Next it ordered German museums and galleries to be purged of all modernist works and anything else deemed inconsistent with Aryan and Germanic culture. In 1937, the Nazis mounted an exhibit of this allegedly degenerate art in Munich, featuring works by such modern masters as Marc Chagall, Vincent van Gogh, Wassily Kandinsky, Paul Klee, Piet Mondrian, and Pablo Picasso. Although intended as derogatory, the exhibition drew enthusiastic crowds. The works had been confiscated from Germany's leading museums. Most of them were destroyed after the exhibit.

Anticipating his conquests, Hitler set up an apparatus with which to gather artworks. As the Nazi armies swept across Europe, Hitler's art collectors seized promising works from newly conquered "enemies of the state." Germany's

own citizens and her allies were not immune. Many of the great artworks of Italy were carried off to Germany "for safekeeping" or bought at fire-sale prices. Such was the fate of an entire eighteenth-century painted ceiling from a Venetian palace, which was carted off to Berlin. As designated enemies of the state, Jews everywhere had their property, including works of art, confiscated.

Dubbed Special Assignment Linz, with headquarters in Paris and Munich, Hitler's art-collecting operation was meant to be a smooth-running machine. In fact, like much of Nazi Germany's bureaucracy, it was an organizational shambles, riddled with corruption and infighting. Nazi officials high and low scrambled to take their personal cut of the prizes. Reichsmarschall Hermann Göring, head of the Luftwaffe and Hitler's right-hand man, was among the most

rapacious. "Whenever you come across anything that may be needed by the German people, you must be after it like bloodhounds," Göring exhorted the occupying armies. Bloodhound Göring—who made a great show of observing legal technicalities—diverted many of the finest works into his personal collection. His palatial estate was furnished with works by Leonardo, Tintoretto, Rembrandt, Velázquez, Van Dyck, Goya, Hals, and Rubens, among others.

As the tide of war turned against Germany, the looted art treasures suffered. Works by Rubens, Van Dyck, and Michelangelo were destroyed in the Allied bombing of Berlin. As a result, the Nazis began storing their booty in more secure locations. One of the largest caches was in the salt mines of upper Austria. Nearly twenty-seven thousand prints, drawings, coins, books, paintings, and sculptures ◊

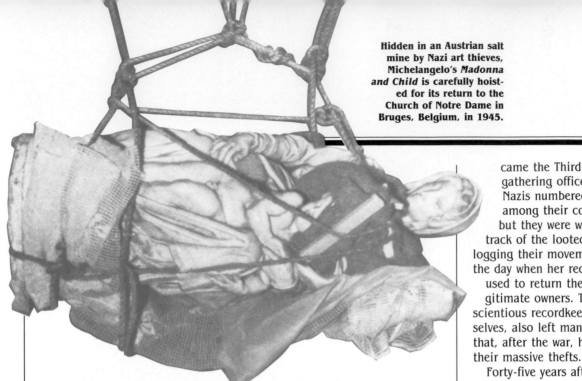

were placed there, including Michelangelo's marble masterpiece *Madonna and Child.* So were eight large explosive charges, strategically located so that the collection could be destroyed at the flick of a switch if it seemed about to fall into the hands of the advancing Allies. Only quick action by Austrian resistance fighters in 1945 averted this act of gratuitous vandalism.

As it was, millions of artworks were dispersed among untold numbers of hiding places, making the postwar task of recovering, identifying, and returning them to their proper owners an immense undertaking. One of the heroes of the effort was a patriotic Frenchwoman, Rose Valland. An art historian, Valland had worked at the Jeu De Paume, one of France's most important museums, after it be-

came the Third Reich's art-gathering office in Paris. The Nazis numbered Valland among their collaborators, but they were wrong. She kept track of the looted artworks, logging their movements against the day when her records could be used to return the art to its legitimate owners. The Nazis, conscientious recordkeepers themselves, also left many documents that, after the war, helped undo their massive thefts.

Forty-five years after Hitler's fall, pieces of stolen art continued to surface. In 1945, a cache of 362 Old Master drawings was rescued by a Russian officer from the basement of a castle outside Berlin. The Russian safeguarded them in his home near Moscow until the lifting of the Iron Curtain in 1990, when he was finally able to return the treasures to Germany.

"The war was an episode," he said, "but the art is eternal." □

Nazi Gold

Between 1938 and 1943, as the Nazi war machine rolled across Europe, squads of soldiers plundered the occupied countries on a massive scale. The gold reserves of each fallen nation were a particular target of the looters. From the Netherlands, Belgium, France, Austria, and elsewhere, captured gold was shipped to Berlin. There, within the imposing walls of the German Reichsbank, the bullion was recast into bars bearing the Third Reich's imprint. The Reichsbank also took on the grisly task of turning into bullion the fortune in

gold jewelry, coins, and even tooth fillings taken from the victims of Nazi concentration camps.

With assets scattered in more than four thousand branches throughout Germany, the Reichsbank was also the circulatory system of the Third Reich's economy, with the central office in Berlin as its beating heart and main treasure house. Toward the end of the war, the Berlin Reichsbank alone held gold bullion worth more than $256 million—this at a time when the price of gold was fixed at $35 per ounce. In more recent times the price has fluctuated between ten and twenty times that value.

The stage for the dispersal of the Reichsbank gold was set on the morning of February 3, 1945, when Berlin reeled under the heaviest bombing the war had yet seen; nearly one thousand American bombers dropped two thousand tons of explosives on the city. When the Reichsbank's five thousand employees emerged from the bunkers beneath the bank, they found the outside of their building blasted away and its vaults and strongrooms exposed.

It was clear that most of Germany's bank balance could blow away with the next raid, so Nazi officials undertook to move Reichsbank reserves to safety in outlying areas. Less than a week later, the first shipments began. First the paper money—including one billion German marks and four million U.S. dollars—was sent to a potassium mine at Merkers, two hundred miles southwest of Berlin. Three days later, the paper money was joined by one hundred tons of gold, carried on thirteen railway flatcars. The wealth rested deep within Merkers's thirty miles of tunnels for seven weeks until advancing American forces occupied the area. Although the Germans tried desperately to remove the cache, they had to abandon most of it—nine-tenths of the official reserves of the Berlin Reichsbank—to the Allies.

Hitler's officials then tried to gather the remains of the nation's wealth from Reichsbank branch offices around Germany. The bullion was consolidated in Berlin, then shipped in two special trains headed for Munich. The gold was to be distributed among Reichsbank branches in southern Germany. Much of it never completed the journey. All the time that the gold was in transit, bits of it trickled into the pockets of its guardians.

Hitler died in his Berlin bunker on April 30. The Third Reich was disintegrating. Confronted with chaos, Reichsbank officials were reduced to hiding what remained of the trainloads of bullion in the mountains of Bavaria and Austria.

Meanwhile, henchmen of SS chief Heinrich Himmler were busily scooping up the sizable crumbs of the crumbling empire. One band lifted Himmler's personal fortune of two million dollars from the Munich Reichsbank and salted it away in a barn near Salzburg, Austria. Others robbed the Berlin Reichsbank at gunpoint, then slipped through the tightening Allied ring around the city. Some of the money was distributed to other Nazis. The rest was buried under trees on a Tyrolean hillside, where it was eventually found by American authorities. It is uncertain, but unlikely, that Himmler ever saw the money.

The looting of the Berlin Reichsbank was completed on May 15, 1945, when an officer of the Russian Army took charge of the bank's remaining assets—some $3 million in gold bullion and $400 million in negotiable bonds. The gold was never seen again, but the bonds and rumors of their whereabouts have surfaced from time to time. As recently as 1982, a Gibraltar-based insurance company carried a substantial number of them in its portfolio.

After the war, the hills of southern Germany were alive with gold hunters. Nazis, Allied occupiers, and ordinary fortune seekers all sought to claim a piece of the Reich's riches.

At least two billion dollars' worth of the Reichsbank's assets—some estimate that the figure is far higher—remains unaccounted for. Great fortunes may lie wherever they were hidden by desperate Nazis in the last frantic days of the Third Reich. □

Perched atop bags of gold stashed in a mine by Germany's Reichsbank in 1945, a U.S. Army officer holds forth a single $20,000 bar.

Mussolini's Treasure

As they fled the advancing Allied forces in the final days of World War II, the Italian dictator Benito Mussolini and his fugitive retinue carried treasures of two sorts: one a hoard of gold, art, and cash; the other an endowment for historians—the documents, letters, and other artifacts of Mussolini's reign.

Mussolini was captured near the northern town of Dongo on the shore of Lake Como on April 27, 1945. He and his mistress, Claretta Petacci, were shot and their bodies hung in a Milan square as public proof of their deaths. But the disposition of the gold and documents was far less public; neither has ever surfaced. Rumors and tantalizing tales are many, however.

The Treasure of Dongo, as the hoard became known, was carried in a German-escorted convoy of cars bearing Mussolini, his ministers, and his mistress toward the Swiss border. The stash included American, British, and European bank notes worth thirty million 1990 dollars and quantities of gold, including three bags of wedding rings donated to the war effort by Italian citizens.

The true value of the fortune was never revealed—if it was ever known—and its disposition remains a mystery. The partisans who captured the convoy made several detailed inventories of what was taken, but each conflicted with the previous one. Some of the swag was deposited in banks—and almost immediately withdrawn. Most historians believe that the bulk of the wealth found its way into the coffers of postwar Italian political parties, particularly that of the Communists.

However, tales persist that bits of the fortune still lie in Lake Como. According to one story, two of Mussolini's German escorts tossed two suitcases of loot into the lake to be retrieved later on. In another, a local fisherman is said to have found pieces of gold near Lake Como's shore, together with a suitcase containing more than a pound of gold scrap. He turned his find over to Italian authorities, but the goods soon disappeared.

Whatever became of the Treasure of Dongo, Mussolini himself apparently had little interest in it. Instead, he was morbidly preoccupied with the documents he carried, poring over them and feverishly covering them with notes, apparently believing that they would acquit him of any wrongdoing during the war.

But the papers, like the gold, disappeared more quickly than the memory of Italy's wartime dictator, leaving the world to speculate on the true contents of both treasures.

In 1957, several former partisans and some Dongo residents were charged with embezzlement and murder in connection with the hoard's disappearance. The mystery remained, however, when the proceedings were declared invalid after the suicide of a juror. □

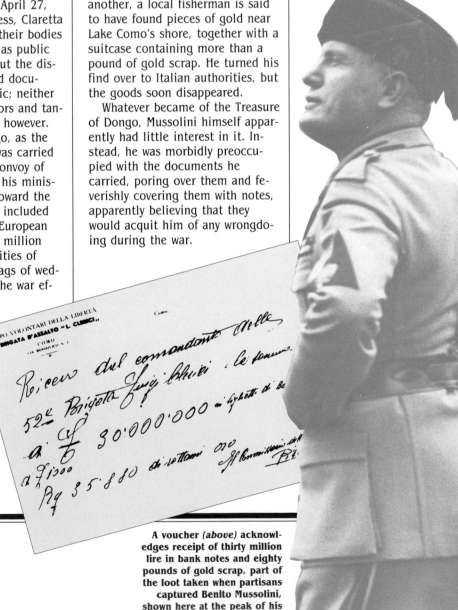

A voucher *(above)* acknowledges receipt of thirty million lire in bank notes and eighty pounds of gold scrap, part of the loot taken when partisans captured Benito Mussolini, shown here at the peak of his reign over Italy.

Yamashita's Gold

It is often said that behind every great fortune lies a great crime. The twisted tale of Yamashita's gold, allegedly buried in the Philippine Islands, is a story of a great fortune and many crimes that became inseparably intertwined.

The chronicle begins with Japan's plundering of its neighbors before and during World War II. As the Germans did in Europe, the Japanese squeezed vast fortunes from their Asian domain, creating a river of riches flowing toward the homeland. There were gems, golden Buddhas, coins, and precious metals of immense value. In 1940, the treasures may have amounted to three billion dollars' worth of material.

But, some say, not all the empire's riches reached the home islands. There are several stories about how the bulk of the booty was diverted. One of the more creditable tales goes like this: The flow of loot from the far-flung Japanese holdings was interrupted in the Philippines—a natural and necessary transshipment point—and buried there. This happened, so the story goes, toward the end of World War II. The Allies were gaining control of the Pacific, making it increasingly difficult for the Japanese to ship soldiers and supplies—much less stolen gold. So, naval officers charged with moving the booty began to hide it instead.

They created some of the hiding places by using Allied prisoners to dig pits in the mountains outside Manila. The officers also blasted caves in coral reefs, and they sank entire shiploads of valuables in the sea around the islands.

Arriving in the midst of this frenzied activity was the Philippines' new military governor, General Tomoyuki Yamashita, "the Tiger of Malaya"—a nickname he had won by conquering that complacent and ill-defended British colony. When Yamashita arrived in October 1944, he may or may not have known the details of the navy's treasure operation. Nonetheless, his name has become linked with the legendary hoard.

Not all authorities agree, however, on the existence of Japanese treasure hoards. Some believe that weapons and ammunition, not gold and silver, were consigned to caches in the jungle—intended for the Japanese occupiers of the Philippines, who planned to retreat into the jungle and defend the islands against the approaching Allies.

The debate notwithstanding, the existence of the Japanese trove has become widely accepted as fact. The story has lured legions of wealth seekers—and a few claim to have found some of the riches.

One searcher was a young Filipino politician named Ferdinand Marcos, who became successively a congressman, senator, president, and finally dictator of the islands before being overthrown in 1986. It was rumored that his rise in politics was financed in part by Yamashita's hoard. One of many stories about Marcos places him with a party of Japanese who hid gold in a cave at the end of the war. Later, when explaining his accumulation of wealth, Marcos sometimes denied charges of corruption by coyly referring to this and other presumed links to the treasure.

Whether the dictator ever found Yamashita's gold, he apparently searched diligently, freely using his presidential powers and the nation's armed forces in the hunt. When he declared martial law in 1972, Marcos took full advantage of the clout it conferred to step up his treasure-hunting efforts. He tried to employ unearthly powers as well, consulting Swedish psychic Olof Jonsson, who provided tantalizing hints of the hoard's location.

In 1975, Marcos awarded himself a monopoly on underwater recovery efforts, decreeing that all ▷

future salvage operations in Philippine waters would require his personal approval.

From time to time, scraps of information leaked from the Marcos inner circle indicating that the dictator did indeed find some sort of treasure. In the 1970s, Marcos hired an American, Robert Curtis, to search for buried treasure and remelt bullion to hide its origins. Curtis later told of seeing bars of gold "stacked from floor to ceiling" in one of the dictator's provincial palaces. Various Marcos intimates gave similar reports. The ingots, they said, were of a distinctive shape used around the time of World War II.

In 1981, a group of wealthy Americans, inspired by such reports, offered to purchase Yamashita's hoard. They were turned down; there was no such hoard, said palace spokespeople.

Or maybe there was. After he was deposed, Marcos boasted that he had fourteen billion dollars in gold tucked away in the Philippines. When that claim was made public, he denied all.

Nevertheless, gold and Marcos seemed inextricably linked. Officials of the government of Corazon Aquino, who became president of the Philippines after Marcos's overthrow, believed that her predecessor's loyalists had assembled a stockpile of seventeen tons of gold bullion and were looking for black-market buyers.

Mere rumors of Yamashita's treasure are still enough to tempt fortune hunters. In the first four years of its rule, the Aquino government issued no fewer than eighty-seven permits to treasure seekers. None of the searchers reported any success.

Nor did the legendary treasure-trove confer any benefits upon General Yamashita himself. He was convicted of war crimes and hanged in 1946. □

Ferdinand Marcos waves triumphantly at his inauguration as president of the Philippines on December 30, 1965. With him, from left, are his wife, Imelda, daughter Irene, son Ferdinand, Jr., and his mother, Josefa Marcos.

THE HUNTER'S HEART

T reasure lies in the mind and heart of the hunter, whose quest for riches is an obsession transcending all obstacles. The pursuit of the prize—a hidden wreck, a forgotten mine—requires courage to overcome raging seas, desiccating heat, and hostile rivals; persistence to carry on in the face of temporary failure; and faith to sustain both. But courage, persistence, and faith count for nothing without the hunter's passion, an appetite satisfied only by the fruit of discovery.

The Dream of Treasure

In the shallow waters off Cape Cod, Massachusetts, lie the bones of more than three thousand ships. The stories of many of these wrecks—exciting tales of derring-do and treasure—are as familiar as fairy tales to local youngsters. But when Barry Clifford was growing up in Hyannis, only one tale mattered: that of the pirate ship *Whydah* and her buccaneer captain, "Black Sam" Bellamy.

Eight-year-old Clifford sat wide-eyed as a favorite uncle first told him the ship's story: Named for one of West Africa's busiest slave ports, the *Whydah* was herself a slaver, a three-masted British galley. She was captured by Bellamy in February or March 1717, as she sailed for England after discharging her human cargo in the Caribbean. Over the next several months, Bellamy and his brigands plundered at least half a dozen more ships before heading north. They may have intended to prey on British ships bound for the colonies, sell guns to the French in Canada, or trade with some of New England's less scrupulous merchants. Romance, too, could have been their goal, for the buccaneer captain reputedly had a mistress on Cape Cod.

Whatever their ultimate intention, the pirates did business as usual on their way to the Cape. They boarded the *Mary Ann,* a merchant vessel bearing Madeira wine among her cargo, and that proved to be Black Sam's undoing. Drunk with the contents of the *Mary Ann's* hold, the men of the *Whydah* failed to control their own ship in a sudden storm. She smashed into a sand bar a quarter-mile off the town of Wellfleet on April 26, 1717.

Enraptured by the story, Clifford began hunting for the ship as a child. He dived time and again, exploring the sea bottom for signs of the ill-fated *Whydah*. In those days, Clifford recalls, there was no urgency to his mission: "I'd pretend I was a time traveler wandering in liquid space."

As a teenager, Clifford hung out in seamen's taverns, soaking up more *Whydah* lore. One tale he heard concerned Black Sam's mistress, Maria Hallet, whose anguished voice is said to cry today when storm winds screech over the Cape's outer dunes, wailing for a lover who will never return. But the most tantalizing yarn of all was that the *Whydah's* rich booty—gold, silver, and rubies as big as hens' eggs—still lay within reach, within sight of Wellfleet.

Clifford's search of the written record at first produced a different, less promising story. Numerous accounts of the *Whydah's* sinking quoted Captain Cyprian Southack, a Boston mapmaker sent by the governor of Massachusetts to salvage the vessel. Arriving within a week of the wreck, Southack reported that "there have been 200 men from twenty miles distance plundering the wreck." The implication was that whatever treasure had been aboard was carried off by the scavengers.

Clifford was skeptical of that interpretation. He felt that it would have been impossible to work in the surf after a major storm, especially in the frigid waters of April. That single observation, based on a lifetime on Cape Cod, inspired Clifford to press on with his research.

Eventually, the effort paid off—literally. As Clifford accumulated Southack's letters and logs, his suspicions were confirmed. And he discovered that Southack's frequently quoted statement was incomplete. Southack actually wrote that the wreck indeed was unreachable in the cold, pounding surf but that two hundred men had been "plundering the wreck *of what came ashore.*" To Clifford, this meant that the bulk of the treasure still lay beneath the sea.

Captain Southack's logs also included precise coordinates for the wreck; unfortunately, they related to landmarks that had long since vanished. Once again, careful research was required to pinpoint the site by reconstructing the scene as Southack had found it. At last, in 1982, Clifford was ready to begin his long-anticipated salvage of the *Whydah*.

By then he had developed the skills and contacts necessary to mount such an effort. Clifford had been a ski racer and rodeo rider, a high-school history teacher and football coach, and finally a successful builder and restaurateur. He had money of his own, and he was able to borrow more from various friends.

A tall, boyishly handsome figure who sported a baseball cap emblazoned with a golden skull and crossbones, Barry Clifford was also a born spellbinder and publicist. Young John F. Kennedy, Jr., a summer Cape Cod resident then in his early twenties, signed on for the first months of the *Whydah* treasure expedition. Other celebrity friends and neighbors, from former secretary of state Henry Kissinger to singer Carly Simon, cheered Clifford on from the sidelines.

Fittingly, a television news crew was on hand when the remains of the *Whydah* were located with certainty. Widely scattered and buried under ten feet of sand, the treasure was all Clifford had dreamed of: in excess of $20 million worth of coins, ingots, and jewelry.

The *Whydah* was the first authenticated pirate vessel ever salvaged. Painstakingly excavated over the following six years, the ship's artifacts yielded fascinating details of eighteenth-century pirate life. Pairs of pistols joined with silken scarves told researchers that pirates did not stuff their weapons into their belts—as Errol Flynn and other movieland pirates did in the twentieth century—but slung them from sashes around their necks. The large number of fine navigation instruments suggests that such items were particularly prized in

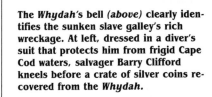

The *Whydah*'s bell *(above)* clearly identifies the sunken slave galley's rich wreckage. At left, dressed in a diver's suit that protects him from frigid Cape Cod waters, salvager Barry Clifford kneels before a crate of silver coins recovered from the *Whydah*.

the New England black markets where pirates such as Sam Bellamy fenced their loot.

To Barry Clifford, one of the biggest thrills was a private one. Thirty years after his Uncle Bill told him bedtime stories of the *Whydah* and other Cape Cod wrecks, Clifford sat on the edge of his aged uncle's bed. "This time it was my turn to tell him a pirate story," he said. "His eyes sparkled like a child's in anticipation. Uncle Bill died later that night. I'm sure he dreamed of treasure." □

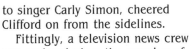

Finders Losers

Jack Slack thought he was immune to treasure fever. In fifteen years of earning a laid-back living as a spear fisherman, underwater photographer, marine surveyor, and water-ski instructor, the thirty-three-year-old Floridian had observed so many futile treasure hunts that he had long ago concluded that shipwrecks were "more closely synonymous with junk than with gold."

Then, on August 27, 1964, less than two months after he and three similarly happy-go-lucky friends had launched a watersport business in the Bahamian city of Freeport, one of his partners discovered a heap of silver coins just offshore, opposite the plush Lucayan Beach Hotel.

Further search led to a stupendous treasure that included more than 16,000 Spanish coins struck between 1548 and the late 1600s. The four excited Americans began hauling their find ashore in burlap sacks and ice chests, and soon Slack's small ocean-side apartment was so crammed with silver that

the building's beams began to groan. His wife complained that she no longer had room to vacuum. The Lucayan Silver Wreck, as it became known, was the remains of an unidentified ship, probably Dutch. At the time it was found, the wreck yielded one of the largest underwater treasure-troves ever raised.

But Slack's was a star-crossed discovery. Difficulties accumulated like grains of beach sand. "We un-

leashed a monster," Slack later wrote in his aptly titled book about the quartet's misadventures, *Finders Losers*. Recovery of the seemingly endless stream of coins required nearly two years. During that time, salvage pirates repeatedly raided the site, and the Bahamian government delayed decisions over the legal status of the coins, meanwhile prohibiting their sale. The partners made one ill-advised move after another—from acquiring dubious business partners to spending pieces of eight in local bars.

Outstanding bills mounted quickly, reaching hundreds of thousands of dollars. The government and various creditors laid claim to more than 70 percent of the treasure, and the four original partners—once carefree friends —became bitter contestants for the rest of it.

Jack Slack, his cynicism about treasure hunting amply confirmed, finally bailed out of the enterprise, relinquishing for just a few thousand dollars his share in a treasure that was estimated to be worth some nine million. □

The Treasure of *Le Chameau*

Since August 26, 1725, when the 600-ton French transport *Le Chameau* struck a reef during a storm off Nova Scotia's rock-strewn Atlantic coast, the ship and the remains of the 310 souls who perished aboard her had rested almost undisturbed. The ship's position was well known; in fact, the reef on which she foundered was dubbed Chameau Rock. On clear days, fish-

ermen from nearby Louisbourg could see her jettisoned cannon lying thirty feet beneath the surface of the water.

Although everyone knew *Le Chameau* was there, for 240 years the ship and the cold, treacherous waters in which she lay had stymied all efforts to locate her reputed treasure: 300,000 French livres in gold and silver—a year's pay for

all the king's troops in New France. It took the imagination and perseverance of a nearly penniless young immigrant to finally land the prize.

Alex Storm was tempered by adversity early in life. Born in 1938 to Dutch parents living in Java, a Dutch colony that was overrun by Japanese troops at the start of World War II, Storm spent five

years of his childhood in a Japanese concentration camp. When he returned to the Netherlands after the war, he learned deep-sea diving, then sailed a small boat around the world and salvaged an ancient wreck off Ceylon. Storm immigrated to Canada in 1959, taking a job as a scuba diver for a salvage firm located in Nova Scotia.

Diving one day off Cape Breton Island, Storm found a 1724 silver livre from *Le Chameau*. Soon he was researching centuries-old French naval documents to figure out precisely how the wreckage had dispersed when the ship broke apart. Eventually he concluded that the part of the hull containing the treasure lay not near Chameau Rock—as had been presumed for centuries—but more than a half-mile closer to shore.

Storm shared his theory with two friends, and in the summer of 1965, the three men covered the targeted site with an underwater rope grid anchored with numbered, cement-filled beer bottles as reference points. Working weekends, they methodically searched each section, discovering a pattern of wreckage that supported Storm's reasoning. In September, the treasure hunters struck pay dirt: a pocket of silver and gold coins lodged in a crevice beneath one of the ship's guns.

By the time they made their discovery public the following April, they had recovered coins worth approximately $700,000— the biggest treasure find in Canadian history.

Predictably, rival claimants immediately materialized, from old business partners of Storm's to the Canadian government. By 1968, when the partners had fended off the last challenger, Storm was already putting the expertise he had gained while salvaging *Le Chameau* to good use diving on wrecks in other parts of the North Atlantic. But the legal wrangling had taught him a lesson common to all successful treasure hunters: "Everyone," he says, "wants to go treasure hunting without getting their feet wet." □

The Pied Piper of *Atocha*

The trim and tidy Key West Yacht Club had seldom seen anything quite like the *Virgilona* when she tied up there one June morning in 1970. Battered and heavily laden with the paraphernalia of the salvage trade, the *Virgilona* was clearly a working boat. Perhaps, some thought, her work was not always legitimate. So the small knot of bystanders watched suspiciously as a tall figure stepped onto the dock. Striding over to a bait box, the new arrival pulled gold bars and old coins from his pocket and laid them out. "Then he told us how we could get into the treasure hunting business," recalls one person who watched the performance.

And a performance it was, for the tanned stranger was Mel Fisher, an engaging wheeler-dealer who had come to Key West in pursuit of one of the greatest prizes of the Spanish Main, *La Nuestra Señora de Atocha.* The rearguard galleon of the 1622 armada bound for Spain with riches from South America, the *Atocha* had sunk during a hurricane. She carried to the bottom with her the bulk of the fleet's treasure.

Spanish salvage boats sped to the scene as soon as the storm abated and easily found the wreck. The *Atocha*'s mizzenmast protruded above the water and her hull was visible fifty-five feet below. Her hatches and gunports, however, had been securely sealed against the storm, and divers could not get into the hull. By the time the salvagers returned with the heavy tools and explosives needed to break in, the ship was gone. A second hurricane had dismembered

Draped with gold chains retrieved from Spanish ships, treasure hunter Mel Fisher displays still more booty: sand-cast gold bars in his left hand and a flower-shaped gold cup in his right.

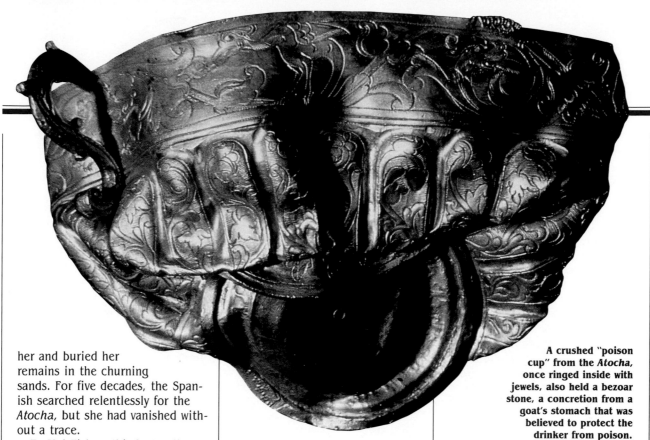

A crushed "poison cup" from the *Atocha*, once ringed inside with jewels, also held a bezoar stone, a concretion from a goat's stomach that was believed to protect the drinker from poison.

her and buried her remains in the churning sands. For five decades, the Spanish searched relentlessly for the *Atocha*, but she had vanished without a trace.

To Mel Fisher, this lost galleon and its immense treasure promised all the romance and adventure that he had craved since his Indiana boyhood. As a youngster, Fisher was sea struck. Once, he nearly drowned in a diving helmet that had been rigged from a bicycle pump and an empty paint can. As an adult, Fisher studied engineering, served in World War II, spent four years spearfishing in Florida, and ran a chicken ranch with his father. In 1951, Fisher opened California's first dive shop in the ranch's feed shed.

By the early 1960s, Fisher had developed a reputation as an underwater filmmaker and the guru of a generation of crack California scuba divers. He was always ready for a new challenge. So, when Kip Wagner asked him to help salvage the wrecks of the 1715 Plate Fleet *(page 111),* Fisher eagerly packed his wife and their four small children into a car and headed east. "I sold my business, my yacht, my

home, my extra car, everything I had and just cashed out," he recalls. Six members of the diving club he had founded gave up their jobs to go with him.

In less than a decade, the group that Fisher founded, Treasure Salvors Inc., turned into the largest treasure-hunting organization in existence. Its vessels ranged up and down Florida's east coast, locating more than five hundred wrecks in the 1960s and recovering some two million dollars in treasure. There were full-time researchers, electronics experts, and archaeologists on the payroll. A retinue of accountants and lawyers sorted out the complex financial schemes that kept the business afloat and fended off claims of state and local governments and rival treasure hunters.

Presiding over this small empire from the decks of the *Golden Doubloon,* a replica of a Spanish vessel, Fisher gained repute as an

irrepressible salesman with a penchant for exaggeration—the "Fisher factor," his crews called it.

Never was the Fisher factor more evident than in the search for the *Atocha.* "Just wait until you see the main pile," he declared. "There'll be stacks of silver bars lined up like a brick wall on the ocean floor. There'll be bars of gold and treasure chests filled with gold and silver coins. It's all there. Believe me," said Fisher. And his divers did believe him—frequently going for weeks without pay when the times were lean. The trouble was, the fabled galleon was nowhere to be found.

The 1622 disaster had been the subject of voluminous and heated correspondence between various seventeenth-century bureaucrats and the mariners who had searched for the wreck. Records seemed to indicate that the *Atocha* had gone down at the head of the Florida Keys, but extensive magnetom- ⟡

eter surveys and test digs in the area produced no sign of her.

In 1970, two years after the search had begun, new research suggested that the exploration was about one hundred miles off the mark. The Spanish galleon *Atocha* had evidently gone down in the Marquesas, some twenty miles from Key West.

Following that discovery, the group closed in on the prize. In July 1975, Fisher's eldest son, Dirk, then twenty-one and captain of the salvage tug *Northwind,* found nine brass cannon from the *Atocha.* But the jubilation over the find was short-lived. Three days later, Dirk, his young wife, Angel, and diver Rick Gage all drowned when the *Northwind* capsized. Their deaths nearly extinguished

Fisher's resolve. "I thought, 'Maybe it just ain't worth it,' " he remembers. "But my son would have wanted me to complete the search, so I said, 'Okay, I'll keep it up until I find her.' "

And Fisher did keep it up, pressing onward through a decade of tantalizing but unrewarding individual finds—an olive jar here, a silver bar there. It was July 20, 1985, the tenth anniversary of Dirk Fisher's death, when his brother Kane radioed Key West with an exultant dispatch: "Throw away the charts! We've got it. We've got it."

The *Atocha* yielded a bonanza that was unmatched by any previous ancient shipwreck. Fisher proclaimed it to be worth a total of $400 million. Many experts believed the figure was inflated, but

it was impossible to tell. The treasure would continue to rise from the sea for years to come, and only a fraction of it would ever appear on the open market.

In October 1986, a computer labored for sixteen hours to divide the 2,700-page inventory of artifacts among six hundred divers, crewmen, and investors in Treasure Salvors Inc. Fisher vowed that his own five percent share would never be sold, but would reside in a Key West museum.

For him, the thrill of the hunt was over, so the prize had lost much of its glitter. Not long afterward, Mel Fisher dissolved his company, sold his own interest in the *Atocha,* and began scheming and dreaming of other treasures lying in other seas. □

A Pioneer in Two Realms

Above and below the sea, the inventive mind of industrialist Ed Link proved to be more than a match for technological challenges. Link originally won fame in 1934 as the inventor of the Link trainer, aviation's first flight simulator. The device mimicked the movements of aircraft, providing training for pilots without the hazards and costs of actual flight. Descendants of his invention are now used to coach astronauts and airline pilots.

But in 1949, Link quit the company he had founded and sought other challenges for his fertile imagination. He became a treasure hunter, and his retirement allowed him to devote full time to this

passion. His gleaming, bald head and thick, horn-rimmed glasses became a familiar sight in ports throughout the world. For nearly a decade, Link built a reputation as an amateur archaeologist, exploring the pirate stronghold of Port Royal, Jamaica, salvaging ancient wrecks off Greece and Sicily, and excavating Caesarea, the sunken seaport of Herod the Great. In 1958, off Haiti, he discovered an anchor that some experts believed came from Columbus's caravel, the *Santa Maria.*

Link the engineer applied his inventive talents to his retirement hobby, developing devices to ease the salvager's job and protect valuable artifacts from the rigors of

excavation. One notable invention, unveiled in 1955, was a deep-diving shelter. In it, workers could live on the seafloor for many days, safe from the cold, watery surroundings and the hardships of repeated ascents and descents.

The seafloor chamber was the linchpin of Link's Man in the Sea Project, a breakthrough effort that enabled explorers to work hundreds of feet below the surface for extended periods of time. Because of Link, other innovators were encouraged to follow with a stunning series of inventions—from mini-submarines to remotely piloted vehicles—that have vastly extended the range of undersea archaeologists and treasure hunters. □

Inventor Ed Link emerges from one of his experimental decompression chambers after a test conducted on the French Riviera in 1963.

The Double Cross of "The Tres"

Spaniards of the eighteenth century had called the ship *Los Tres Puentes*—"The Three Decker." To the Florida treasure-diving community of the twentieth century, she was simply "The Tres," one of the most elusive wrecks in the Keys.

The great merchantman sank in a storm in 1733, together with eighteen other ships sailing to Spain with the king's long-awaited shipment of New World riches. She was clearly shown on charts locating victims of the disaster. But she frustrated two centuries of reclamation efforts until one hot summer day in 1962, when Miami building contractor-turned-treasure hunter Martin Meylach spied her ballast heap from the window of a small airplane.

"A virgin galleon," he crowed to himself as he and his three partners made plans to salvage the ship in the spring. In the mean-time, they agreed, they would stay clear of her to throw any claim jumpers off the trail. The scheme failed. When Meylach and his friends returned to The Tres that spring, there appeared to be nothing left but a big hole where rival divers had torn the wreck apart. "Our virgin galleon was a shambles," Meylach recalls.

But as the divers poked mournfully at the matted grasses on the edge of the depression, their spirits began to lift. In the years since her sinking, *Los Tres Puentes'* three decks had collapsed on one another, stacking their contents neatly amid the beams, spikes, and rods of the ship's structure. The winter's looting had skimmed the treasure of the upper decks but had left untouched the most valuable portion of the treasure. The real booty was buried deep below, just barely visible to Meylach and his colleagues. A triumphant Meylach had the last laugh on the looters. He and his friends retrieved a trove of silver ingots, gold ornaments, porcelain, and other riches that had been stored on the third and lowest deck of *Los Tres Puentes.*

The poachers, concentrating on the ballast mound, had stopped digging less than two feet from the ship's main treasure. □

Notations of modern treasure diver Tom Gurr mark an antique map showing where ships of Spain's 1733 fleet sank off the Florida Keys. Number nine on the map is *Los Tres Puentes.* Art McKee's *Capitana* and Gurr's *San José (page 96)* lie close by.

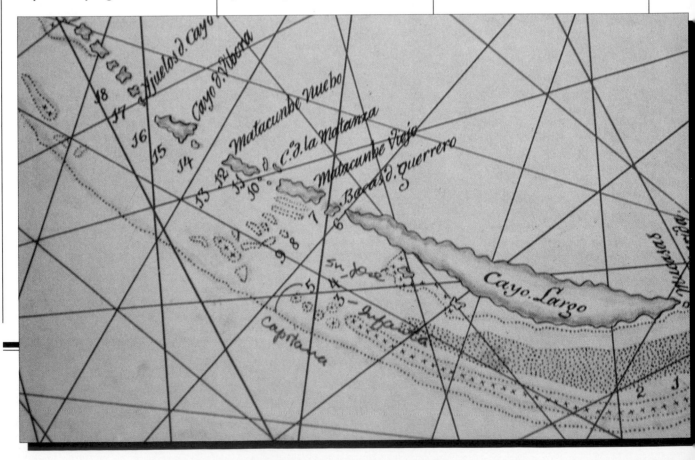

The Birth of the Boom

Before people could strap on scuba gear and swim through the water as freely as fish, the ocean floor remained as remote as the moon to all but the hardiest, best-equipped divers. So, when a twenty-four-year-old commercial diver from New Jersey named Art McKee took a job tending an underwater pipeline near Key West, Florida, in 1934, he had the local waters almost entirely to himself.

Although Art McKee had no inkling of it at the time, the reefs and shoals that became his backyard harbored the graves of galleons lost two centuries earlier in one of the greatest disasters of the Spanish Main.

On July 15, 1733, the treasure fleet that sailed each year from Havana to Cádiz was making its way up through the Straits of Florida on the first and most dangerous leg of its journey when it encountered a hurricane. Nineteen ships, including the four galleons carrying the king's annual silver shipment, were sunk or stranded along eighty miles of jagged, coral-fringed coastline between Key Largo and Key Vaca.

The loss of an entire fleet was a staggering calamity, and the Spaniards wasted no time launching a massive salvage operation that would last several years. But the operation proved to be an embarrassment to colonial officials, for Indian divers recovered more cargo than was listed on the official manifests—incontrovertible evidence that the ships were smuggling large quantities of riches traveling "unofficially."

Triumphant Art McKee points to the chalked sign left by burglars who tried and failed to enter the strongroom of McKee's museum.

The disaster was duly recorded in official documents that were transferred to Spain, filed, and forgotten. Like the documents, the ships also lay unremembered, covered with a mantle of sand, sea grass, and coral.

Centuries passed. Then, in 1938, Art McKee, who had made a hobby of searching the reefs for salvageable brass and iron to sell to scrap-metal dealers, came upon a one-hundred-foot-long, fifteen-foot-high mound of stones. It was the ballast of an ancient ship. The mound was pointed out to McKee by a friend named Reggie Roberts, who suspected the wreck might be valuable. Roberts, however, lacked the expertise to salvage it.

The discovery stirred McKee's imagination and energies. He combed local libraries for information about old shipwrecks in the area. Finding nothing of note there, he wrote to the General Archives of the Indies in Seville, the repository of Spain's voluminous New World files. Months later, he received a thick packet containing copies of the documents chronicling the loss of the 1733 treasure fleet. Written in the flowing, nearly illegible Spanish script called *procesal,* they were difficult to read, but McKee could make out enough to conclude that his pile of ballast had come from the fleet's flagship, its *capitana.*

In the following months, McKee and a group of friends shifted nearly 250 tons of ballast by hand in order to uncover whatever the Spanish salvagers had left behind. Using an airlift—an underwater excavation device that functions like a huge vacuum cleaner—they uncovered a prodigious haul: more than one thousand silver coins, as well as cannon and other weapons, silver statues and religious medals, candlesticks, and crockery. Although the monetary value of ◊

95

the treasure was not great—certainly nothing compared to the treasure of wrecks discovered in later years—the find caused a sensation. *"El Capitana,"* as McKee called the galleon, was featured in magazines and documentary films, and tourists flocked to the Keys to gaze at her remains from a glass-bottomed boat.

During his lifetime, Art McKee and his partners salvaged more than thirty wrecks along the Florida coast. He ventured throughout the Caribbean, amassing a record of exploits that read like pages from the novels of his crony, tough-guy adventure writer Mickey Spillane. McKee's discoveries started a treasure-hunting craze that lured other divers to Florida, but, ironically, the recognized father of Florida treasure hunting never struck it rich himself. The great mother lode of intact treasure— the dream of every fortune hunter—eluded McKee throughout his life. He supported himself with the proceeds of a treasure museum he opened in 1949 to display the artifacts of his expeditions. His ventures were usually financed by high rollers willing and able to pay for the privilege of associating with McKee. Although treasure hoards were not always forthcoming, the investors were seldom disappointed—nor was McKee.

To him, the absence of material rewards seemed insignificant compared to the allure of the dangerous, exhilarating, heartbreaking profession he had pioneered. "You never get enough," he reflected shortly before his death in 1980. □

Throwing It All Away

During the summer of 1968, Tom Gurr, a south Florida engineer who had once been a Navy diver, culminated a passionate, four-year pursuit of riches by discovering the remains of the *San José de las Animas.* The galleon was one of the many Spanish merchant ships that sank off the treacherous coast of Florida in 1733.

To Gurr, the find was the climax of a dream. But its aftermath would soon turn into a nightmare, one that he brought to an end in a startling, novel way.

The salvaging of sunken ships off the Florida coast was once a simple, if strenuous, process. Although the assembly of skilled workers and adequate equipment to recover a wreck could be costly, risky, and time-consuming, the essential rule was finders keepers. No state, local, or federal government interfered or claimed any part of a treasure. However, as the volume and value of salvaged treasure grew during the 1950s and the 1960s, Florida lawmakers enacted increasingly restrictive regulations governing the salvagers' work with the intention of preserving historic artifacts and gaining for

the state a share of the prizes.

State jurisdiction ended three miles offshore—generally interpreted to mean three miles from the beach—so many salvagers, Gurr included, confined their explorations to areas beyond that limit. But the rules changed soon after the discovery of the *San José:* A judge ruled that Florida's territory extended not three miles beyond the shoreline but three miles past the outer reefs. Overnight, Gurr's prize became subject to Florida law, and the state claimed 50 percent of his find.

Five years of costly court battles followed, and Tom Gurr went broke. Although the treasure he

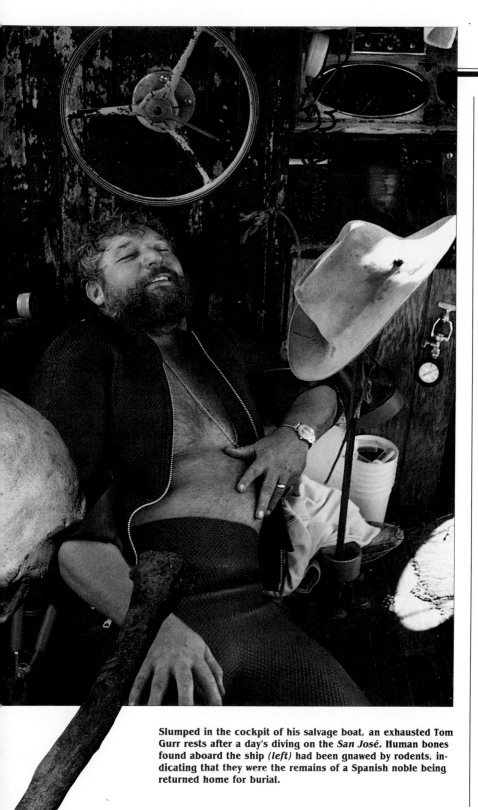

had found was estimated to be worth three to four million dollars, he was forbidden to sell a single coin. His defeat was nearly complete; Gurr's salvage ship even sank at dockside.

Frustrated and angry, Gurr tried to end the nightmare—and thumb his nose at the state—by returning the treasure to the sea. On New Year's Eve, 1973, on the fifth anniversary of the state's claim, Gurr began dumping the treasure back onto the wreck site. As CBS television cameras rolled, barrel after barrel of artifacts, gold, and silver went over the side. Finally, Gurr's own small boat sank beneath his feet, and he had to be rescued by the TV camerapeople.

But the nightmare did not end there. State officials charged Gurr with grand larceny on the ground that the treasure was not his to dump. They also claimed that Gurr had illegally sold some items. Eventually, an agreement was reached: Florida would drop its charges, and Gurr would help retrieve the *San José*'s treasure for a second time. He did, but the riches that he had once hoped to realize from the find continued to elude him. Much of the prize was consumed by the fees of lawyers, divers, and others involved.

Gurr put treasure hunting behind him and became a successful engineering executive. He calls his life as a salvager "a long vacation. I'm glad I did it, but I would never want to do it again." □

Slumped in the cockpit of his salvage boat, an exhausted Tom Gurr rests after a day's diving on the *San José*. Human bones found aboard the ship *(left)* had been gnawed by rodents, indicating that they were the remains of a Spanish noble being returned home for burial.

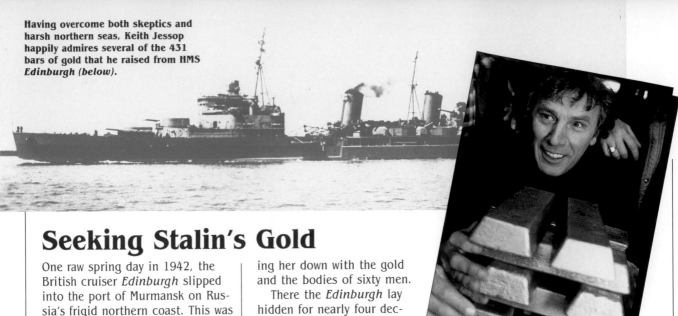

Seeking Stalin's Gold

One raw spring day in 1942, the British cruiser *Edinburgh* slipped into the port of Murmansk on Russia's frigid northern coast. This was the Allies' darkest year of World War II, and the ship's mission was shrouded in extraordinary secrecy. Soon, the *Edinburgh*'s crew began hoisting aboard numbers of small but heavy wooden crates. The contents, according to the cargo manifest, were beans. But the watchful eyes of heavily armed Red Army soldiers made it plain that the boxes held some other, far more valuable consignment.

With dramatic suddenness, the ship's mission was revealed to the laboring sailors: One case slipped from its hoisting sling and crashed to the deck, splitting open and spilling its contents. Gold gleamed in the slanting northern light.

The secret shipment consisted of ninety-three crates containing 465 outsize ingots, each weighing twenty-eight pounds. Stalin was sending the bullion to the United States to pay for American weapons and supplies, sorely needed by Russia's beleaguered defenders. But the gold was not to reach its destination, for on April 30, 1942, five days after it was loaded and 250 miles out in the Barents Sea, the *Edinburgh* was struck by two well-aimed torpedoes fired by a German U-boat.

Two days later, a small flotilla of British minesweepers rescued the cruiser's surviving crew and scuttled the ship with a torpedo, sending her down with the gold and the bodies of sixty men.

There the *Edinburgh* lay hidden for nearly four decades, tipped on her side beneath eight hundred feet of water. British, Russian, and Norwegian salvagers tried repeatedly to locate her in the 1950s and 1960s, but without success; the site of the warship's sinking had been incorrectly recorded by the Germans and the British at the battle site.

Thus, it seemed likely that failure would greet a Briton by the name of Keith Jessop when he set out to find the *Edinburgh* and recover the gold in the late 1970s. Although Jessop had few initial resources other than his little company's registered capital of one hundred pounds sterling, he was a veteran cold-water diver, with experience in the North Sea. Jessop also had the determination and skill to raise money—an elemental necessity, as he and his backers were to discover. They would spend some $10 million on their operation, employing such sophisticated equipment as a remote-controlled robot submarine that could send back video pictures of likely finds, and a salvage vessel whose computers could keep her hovering over one spot despite buffeting winds and currents.

The equipment soon proved its worth. A wreck was pinpointed with sonar during rough weather on May 14, 1981, and two days later the robot sub sent up confirming video pictures of the *Edinburgh.*

Jessop also had the help of brave and skillful divers, who had to work at a depth of eight hundred feet in near-freezing water under a crushing pressure of 350 pounds per square inch. The divers spent two days in a shipboard chamber to become acclimated to the pressures. They also worked in shifts while living in a diving bell at the sea bottom, wearing suits heated by hot water and breathing a mixture of oxygen and helium formulated for use at great depths. The divers' return to the surface consumed seven full days of gradual decompression.

The doggedness, intelligent planning, and courage paid off. The crew raised 431 of the 465 bars loaded on the *Edinburgh*— five and one-half tons of gold worth about $81 million. With the precision of accountants, they apportioned the find: Great Britain and Russia shared 55 percent, while the salvagers and their investors kept 45 percent.

Jessop's personal share amounted to more than $3.5 million worth of gold. □

Going for *DeBraak*

On May 25, 1798, a sudden storm overtook the British warship *De-Braak* as she approached the mouth of the Delaware River. She sank, taking with her thirty-four members of her eighty-two-man crew. Captain James Drew was among those lost.

When she went down, the *De-Braak* was escorting a captured Spanish merchant vessel, an unremarkable sight, if not a frequent one. But when some of the wreck's survivors began paying for their lodgings with Spanish coins, the bayside towns gave this simple fact new and provocative significance. The *DeBraak*, it was rumored, had been plundering Spanish treasure ships, and, according to the irresistible logic of greed, her sunken remains must be filled with a fortune in booty.

Over the years, the legend persisted and grew. The bounty's reputed worth became $5 million, or $50 million, perhaps $500 million in bullion, jewels, and coin. For 186 years after she slipped to the bottom of Delaware Bay, the *De-Braak* and her reputed treasure inspired one fruitless salvage attempt after another. Fierce tidal currents and turbid waters thwarted all attempts to find the ship until the summer of 1984, when a graying, soft-spoken commercial salvager named Harvey Harrington took up the quest.

Using modern electronic search tools, Harrington found the *De-Braak* after just three weeks of searching. That part, he said, was "embarrassingly easy." But it was all uphill from there.

Harrington, a professional diver with twenty years' experience on underwater construction and maintenance jobs, had spent years planning and raising money for the salvage operation. Within a year after finding the wreck, however, Harrington's company, Sub-Sal, was broke, having spent $500,000 on legal fees and unproductive salvage efforts. Sub-Sal passed into the hands of New Hampshire real-estate developer L. John Davidson. He renewed the salvage effort on the *De-Braak* but retrieved ◊

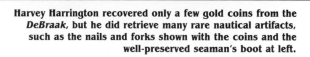

Harvey Harrington recovered only a few gold coins from the *DeBraak*, but he did retrieve many rare nautical artifacts, such as the nails and forks shown with the coins and the well-preserved seaman's boot at left.

virtually nothing of value. Davidson spent more than one million dollars before quitting in 1986.

Both men's efforts were rich in controversy, if poor in gold. According to a disgruntled ex-employee, Sub-Sal illegally raised historic artifacts and spirited them away. It was also alleged that Harrington ordered his divers to suppress news about archaeological finds, fearing that such information might prompt government intervention and thus slow down the operation.

The wreck was virtually devoid of conventional treasure. Early on, one hundred gold and silver coins were unearthed—and used by Harrington as collateral to raise money to search again. Finally, cables were slung beneath the ship, and she was hauled out of the water, together with three hundred truckloads of mud, sand, and silt. Out of all that debris there emerged one gold coin, seven silver dollars, and a handful of copper pennies.

The real treasure aboard the *DeBraak* was the rich store of archaeological items that were ignored in the salvagers' dogged search for gold. In three years, the wreck yielded 20,000 artifacts that have since provided historians with a detailed picture of eighteenth-century shipboard life.

Although the record supports skepticism regarding the *DeBraak*'s status as a treasure ship, true believers remain faithful to the legend. As he reluctantly shut down his unprofitable operation, John Davidson predicted that, even though the *DeBraak* has been raised from the water, "someone will come along . . . and start looking for the treasure all over again." □

Treasure without Greed

One of the most successful and sophisticated organizations to seek treasure under the sea is not motivated by a lust for riches; instead, it is a labor of love for the best-selling novelist who finances it.

American author Clive Cussler has used his considerable earnings from adventure novels such as *Raise the Titanic* and *Dragon* to create and fund a nonprofit enterprise called the National Underwater and Marine Agency (NUMA). Aided by dozens of skilled volunteers and employing the best available high-tech equipment, Cussler and his organization have scored successes that some people say have ushered in a new era in underwater exploration.

Rather than raising a wreck, NUMA and Cussler turn over sonar pictures and other information about their finds to the national authorities involved, keeping nothing for themselves except the thrill that accompanies a significant discovery.

Their finds are notable as much for their historical significance as for their monetary value. In 1984, NUMA's explorers discovered the remains of the German submarine *U-20*, which had helped bring the United States into World War I by sinking the British liner *Lusitania*. The *U-20* itself ran aground and sank in a fog off the coast of Denmark in 1916.

During the same expedition that turned up the German U-boat,

NUMA located the wreck of the freighter *Montclair* off Weymouth, England. This ship was thought to have carried a fortune in gold out of France virtually under the noses of the invading Germans in 1940. NUMA was also responsible for identifying the remains of another World War II ship, the *Leopoldville*, which was sunk by a German torpedo near Cherbourg, France, on Christmas Eve, 1944. Some 800 of the 2,200 American troops on board the Belgian liner died when she went down.

Cussler and his researchers found the *Leopoldville* literally on the run. They made a quick sonar pass over her suspected resting place in their search vessel while being hustled away by French authorities who had denied them a search permit.

Since the late 1970s, Cussler has engaged in twenty to twenty-five other expeditions. He has located Union and Confederate ships from the Atlantic coast to the Mississippi River. Once—while vainly searching for the *Bon Homme Richard*, the ship of Captain John Paul Jones, the father of the United States Navy—NUMA located a sunken Russian spy ship.

Despite the praise he has received, Cussler calls himself a "dilettante." And he will continue to seek wrecks without riches. "It's fun," he says, "because I don't have to hire attorneys to claim anything I find." □

American author Clive Cussler displays sonar photos of the World War II wreck *Leopoldville.*

Bermuda's Swashbuckler

The treacherous reefs surrounding the "still-vex'd Bermoothes," as Shakespeare called storm-swept Bermuda in his play *The Tempest,* have drawn treasure hunters since the first Europeans arrived in the sixteenth century. Teddy Tucker, the island's most renowned salvage diver, is only the latest among many—if one of the most colorful and inventive.

Tucker once provided a magazine writer with this thumbnail autobiography: "I have been a British Navy deserter, a soldier of fortune, a gold smuggler, a stowaway, and a good-natured brawler. I have been in so many jails throughout the world, from Belfast to Saigon, that I can't count the number of times the gendarmes have locked me up or remember their reasons for doing it. Nowadays my troubles are more respectable, but they are as exciting as ever. My business is treasure hunting."

The facts indicate that Tucker was not guilty of hyperbole. The black sheep of one of the island's most prominent families, Tucker pulled off his first salvage job at the age of fourteen, when he and a school friend filched two cases of wine from a Spanish ship that had run aground a few miles northwest of Bermuda. The two boys sold part of the cache and drank the rest, passing out while drifting through busy Hamilton harbor in their rowboat.

A year later, Tucker stowed away on a merchantman bound for England, where he lied about his age and joined the British Navy in time for World War II. After a checkered postwar career, he returned to Bermuda in 1948 and started a commercial salvage business with his brother-in-law, Bob Canton.

In 1950, the two men found the wreckage of an old ship but waited six years before they began exploring it. The ship was later identified as the *San Pedro,* a Spanish merchant vessel lost in 1596, and out of its ruins first came a sixteenth-century bronze apothecary's mortar and a small gold cube. More gold and silver artifacts were found, including an emerald-studded cross once worn by a bishop of Lima, Peru. The cross, valued in 1972 at $200,000, is still considered to be one of the most valuable single items ever recovered from a shipwreck.

The *San Pedro* provided Tucker with his first taste of the bureaucratic turmoil that often plagues treasure hunters—and furnished the bureaucrats with their first taste of Tucker's style. When the government threatened to confiscate the found objects because they had been discovered in territorial waters, an angry Tucker stuffed the treasure into a potato sack, hid the sack in an underwater cave, and vowed to leave it there rather than relinquish it to the authorities.

The imbroglio was settled in 1961 when the *San Pedro* treasure was sold to the government for $100,000, less than half its esti-mated value at the time. But the agreement smoothed ruffled feathers and led to an amicable arrangement by which Tucker and the government could share in the spoils of his work.

By then, Tucker was well on his way to becoming one of the world's most successful underwater treasure hunters. Over the years, using such offbeat but effective methods as dangling from a helium-filled balloon to scan the coastline for clues, Tucker and his colleagues have found more than one hundred wrecks dating from the sixteenth through the nineteenth centuries.

Finally enjoying a career that suits his restless, swashbuckling temperament, Tucker comments, "The hazards are great, but the rewards are high, so I plan to pursue undersea treasure for the rest of my life." □

Bermuda's innovative Teddy Tucker dangles from a helium balloon to scout for treasure. One of his first finds *(above, left)* was an emerald cross worn by a bishop of Lima, Peru.

The Phantom Galleon

It was midnight, January 4, 1656. Beneath a moonless sky, the twenty-two ships of the marquis de Montealegre's Madrid-bound Tierra Firme Armada were nosing through the treacherous Bahama Channel when a blast of cannon fire shattered the enveloping silence. It was a warning shot fired from the *Nuestra Señora de los Maravillas,* the fleet's rearguard galleon, to caution the other ships that shallow water lay all around them.

The result was pandemonium. In their panic, ships lumbered right and left without regard for one another. It was every ship for herself, and in the melee, the *Maravillas* was struck broadside and broken in two. Her forward section snagged on reefs in thirty feet of water. The rest of the ship was swept away by the currents. As it dragged across the ocean floor, the stern section spilled coins and other treasure like change from a ripped purse.

The *Maravillas* carried one of the richest cargoes ever shipped aboard a single Spanish treasure vessel: 260 tons of silver, along with consignments of gold and gemstones. Spanish salvagers recovered a few tons of the silver and forty pounds of small gold bars, all from the bow. The richly laden stern and all of the spilled cargo seemed lost forever.

The *Maravillas* remained lost for three centuries, although she periodically offered tantalizing tokens of her presence in the form of black clumps of sulfided silver coins turned up occasionally by fishermen. Every few decades, a passing ship would spy ancient timbers or lumps of gray metal that, when retrieved, turned out to be huge silver ingots. But treasure hunters who followed up on these clues invari-

ably found that all traces of the ship had vanished under the shifting, sandy bottom.

In 1960, this elusive phantom captured the imagination of a young adventurer named Robert Marx. Still in his twenties, Marx had already filled his life with more excitement than most people three times his age. When he was twelve, Marx ran away from his Pittsburgh home four times. On his last sojourn he headed for Jamaica by bicycle to search for treasure in the sunken city of Port Royal. The journey was interrupted in Richmond, Virginia, where Marx was hit by a truck. After he got out of the hospital, he was consigned

Diver Robert Marx displays pieces of eight he found in the *Maravillas.* Above are some of the emeralds, gold bars, jewelry, and coins given up by the seventeenth-century wreck.

Emerald-studded jewelry, gold bars, and silver coins were raised from the *Maravillas* by Herbert Humphreys, Jr. *(right).*

to a juvenile detention farm.

In 1955, after a three-year hitch in the Marine Corps, Marx flung himself into a hectic career as a self-taught marine archaeologist. In Seville, Spain, he buried himself for months at a time in the archives of the West Indies trade, filling crates full of notes on Spanish ships and shipwrecks. He sailed a replica of Columbus's smallest ship, the *Niña*, across the Atlantic, explored the Yucatán, and dived on shipwrecks in the Mediterranean and the Caribbean. All the while, he churned out a stream of books and magazine articles describing his exploits. Eventually, Marx realized his childhood ambition by helping to excavate the remains of Port Royal.

But Marx's personal grail was the elusive *Maravillas*. In 1968, he joined Kip Wagner's Real Eight company *(pages 110-111).* From then on, whenever he was not actively working the 1715 wrecks that were Real Eight's franchise, he pursued the *Maravillas*. In 1972, after obtaining backing from a group of Wall Street financiers, Marx and a partner took the Real Eight's salvage ship, the *Grifon*, on an exhaustive search. After four fruitless months, they were weighing anchor to leave for home when two

smooth, Spanish-style ballast rocks emerged from the sea wedged tightly in the flukes of the *Grifon*'s anchor. Further search revealed artifacts—including a 1655 coin—that indicated the *Grifon* had anchored directly over the bow of the Spanish galleon *Maravillas.* During the next six weeks, Marx and his divers brought up silver bars, specie, and artifacts worth between $15 million and $20 million. So abundant was the trove that they filled a jellybean jar with gemstones.

Marx soon embarked on a search for the rest of the *Maravillas*. It turned up three miles away, marked by the tip of an anchor protruding from the seafloor. But before Marx could move to the new site, Bahamian government officials—suspicious that he was sneaking recovered treasure out of their waters—threatened to arrest him and confiscate his ship. Marx fled to Florida, but not before dragging the *Maravillas*'s anchor away from the potential riches of the ship's stern section in order to hide its location.

Marx was not allowed to return to the area for several years. Without his knowledge of the stern's

whereabouts, the *Maravillas* was a ghost once more.

The elusive galleon might have remained hidden, but for the arrival in 1986 of a ghost buster named Herbert Humphreys, Jr. Armed with an arsenal of high-tech devices—and a Bahamian government permit to search 161 square miles of ocean and shoreline—Humphreys located the ship and raised emeralds, amethysts, Ming dynasty porcelain, weapons, jewelry, gold bars, military decorations, and silver coins and ingots.

Humphreys may have succeeded where others failed because, after three centuries of concealment, the skeleton of the phantom *Maravillas* was showing signs of rising from the depths on her own, aided by nothing but the currents that had buried her in 1656. □

1961: A Sea Odyssey

"Nothing, except perhaps the landing of a flying saucer in one's backyard, is quite so disruptive of everyday life as the discovery of sunken treasure," wrote Arthur C. Clarke in 1964.

It was an apt analogy for Clarke, the best-selling author of *2001: A Space Odyssey* and other stories of science fiction and fact, for this genial British writer once participated in a real-life adventure under the seas off the coast of Sri Lanka, where he has lived since 1956.

Also involved in the episode was Mike Wilson, Clarke's partner in a diving and undersea documentary business. In 1961, Wilson returned from filming in the Great Basses, a wave-swept line of submerged rocks on the south coast of Ceylon, as Sri Lanka was then known. He was carrying a small trunk into which he had packed musket balls, clumps of blackened silver coins cemented together by corrosion and coral, and two small brass cannon, burnished by centuries of being rolled in the sand. Clarke's first look into the trunk, he wrote later, "was was one of the unforgettable moments of a lifetime."

When the men cleaned the coins with battery acid, they discovered Persian rupees minted in 1702—possibly part of the cargo of an old trade vessel that was blown onto the Great Basses by a monsoon as she rounded Ceylon's south coast on the old and heavily traveled Spice Route to India.

They salvaged the ship during the next three summers, donating most of the coins and artifacts to the Smithsonian Institution and the governments of Great Britain and Sri Lanka.

For years afterward, Clarke kept the now-empty trunk in his office, where he could see it every time he raised his eyes from his typewriter. "Out of the chest wells a curious metallic tang as of iodine and seaweed—not at all unpleasant," he once wrote. "It is now one of the most evocative smells I know; for the rest of my life it will bring back vivid memories of the sea, and of spray-drenched rocks glistening beneath the equatorial sun. It is the scent of treasure." □

Clad in a native sarong, science-fiction author Arthur C. Clarke relaxes on the patio of his home in Colombo, Sri Lanka. Above is a Persian rupee that Clarke found in the Great Basses off the coast of Sri Lanka.

The Hare's Tale

Many people dream of finding lost treasure, but few ever have the chance even to look for it. That changed briefly in 1979, when a whimsical British author and artist by the name of Kit Williams gave anyone with the price of a book the opportunity to become a bona fide treasure hunter.

The book was *Masquerade.* It told the story of a magical hare's journey through the realms of earth, air, fire, and water. Superficially resembling a children's fairy tale, the book was actually a treasure map. Its beguiling color pictures and short, cryptic text were intricate clues leading to a bejeweled, eighteen-karat gold figure of a hare that Williams had encased in terra cotta and buried somewhere in the British Isles.

The book sold more than a million copies, inspired an opera, and launched a frenzied twenty-seven-month-long search of the English countryside that ended in 1982 when the hare was located in a Bedfordshire park. The finder was a retiring fellow named Ken Thomas, who admitted to having only partially solved the puzzle. He modestly credited his dog with pinpointing the treasure.

Thomas's success seemed to bear out an old truth, that luck is the essential ingredient in treasure hunting. But six years later, in 1988, it was revealed that the discovery of the hare represented a shadier tradition: outright chicanery. "Ken Thomas" was really Dugald Thompson, the business partner of a man named John Guard. And Guard was the paramour of Veronica Robertson, a former girlfriend of artist Williams. Although

Williams had never told Robertson where he buried the hare, she knew enough to deduce that it was somewhere in Bedfordshire's Ampthill Park. Dead-of-night searches with a metal detector had done the rest. □

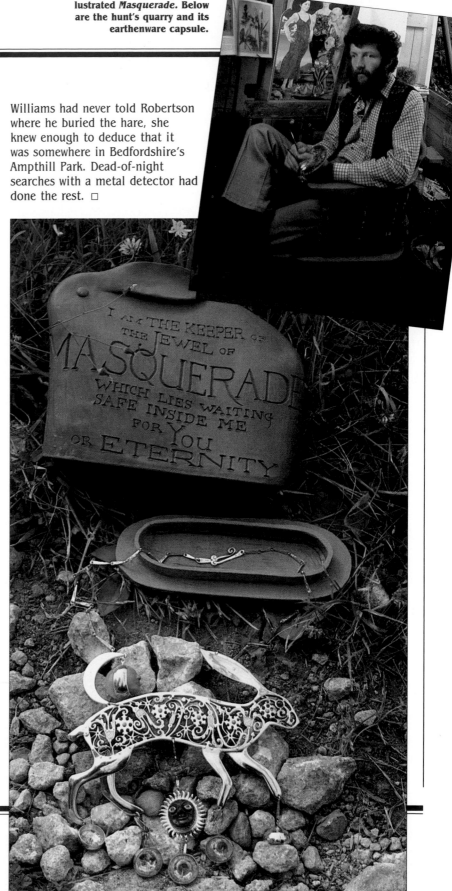

The Indispensable Homewrecker

When it was first published in 1960, *The Treasure Diver's Guide* was greeted as just another entry in the dubious file of treasure hunt intelligence. The book purported to describe all the world's richest sunken treasures and provide their locations and other information to guide would-be fortune hunters. Predictably, professional treasure salvagers were skeptical. "Who would be crazy enough to give real locations of treasure wrecks?" asked one old pro. He and others figured the book would be about as reliable as a whispered tip in a dockside barroom or a crumbling map with *X* marking the spot.

But as both professional and armchair shipwreck enthusiasts soon discovered, *The Treasure Diver's Guide* was the real thing—a legitimate labor of devotion and scholarship. Its author, John S. Potter, Jr., spent several years in the late 1950s interviewing two hundred treasure divers and examining archives—especially those of Spain—to catalog every major shipwreck since biblical times. There were details about each vessel's cargo, the circumstances of her loss, and whatever was known about her whereabouts.

The book became as indispensable to treasure hunters as their airlifts and underwater metal detectors. People got rich excavating ships that they initially read about in the *Guide*. The book supposedly inspired so many expeditions that it acquired the nickname "the Homewrecker."

Although he is without peer as a documentarian, Potter was unsuccessful as a treasure hunter. In 1955, he organized the Atlantic Salvage Company to recover one of the biggest prizes: three hundred tons of silver thought to be lying at the bottom of Spain's Vigo Bay. There, in 1702, the Plate Fleet commanded by Don Manuel del Valesco was sunk by Dutch and British warships as it unloaded its cargo of New World treasure.

Potter's divers combed the wreck site for five years without reward, as scores of other treasure hunters followed the pages of his book toward their own rich finds.

The author harbors no jealousies, however. His guide, since revised, remains the standard reference of the treasure trade, and Potter is a successful businessman in Hong Kong. □

In a gathering storm *(top)*, divers search Spain's Vigo Bay from John Potter's salvage vessel, the *Dios Te Guarde*. Below, the salvage frogmen, from left, are Mike Gaynor, Potter, Owen Lee, Florent Ramaugé, and Robert Sténuit.

A Mystery Solved

The nautical court of inquiry that convened in Auckland on November 28, 1902, captured the attention of all New Zealand. Nineteen days earlier, the 2,585-ton passenger steamship *Elingamite* had plowed headlong into the rocky cliffs of West King Island at the country's remote northern tip. Forty-five lives were lost, and the 144 survivors had endured five hellish days drifting in inadequately provisioned lifeboats or clinging to windswept rocks before finally being rescued. Now, New Zealand's grieving, angry citizenry would find out just what had gone wrong—and who was to blame.

The court's verdict, delivered on January 19, 1903, found that the ship's master, Captain Ernest Attwood had, among other transgressions, bungled both navigation and evacuation. But blame for the collision itself went to the *Elingamite*'s chief engineer, a Mr. Fraser, who had died in the wreck.

Captain Attwood claimed that moments before the ship struck the cliff, he had ordered the engines reversed in order to back away from the looming disaster. But the engine-room crew could not make the propeller respond. Attwood's attorney argued that Fraser's handling of the engines was inept. However, surviving crewmen claimed that the ship had already struck the reef.

With the *Elingamite* resting at the bottom of the sea, there was no way to prove the crew's assertion. Blame was partly assigned to the dead engineer, and Attwood was able to avoid a possible manslaughter charge.

A subsequent inquiry nine years later found that the rocks had been improperly charted and held that Captain Attwood was blameless. But the cloud remained over the reputation of engineer Fraser, who lay with the ship in 150 feet of water off West King Island.

So matters stood until 1965, when Wade Doak, a schoolteacher and energetic founder of the magazine *Dive South Pacific,* happened on the wreck while spearfishing. Doak *(left)* and a group of fellow divers formed a syndicate to find *Elingamite*'s treasure—a consignment of gold and silver coins intended for the New Zealand branch of an Australian bank. Several earlier salvage attempts had netted a few thousand dollars' worth of treasure, but the salvagers' enthusiasm had waned after three of their number died from the effects of working in the frigid depths where the *Elingamite* lay.

Nonetheless, Doak's group, whose members were experienced cold-water divers, eventually raised a substantial number of coins. Doak's share allowed him to quit his teaching job and concentrate on exploring and studying marine subjects full-time.

Nearly as gratifying was his opportunity to find evidence exonerating the *Elingamite*'s engineer. In January 1969, Doak salvaged the four great blades of the ship's propeller. "Bent like bananas, huge chunks have been smashed from the leading edges," Doak wrote. "They were certainly turning when the *Elingamite* hit!" The propeller was the missing link in the 1902 inquiry. It proved what some of Fraser's subordinates had claimed: There had been no mechanical problems. The captain's order had come too late. After sixty-six years, Fraser was proved blameless. □

A Three-Century Search

All London was agog when the two-hundred-ton *James and Mary* docked at the Royal Shipyard in Greenwich in April of 1687. There was good reason, for the ship carried more than twenty-five tons of silver and a small fortune in gold and gemstones. The bounty had been recovered from the wreck of a Spanish ship, *La Nuestra Señora de la Concepción.* Not only was it the richest trove of sunken treasure ever recovered, but it had been snatched from a Caribbean reef under the very noses of the Spanish, who were England's archrivals for New World domination.

The man responsible for this breathtaking coup was the *James and Mary*'s thirty-seven-year-old captain, William Phips, a brawny giant who strode the decks that day sporting a gold hatband and a yard-long gold neck chain. Although Phips's accomplishment was great, his loot represented only a fraction of the *Concepción*'s cargo. Nearly three hundred years would pass before the rest was raised.

Phips's search for the *Concepción* had begun in the early 1680s when he sailed to the Bahamas to make his fortune as a "wracker"—one of the English or Dutch freebooters who preyed on Spanish ships in the Caribbean. In a Nassau tavern he met an old Spanish seaman who claimed to be a survivor of the *Concepción,* the most famous wreck of her day.

In 1641, the galleon had left Havana dangerously overloaded with one of the largest cargoes of silver ever shipped to King Philip IV of Spain. Severely damaged in a hurricane less than forty-eight hours out of port, the *Concepción* turned toward Puerto Rico for repairs. But she soon smashed into an uncharted reef north of the island of Hispaniola. Repeated Spanish salvage expeditions failed to locate her remains.

Even so, the old Spanish barfly said he knew where she lay. Phips believed him and sailed at once for England to seek backing. He talked his way into an audience with King Charles II, spun a captivating tale, and left London in charge of an eighteen-gun frigate loaned by the king in exchange for one-quarter of the anticipated treasure.

In truth, Phips's Spanish source had given him only the vaguest notion of where to look for the wreck, and the adventurer returned to England empty-handed. Undeterred, Phips talked his way into new backing, sailing once more in

William Phips *(above)* first found and salvaged the *Concepción* in 1687. Three hundred years later, Burt Webber, wearing a yellow life vest, and Jack Haskins admire a ceramic jug they raised from the once-lost wreck.

1686 with two well-equipped salvage ships. It was the smaller of the two, the *Henry of London,* that happened on to the *Concepción.* She was wedged between rocks forty feet down, sixty miles north of Hispaniola. Indian divers picked the wreck clean of all visible plate and bullion in little more than a month. This was only a small portion of the galleon's fabulous cargo. But it was enough to awe London, make Phips rich and famous, return his backers a hundredfold profit, and launch a British treasure-hunting craze that sent dozens of ships to the New World to angle for Spanish treasure.

Phips was idolized by the British as no seaman had been since Sir Francis Drake. He was knighted and eventually named governor of Massachusetts, where he earned the enmity of the commonwealth by putting a halt to the popular Salem witch trials. By the time Phips died in 1695, the memory of the *Concepción* had faded, and with it most clues to the galleon's location. Only the name of the vaguely charted area where Phips had found her persisted—the Silver Shoals.

The ship may have been lost, but its bounty was not forgotten. Beginning in the 1930s, the *Concepción* again became a target for treasure hunters. Dominican dictator Rafael Trujillo, speedboat champion Sir Malcolm Campbell, industrialist Ed Link, and playboy Porfirio Rubirosa were among a glittering array of celebrities and adventurers who vainly pursued the galleon's riches. In 1968, French mariner Jacques Cousteau sent a team of divers into what he thought was a promising location. They returned with a diver's weight belt labeled ''Mel's Aqua Shop''—a relic of an earlier visit by wreck hunter Mel Fisher.

Finally, the *Concepción*'s mystery yielded to an intense young professional treasure hunter with the paradoxical reputation of being the best prepared and least fortunate man in the business. Burt Webber, Jr., the son of a Pennsylvania car dealer, had gone on his first treasure hunt in 1961. Then only nineteen years old, Webber scraped up one thousand dollars to accompany the legendary Art McKee *(pages 95-96)* on one of McKee's pay-to-hunt adventures. More than a dozen other treasure trips followed, none of which produced anything more valuable than adventure tales.

To support himself and his family, Webber sold encyclopedias and laid bricks. In his spare time, he studied everything he could lay his hands on that pertained to treasure hunting: charts, maps, naval histories, technical manuals, and Spanish records. He became a recognized authority on the use of ◊

A mariner's compass from the *Concepción* lies across an ancient Spanish chart of Hispaniola. A few priceless porcelain cups *(above, left)* were recovered from the galleon.

electronic detection equipment. But he never found treasure.

In 1972, Webber suffered the most devastating defeat of his career when rival treasure hunter Mel Fisher beat him to the grave of the Spanish galleon *Atocha*, which Webber had sought for five years *(pages 90-92)*. Webber's backers deserted him, leaving him broke and in despair.

But by 1976, Webber was ready for one last try. His friend Jack Haskins, a corporate pilot and self-taught scholar of archaic Spanish documents, convinced Webber that he had narrowed the location of the *Concepción* down to a single seventeen-mile stretch of the Silver Shoals. Once more, Webber found investors and led a meticulously prepared expedition into the sea off Hispaniola.

Despite Haskins's certainty, five months of searching the target area revealed no sign of the elusive ship. Then Haskins called with electrifying news: The logbook of the *Henry of London* had been found in a library in Maidstone, Kent, where it had been deposited by a descendant of one of Phips's backers. In the log were compass bearings—records of the *Henry of London's* course just before she came upon the wreck—written three centuries earlier by the *Henry's* captain, Francis Rogers.

With that information in hand, Webber and his crew needed just three days to locate the galleon. Nine months' labor was required to raise her treasure, valued in the tens of millions of dollars. After seventeen years, Burt Webber's luck had finally turned. □

Real Eight

One of the earliest twentieth-century fortunes founded on sunken treasure had its beginnings on a rainy day in 1949 when Kip Wagner, a Sebastian, Florida, building contractor, helped sober up a drunken employee by walking with him along the beach. There, the man confided boozily that he often found old coins lying on the sand after storms. To Wagner's astonishment, the man proceeded to pick up seven lumps of black metal—silver coins that had been corroded by salt water. The chance event forever altered Wagner's life.

Fascinated by the discovery, Wagner borrowed a war-surplus mine detector and took up beach-combing in his spare time. The solitary hobby suited Wagner's mild, patient nature, and over the next few years, he found so many old coins that he began melting them down to make toys for neighborhood children.

A local history buff assured him that his finds most likely came from a cache buried somewhere on shore, but Wagner became convinced that they were washing in from an old wreck lying in ocean waters near Sebastian Inlet. The inlet was a natural ship's trap of jagged rocks, shallow limestone reefs, and swift currents.

In 1959, Wagner wrote to Spain's General Archives of the Indies in Seville, asking about any shipwrecks in the area in or around

Kip Wagner, organizer of the Real Eight, pores over a chart of Florida and the Bahamas, pointing to the place off Fort Pierce where he and friends uncovered the remains of the 1715 Plate Fleet.

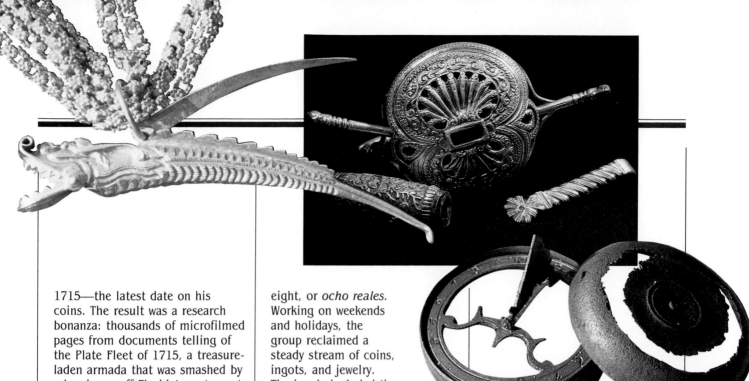

1715—the latest date on his coins. The result was a research bonanza: thousands of microfilmed pages from documents telling of the Plate Fleet of 1715, a treasure-laden armada that was smashed by a hurricane off Florida's east coast. It took a year for Wagner and his partner, Dr. Kip Kelso, to decipher the archaic Spanish text.

To Wagner, a landlubber who did not have a boat and did not know how to dive, the documents' most compelling details concerned a salvage camp that had been set up on the beach off Sebastian Inlet to reclaim valuables from the fleet's wrecks. The camp would be close to the wrecks, Wagner reasoned. Setting off with his metal detector, in short order he unearthed cannonballs, cutlasses, and a diamond ring. All of the items seemed certain to have belonged to the Spanish salvagers.

Thus encouraged, Wagner constructed a crude surfboard with a built-in glass window and paddled it clumsily offshore, searching for the ship. He soon found the marks of a wreck—several cannon lying in shallow water. Realizing that he could never salvage the ship without help, Wagner recruited seven local sports divers and organized a salvage company known as Real Eight. The name was a play on their number and on the Spanish coins they discovered—pieces of eight, or *ocho reales*. Working on weekends and holidays, the group reclaimed a steady stream of coins, ingots, and jewelry. The jewels included the ruby-eyed, dragon-shaped gold whistle that some people say hung from an extraordinary chain of 2,176 ornamented gold links around the neck of the fleet's commander, General Don Juan Esteban de Ubilla.

But progress was slow until 1963, when Real Eight struck a partnership agreement with Treasure Salvors, a small, ambitious group of professional divers from the state of California led by a dive-shop owner by the name of Mel Fisher *(pages 90-92)*.

The Californians injected an invigorating shot of manpower and underwater expertise into the salvage operations, and the two groups opened a staggering vein of treasure: beautifully crafted tableware and religious objects, bejeweled medallions and weapons, and fragile Chinese porcelain still packed in the clay that had carried it safely across the Pacific to Mexico on Spain's Manila galleons *(page 42)*. They discovered more than a ton of silver and found the seafloor carpeted in some places with spilled gold coins.

Treasure worth more than $10

The single most valuable item found by Real Eight in the 1715 wrecks was the gold dragon pendant at top, combining whistle, toothpick, and ear-cleaning tool. Also raised were the remains of an exquisite silver sword *(center)* and a small brass sundial that served as a pocket watch for travelers of the 1700s.

million was eventually recovered from the remains of the 1715 Plate Fleet. Even after the proceeds had been taxed and the state of Florida had taken its 25 percent cut, there was enough left over to make the original partners wealthy. Mel Fisher sank his share into other treasure hunts, repeatedly using gold coins from the sunken galleons as collateral to finance his quest for the fabled *Atocha*.

And Kip Wagner, the mild-mannered beachcomber who followed a trail of coins to a fortune, died in 1972 as modern treasure hunting's first millionaire. □

High-Tech Hunting

The first account of the disaster was delivered to those who survived it—the shivering women and children who only hours earlier had been rescued from the steamship *Central America* as it pitched and wallowed in the seas off South Carolina, mortally stricken by a hurricane. At great risk to rescued and rescuers, they had been transferred in frail rowboats to the passing brig *Marine.*

At about eight o'clock that night, September 12, 1857, as the *Marine* stood by and her crew tried to calm the shocked survivors, the *Central America* abruptly sank with most of its passengers and crew still on board. Hysteria gripped the survivors aboard the *Marine.* "Such a shriek as rose from our midst I hope never to hear again," passenger Almira Kittredge told the *New York Herald.* One woman sprang to the cabin door, insisting she heard her husband's voice calling from the dark sea. Others wept and cried out that if they had known the ship would perish in the storm, they never would have left her.

The sinking of the *Central America* was the worst maritime disaster of the era in the United States. The ship had been en route from Panama to New York, carrying 578 people and three tons of California gold. Many of her passengers were new millionaires, triumphant Forty-Niners who had struck it rich out West and were returning home via the quickest route: down the Pacific coast, across the narrow Isthmus of Panama by train, then through the Caribbean and up the eastern seaboard by fast steamboat.

The *Central America* was one of the most luxurious of the so-called Panama Packets, and one of the busiest. She had made the Atlantic leg of the trip forty-three times in four years, transporting nearly one-third of all gold shipped to the East during that period. She was a symbol of gaudy prosperity in a heady, expansionist age.

The fast steamer was also a crucial link in the nation's economy at that time. Many New York banks, teetering on the edge of insolvency, were counting on deposits carried aboard the *Central America* to shore up their assets. Her sinking set off a wave of bank failures nationwide and helped to launch the Panic of 1857, one of America's worst economic depressions.

But it was the human toll of 425 lost lives that immediately gripped the country's attention. Newspapers and magazines ran long and harrowing first-person accounts of the ship's final forty-eight hours. More than a century after the tragedy, those vivid, horror-filled stories reached from yellowed pages

and led an Ohio engineer named Thomas Thompson to the grave of the *Central America*.

By then the ship had been all but forgotten. But musty newspaper and magazine files proved rich in clues to her location. Between 1983 and 1986, Thompson, a research scientist who had spent seven years studying deep-sea mining technology; Bob Evans, a geologist and an expert in interpreting nineteenth-century scientific data; and Barry Schatz, a journalist, culled details from hundreds of old accounts. They fed the information into a computer to produce an analysis that would help them to locate the wreck site.

The area the computer targeted was 1,400 square miles of 7,000-foot-deep ocean, 200 miles off the coast of South Carolina. Only a few years earlier, anything so remote would have been out of reach of all but the newest military submarines. But computer technology and remote-controlled deep-sea robots promised to make deep-ocean salvage projects economically feasible for the first time.

Thompson assembled a multi-talented team of high-tech treasure hunters who knew how to make the best use of the new equipment. They called themselves the Columbus-America Discovery Group after the Ohio city where many of their 166 investors lived, and they approached the task of finding and salvaging the *Central America* as a research project. To some who took part, the serious scientific goals equaled—even outweighed—the quest for gold. The engineers, mechanics, and computer experts presented a staid image—a sharp contrast to the devil-may-care figure cut by commercial treasure hunters. But there were similarities: After all, Thompson had once worked as a diver for that most rakish of salvagers, Mel Fisher.

The careful science produced stunning success. The wreck, sitting on the bottom of the sea, was located by sonar in a mere forty days in the summer of 1986. Three summers later, fueled by additional investment and scientific support from the Smithsonian Institution, Columbus-America closed in on the target. A state-of-the-art research ship carrying a team of scientists and a remote-controlled, deep-diving robotic vehicle began the process of retrieving the *Central America*'s treasure.

In August and September of 1989, the team raised more than a ton of gold bars and coins. "I never dreamed it would be like this," said an awestruck Thompson. "It's just like a storybook treasure."

The scientists were as thrilled as the treasure hunters, since the wreck proved to be a trove of living treasure as well as booty. ♢

Against a backdrop of gold coins from the *Central America* are Columbus-America project organizers: from left, Thomas Thompson, Bob Evans, and Barry Schatz.

Pulled from the sea were two previously unknown species of marine life, invertebrate animals dwelling in the frigid, deep-water ecosystem that the steamship *Central America* supported.

Estimates of the total value of the steamer's gold ranged as high as one billion dollars, depending on the numismatic worth of thousands of mint-condition coins more than 130 years old. Some individual coins were appraised at one hundred thousand dollars.

But the Columbus-America venture was not entirely golden. After battling with the elements below the seas, the team's treasure hunters had to defend their work in the courts. No sooner had the gold been found than thirty-eight insurance companies, many of them claiming to be descendants of long-extinct firms, brought suit. The companies asserted that, because they had paid off on the 1857 loss, they were entitled to recover their alleged assets.

The claims were rejected on August 14, 1990, by U.S. District Court Judge Richard Kellam in Norfolk, Virginia. The judge pointed out that, in more than 130 years, the insurance companies had made no effort to recover the lost treasure, or even to keep adequate records to justify any claims.

Judge Kellam also ruled that private persons had deep-ocean salvage rights. Before the ruling, such rights had been legally reserved to sovereign nations only. "The decision is a major development in the law," declared Richard Robol, one of Columbus-America's lawyers. "This makes it clear that individuals are free to explore the deep oceans and enjoy the benefits of their discoveries." □

Divining for Dollars

If all the stories concerning Indian gold sealed in caves or coins buried beneath barns were true, the treasures hidden in the state of Georgia would beggar those of the Spanish Main.

Yet despite the exaggeration, there are scores of fabulous finds waiting to be unearthed in the Peach State, according to its resident expert on such matters, Ernest Andrews. One of these, the Waterhouse Treasure, is said to be among the richest. It supposedly consists of six-foot-long, nine-inch-square, solid gold bars stacked as high as a man's head in a cave somewhere in Whitfield County. "Undoubtedly it is the largest hoard of gold in the United States with the exception of Fort Knox," says Andrews.

Although he started looking for it in the 1940s, the Waterhouse Treasure—named after the farmer who first claimed to stumble across it—has steadfastly eluded Andrews, despite the unique tool he chose for his search. He has relied on the ancient art of dowsing. Used since medieval times to locate water or minerals, dowsing employs an instrument called a divining rod—usually a simple forked stick—held straight out from the operator's body. The operator grasps a prong in each hand, and the stem points forward. In the presence of water or metal lying underground, the stem supposedly pulls downward as though drawn by a powerful magnet.

Using an adaptation of the divining rod that he calls a "metaloscope," Andrews claims success of a sort. "I've found a lot of coins, let's put it that way," the octogenarian dowser told an interviewer in 1990. "In fact, mostly what I've found is pennies. Thousands and thousands of pennies."

By the time of his interview, Andrews had quit active dowsing for gold. But his enthusiasm for the hunt—and his faith that fortunes remain for the lucky—was undimmed. "I had a grand time searching," he said. □

Carefully suspending his dowser's pendulum over a map, Georgia treasure hunter Ernie Andrews awaits a gentle tug that will give a clue to buried riches.

Armada Gold

To the clans of the Scottish Highlands, England's defeat of the Spanish Armada in 1588 was a matter of little concern. But the battered remnants of the vanquished fleet, swept by howling gales up the British coast and around Scotland's northern tip, were another matter. More than sixty vessels of Spain's great invasion force were driven onto the rocky shores of northern Scotland and western Ireland. The Scottish Highlanders reacted to the shipwrecked Spaniards as they would to any invaders: They put thousands to the sword.

But Lauchlan MacLean, head of the clan MacLean, saw only opportunity when the 961-ton galleon *Florencia* limped into Tobermory Bay on the isle of Mull. MacLean agreed to provision the ship for the journey back to Spain if her captain, Don Andres Pereira, would lend the MacLeans 100 fighting men to help eradicate members of a rival clan located on the neighboring isles of Rum and Eigg. Captain Pereira was hardly in a position to refuse, and over the next few months the MacLeans and their Spanish allies laid waste the two islands.

There followed a falling-out with tragic consequences for all: Pereira and MacLean quarreled over the payment; the Spaniard took as hostage one of the clan leader's kinsmen and held him on board the *Florencia;* and the captive MacLean, in a suicidal act of retaliation, blew up the ship, sending her to the bottom of the bay. Most of the crewmen were killed, but Pereira escaped and eventually made his way to Spain.

The ship lay undisturbed until 1641, when the eighth earl of Argyll, head of the clan Campbell, acquired the wreck from England's King Charles I in return for one percent of the salvage profits and a crown reputed to be aboard. The earl had been told by his father—who had heard the story in Spain from no less an authority than Captain Pereira—that the *Florencia* was the Armada's pay ship, laden with ducats for the invading forces. In 1683, his own son, the ninth earl of Argyll, hired a diver named Archibald Millar to employ a new invention, the diving bell, to descend to the bottom of the bay and discover the truth.

MacLean clansmen, resentful that a rival Argyll had appropriated their ship, hurled stones at the diver from a nearby hillside. Nevertheless, Millar located the ship, buried in mud to her upper decks, and recovered a few cannon and a ship's bell. Although the find was less than rich, it launched a tradition of sporadic treasure hunting among the Argylls.

Every few generations, the incumbent duke of Argyll—the title was raised from earl to duke in the eighteenth century—has hired divers to search for the legendary treasure. A number of historical artifacts have been recovered, but no hoard of riches.

Townsmen in the little village of Tobermory have adopted a steadfastly skeptical—and practical—attitude toward the *Florencia:* "There's more good money been poured into the waters of Tobermory than will ever be taken out of it," observed one.

But the lure of fortune still beckons the dukes of Argyll: Exhibiting the sensibility of a born treasure hunter, the eleventh duke once declared, "The world is too drab these days. We could all do with a little romance." □

ELUSIVE TREASURE

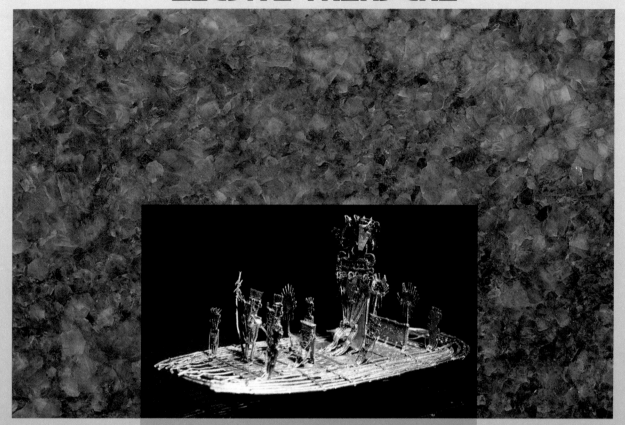

If the pursuit of treasure adds value to the prize, certain lost fortunes are truly priceless. No matter what effort is expended to reach them, some hoards of gold, coin, and precious gems remain just beyond reach of the pilgrim. The buried treasure sinks deeper into the pit; the entrance to the mine leads nowhere; the canyon filled with gold-rich sand remains beyond another mountain. The mystical object, like the Cheshire cat's grin, seems to vanish into air.

The search for such quicksilver riches has yielded a mother lode of tales. But here, too, lies confusion. Told and retold, the stories are so well burnished by imagination that the facts, like the details on the face of an ancient coin, are as elusive as the fortunes themselves.

5

The Money Pit

A Nova Scotia farm boy named Daniel McGinnis probably had pirates on his mind one summer day in 1795 when he rowed out to Oak Island to do a little exploring. McGinnis had heard stories of the notorious Captain Kidd and other pirates who supposedly had hidden their booty along this section of the Atlantic coast.

On the island, the teenager soon found himself at the edge of a small clearing. In the middle of it a large oak tree stood alone, and just below the tree, the ground slumped into a saucer-shaped depression. Young McGinnis's first thought was of buried treasure.

The boy and two friends were back the next day, digging for all they were worth. Two feet below the surface, they found a layer of carefully laid flagstones. The stones protected the top of a circular shaft, about thirteen feet across, that had been scooped out and then refilled with dirt. They continued digging, that day and many more. At ten feet, they found a platform of oak logs wedged into the shaft's walls. Ripping it out, they excavated another ten feet. There they found another platform, then another, ten feet lower. Frustrated by the barriers, the boys returned to their farm chores.

McGinnis and his friends were the first of swarms of treasure hunters to gouge the island's clay soil in search of the riches presumedly lying below. Their efforts have earned the Oak Island shaft the apt name of the Money Pit, marking the millions of dollars spent in the vain exercise of unearthing its mysteries. And the pit has swallowed lives as well as fortunes: Accidents during various digs have killed six men.

After two centuries, the only yield from the pit is the certainty that it is a complex structure, engineered and built in the late sixteenth or early seventeenth century. Its purpose and contents, however, are enigmas, which—like the excavation itself—have deepened over time.

The first well-financed dig at Oak Island was mounted in 1803 by an adult McGinnis and his friends, with the backing of a syndicate of Nova Scotia businessmen who called themselves the Onslow Company. The venture confirmed what the boys had guessed in their amateur scrabblings eight years earlier: Oak platforms had been placed every ten feet in the shaft. The Onslow party had reached a depth of ninety-three feet when, overnight, seawater seeped in and filled the pit. No amount of pumping could remove the water, and the dig was abandoned.

Fifty years later, other explorers realized that the flooding was a booby trap built to protect the Money Pit's secret. Five hundred feet from the excavation, on the shore of Smith's Cove, a cobbled beach concealed an elaborate system of drains leading to a rock-lined tunnel that directed seawater into the shaft. The water was held back by a barrier that was destroyed during the excavation, releasing the water. Later probings revealed another, similar flood tunnel leading from a cove on the opposite side of the island.

The flooding suggested that the pit was more complex than its early investigators had suspected. According to modern construction experts, builders of the sixteenth or seventeenth century would have required 100,000 man-hours—fifty men working steadily for a year—to complete such a complicated job. Many feel it was the kind of task best tackled by a disciplined organization, such as an army, rather than by a band of fractious buccaneers. What government or army would undertake such an extensive project remains unknown.

The booby traps also raised the question of how the builders expected to reclaim whatever it was that they buried. Hunters have theorized that loot was hidden in side tunnels sloping back to the surface and that the Money Pit was nothing more than a complicated decoy. However, no side tunnels have ever been found.

Diggers have tried without success to devise a way to block the

1795 elevation

Flagstones

Present elevation

Charcoal

Ship's putty

Coconut fiber

Timber platform every ten feet

Inscribed stone

Oak chest

Flood tunnel

Parchment scrap

Flood tunnel

A cutaway drawing illustrates the layers of timbers and flood tunnels that have protected the secret of Oak Island's Money Pit from generations of treasure hunters.

Oak Island's mysterious Money Pit and its protective fence are boxed in red in this aerial photograph. On the right, crescent-shaped Smith's Cove conceals the inlet to a flood tunnel.

floodwaters or circumvent the mechanism that triggers their release. To that end, diggers have sunk a vast network of parallel shafts and side tunnels—only to have them inundated. The only upshot of all the digging has been to so weaken the ground around the original Money Pit that the entire area has collapsed, creating a huge depression in the eastern end of Oak Island.

The pit has yielded scant clues to what it may hold. Three links of chain, iron scissors of Spanish manufacture, a carved-bone bosun's whistle, and a scrap of parchment are among the few artifacts to be raised. Coconut fiber has also been found. Although the nearest coconut trees are 1,500 miles away, the fiber was used to pack cargo on seventeenth- and eighteenth-century ships.

One of the most tantalizing discoveries was a heart-shaped stone similar to those found among pirate treasure-troves in Haiti. Another stone, this one with cryptographic markings, was also raised. Dig organizers said that the stone's markings promised that "forty feet below, two million pounds are buried." Quite possibly, the stone was a hoax, planted to pique the interest and pluck the pockets of new investors.

In 1971, a TV camera lowered 230 feet into the murky water captured the grisly image of a severed human hand, half clenched, its flesh preserved by the salty water and the absence of oxygen. The hand has never been retrieved.

The Money Pit's secret has obsessed scores of people. Fred Blair, a Boston insurance salesman whose uncle had taken part in the search in the 1860s, first visited the site as a boy in 1893. He held the lease on the pit area for many years and continued his search until his death in 1951. He explored it through a succession of syndicates, including the Old Gold Salvage and Wrecking Company, whose most famous investor and occasional digger was a young law clerk named Franklin D. Roosevelt. Other searchers and investors have included actor Errol Flynn and explorer Richard Byrd. A group of Canadian and American investors called the Triton Alliance began digging in the late 1960s, expecting to spend $10 million excavating 200 holes in Oak Island.

However, there are those who believe that no amount of money or human effort will force the Money Pit's secret from the land before it is ready to emerge. One legend has it that the search will end only after all the island's oaks are dead, and seven fortune seekers with them. By 1990, six diggers had died. Three oaks remained. □

Max's Millions

The condemned man's gesture had a fine aristocratic flair: Emperor Maximilian of Mexico, standing before a firing squad, entreated his executioners to shoot true and handed each a gold coin. The marksmen obliged, and, on July 19, 1867, bullets ended Maximilian's three-year career as Napoleon III's New World puppet.

Before his overthrow, the emperor had lived lavishly in his colonial empire. An Austrian archduke by birth, he had expensive tastes. So did his wife, Carlotta, and the two were thought to possess great wealth. But Maximilian's assets disappeared with his life.

One story has it that he sent his treasure out of the country when things started to go sour in 1866.

According to this account, the emperor ordered that forty-five barrels be crammed with plate, coin, and jewels. The nest egg was loaded onto a caravan of wagons guarded by a few trusted Austrian soldiers. The wagons were to head for the Texas port of Galveston to be loaded aboard a ship for Europe. Carlotta was already in Europe, and Maximilian would follow.

In wild Texas, the tale goes, troubles began along the trail when Maximilian's men ran afoul of six former Confederate soldiers. The six had been hired to augment the guard. But when they learned the nature of the cargo, the Southerners killed the Austrians, stole the treasure, and buried it near the trail in the vicinity of Castle Gap near the Pecos River.

Legend tells that the six then headed for Missouri to enlist the aid of outlaw Jesse James and his gang to retrieve the loot from hostile territory. But the thieves were attacked by Indians, who killed five of the six. The lone survivor wound up in jail somewhere along the way and died there—but not before telling his tale to a doctor and gasping out directions to the booty. By the time the doctor reached Castle Gap, however, landmarks had changed. The dying soldier's instructions led nowhere, and an archduke's gold may still be hidden somewhere near the Pecos. □

Arkansas's Field of Dreams

Sometime around 1906, farmer John Wesley Huddleston bought a quarter section of land—160 acres—in Pike County, Arkansas. There he planned to raise livestock, grow vegetables, and engage in the pursuits he most loved: hunting, fishing, and prospecting. On a hot August day not long after buying the place, Huddleston went looking for gold and found something far better. Out of the earth emerged two diamonds, one weighing three carats, the other four and one-half.

Before long, Pike County was the site of a diamond rush that resembled California's gold rush a half century earlier. A tent city of prospectors sprang up around Huddleston's farm, and developers laid plans for a new town named Kimberly, after the famous South African diamond mine. The son of an adjoining landowner—diamonds were found throughout the neighborhood—had a diamond embedded in one of his teeth.

But the diamond field seemed destined to grow paupers rather than millionaires. John Huddleston sold his farm almost immediately after the discovery. He was paid $36,000, a sum he figured would

These three intent diamond hunters of
the 1920s are among the thousands
who have scratched the ground of Pike
County, Arkansas, since diamonds were
found there early in the century.

last a lifetime—and establish a $1,000 dowry for each of his five daughters. He was the first man in Murfreesboro to buy a car and, when his wife died, he married a young woman from a carnival. But the new wife disappeared with the car, and Huddleston ran out of money before all his daughters were married. He died broke.

Several would-be diamond miners who followed Huddleston also had bad luck. One, a geologist named Austin Millar, managed to find some diamonds, but his mining plant burned down in 1919.

The cause of all this unusual activity was a volcanic pipe—a vertical column of magma thrust up millions of years ago from deep within the earth, where great temperature and pressure forged diamond crystals out of carbon. The Pike County field is the only place in the United States where diamonds are found in any quantity. It is possible, say geologists, that a rich trove of gems lies 1,000 feet underground there. However, commercial mining ventures have barely scratched the surface. None has sunk a shaft deeper than 205 feet. The average gem weighs about one-tenth of a carat and is about the size of the head of a pin. But in 1924, a huge diamond of 40.23 carats turned up, and other stones, including garnets, opals, and amethysts, have also been found.

In 1972, the state of Arkansas created Crater of Diamonds State Park, the nation's only public diamond mine. For a small entry fee, 85,000 tourists pluck 1,000 diamonds from the dirt every year; the size and quality vary widely. Thanks to the fee, the field is finally turning a profit. □

Hoard of a King

King Lobengula of the Matabele looked and acted the part of a powerful chief. He was tall, muscular, described by some as a "bull elephant" of a man. He had 200 wives. And he was the last of the African chieftains to stand up to the Europeans who colonized the continent in the nineteenth century. Lobengula was also prudent. He was reputed to possess a great hoard of gold and diamonds contributed by his subjects. And so, in 1892, with Britain's Cecil Rhodes thundering at the gates of Matabeleland, Lobengula acted to save what he could.

According to John Jacobs, Lobengula's longtime secretary, the king piled his valuables aboard five ox-drawn wagons. Jacobs— whose stories are not considered to be the whole truth—said there were two safes filled with gold coins, three biscuit tins of uncut diamonds, and an unspecified quantity of ivory. Accompanied by Jacobs, four indunas, or headmen, and several tribesmen, Lobengula headed up the Zambezi Valley, where he had the treasure buried in a great pit. After it was safely interred, he ordered the execution of the tribesmen to protect his secret. Then the sovereign returned to his kraal to await the British.

Within a year, Lobengula's warriors were vanquished, and Matabeleland became part of Rhodesia,

now Zimbabwe. Acknowledging defeat, Lobengula and his second-ranking chief, Magwegwe, went into the Lubimbi Valley, where they swallowed fatal doses of poison. Lobengula's body was sealed in a cave whose location remained a secret for fifty years.

After the king's death, Jacobs might have moved speedily to use his purported knowledge of the treasure's burial ground to reclaim it. It is not quite clear why he did not do so, although some surmise that he was lying about the trove's existence or its location or both.

Jacobs's version of events was that the British jailed him in Salisbury—today's city of Harare, Zimbabwe. He offered to lead authorities to the hoard in return for his release, he said, but instead the British deported him from Rhodesia. In later years, Jacobs sought to lead fortune hunters to the treasure several times, but his parties were turned back at the Rhodesian border each time.

When Lobengula's bones were finally discovered in 1943, the only items found with him were some rifles, a bullet mold, a saddle, and an ornate chair that had been a gift from Queen Victoria.

The great chief's treasure—if there truly is one—remains buried somewhere under the soil he sought to save from foreign domination. □

Artist Thomas Baines put himself in the picture when he sketched pipe-smoking Matabele chief Lobengula in 1870 as the chief reviewed warriors returning from a successful raid on a rival tribe.

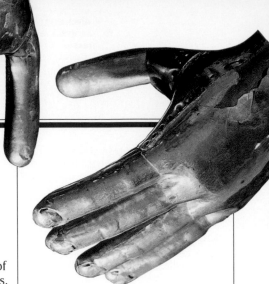

A King's Ransom

Gold, glowing with the color of the sun, surrounded the sixteenth-century Incan emperor Atahuallpa, whose people believed he was the son of the Sun. His plates and cups were made of gold, the litter he rode on was gold encrusted, and he adorned himself with gold earrings and a gilded headband.

Thus glittering, Atahuallpa greeted the Spanish conquistador Francisco Pizarro in 1532. It was supposed to be a diplomatic meeting; it turned out to be an ambush. Atahuallpa was taken prisoner. To Pizarro's great pleasure, the Incan king offered a ransom in gold—enough to fill his prison chamber. It is said the room measured twenty-two feet long, seventeen feet wide, and eight feet high. The king also promised to fill another room twice over with silver.

At Atahuallpa's command, there began what might be called one of the world's great cultural disasters. To pay the king's ransom, thousands of precious artifacts were melted down. The effort produced twenty tons of gold and silver bars. But Atahuallpa's deliverance never came. Fearing that the emperor, once free, would lead his subjects against the small band of Spaniards, Pizarro executed him.

Abruptly, the river of gold ceased to flow. The Inca began to hide vast amounts of treasure in caves throughout the empire. The European invaders unearthed some of the objects, but the rest of the gold remains hidden to this day.

Golden gloves such as these were made to dress the body of an Inca for burial in the time of Atahuallpa.

Untold numbers of treasure hunters have died searching for it, for the size of the suspected hoard is immense. "That which the Inca gave to the Spaniards," an Indian nobleman remarked to a Spanish contemporary of Pizarro, "was but a kernel of corn compared with the heap before him." □

A Bell for Tayopa

Saving the souls of unbaptized savages was the sacred mission that brought Spain's Jesuit priests to the New World in the sixteenth century. But the powerful religious order soon found an earthly vocation as well: mining silver and gold.

Spain prohibited the clergy from owning or operating mines, so the Jesuits did their work in secret. Secrecy also enabled them to avoid the Crown's 20 percent tax on precious metals from America. Many Jesuit bands hoarded their treasure rather than return it to Europe.

Spain expelled the Jesuits from Latin America in 1767, fearing the order's growing power and wealth. By then, legend has it, the order operated many secret mines and held stashes of metals of immense value. Of all the hoards, the richest was said to come from the mines clustered around Tayopa, a town set deep in Mexico's rugged Sierra Madre.

Tayopa itself is elusive, never appearing in official mining records or maps of the region. But oral tradition and tattered rem-

A profusion of Jesuit settlements and possible mine sites dot a 1754 map of Mexico.

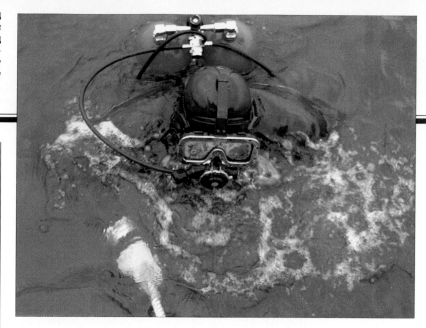

nants of private documents describe a village on the border of Chihuahua and Sonora states, where more than a dozen mines were worked. One scholar found evidence that Tayopa had its own priest and church. The town was abandoned in the late 1600s, he surmised, because of Apache attacks. A U.S. Army officer pursuing Indians in Sonora in 1885 found himself in the vicinity of Tayopa. He was told by a resident that the mines surrounding that legendary place yielded blocks of silver so big that they had to be cut into pieces so mules could carry them.

Many have sought Tayopa and its treasure to no avail. The man who came closest to tracking it down was Henry O. Flipper, the first black to graduate from West Point. Flipper, who became an expert in Mexican mining law after he left the army, was hired at the turn of the century by an American speculator to find Tayopa.

Flipper started out not in Mexico but in Spain. Somewhere in that country, he found directions to the village written in archaic Spanish. In the best tradition of treasure hunting, the instructions laid out an elaborate, if vague, course to follow: In short, the directions were to start at the summit of the mountain called Cerro de la Campagna and travel toward the setting sun for eight days.

Mexico's revolution of 1910 prevented any test of Flipper's cryptic directions. Tayopa remains today only a legend, its secret as closely guarded as any wily Jesuit might have wished. □

The Redcoats' Payroll

A burial ground for abandoned cars, appliances, machinery, and other unsavory debris, New York's East River is arguably the last place anyone would want to look for gold. However, divers have repeatedly risked life and limb in the river's traffic, tides, and pollution, hoping to retrieve a 200-year-old hoard of gold sovereigns and silver coins.

In 1780, during the Revolutionary War, HMS *Hussar*, a British man-of-war bound for Rhode Island, sank in seventy-five feet of water. The *Hussar* had suffered the misfortune of striking Pot Rock in Hell's Gate, the treacherous passage between the East River and Long Island Sound. Word soon spread that the ship carried four million dollars in cash—pay intended for British soldiers in New England. One New Yorker claimed that his father had witnessed the loading of fourteen carts of coins onto the *Hussar*. The British never tried to salvage the ship, claiming that there was nothing of value on board. However, salvage may have been out of the question for a reason unrelated to money: Britain's hold on New York was slipping.

Several non-English salvagers went after the ship in the nineteenth century, but strong currents, murky waters, and a heavy burden of silt proved too much for them. A final complicating factor was the jumble of wreckage in the area. The rocks that claimed *Hussar* also sank other ships. By the 1930s, when a submarine inventor named Simon Lake tried to salvage the British ship, a formidable glut of wrecks had joined the natural obstacles of currents and mud. Lake, the most persistent of the *Hussar's* would-be salvagers, spent six years diving and drilling for the ship without ever firmly establishing her presence.

In 1985, Barry Clifford, who later found the treasure ship *Whydah* off Cape Cod (*pages 86-87*), claimed to have located the *Hussar* using side-scan sonar, a sophisticated device capable of drawing pictures of underwater artifacts. However, divers failed to bring up any convincing evidence. More than two centuries and dozens of salvage efforts later, the *Hussar* and her cargo—whatever it was—remain the property of the East River's turbid waters. □

The Golden One

Stripped to his skin, the man who would be the Muisca Indians' next king was anointed with a sticky substance and sprinkled from head to foot with gold dust. Like a glowing icon, he stood motionless on a raft while his subjects heaped at his feet the gold and emeralds that would be offered to the gods. Several nobles joined him, and the raft moved off into the sacred lake. Over all hung the odor of incense. Music filled the air until the vessel reached the lake's center. Then silence fell. The gilded new ruler and his attendants cast their precious offerings into the water.

The story of the gilded man—the Spaniards' El Dorado—captivated sixteenth-century Europeans encountering the exotic New World. The tale's truthful fabric was embellished at every telling, so wondrous was it that there existed a race of people rich enough to cover themselves in gold.

The gold-mad Spanish conquistadors transformed El Dorado from a person into a place—a valley paved with gold, just beyond some unfordable river or impassable mountain range. The idea of El Dorado probably inspired more exploration than any other of the world's treasure legends. Its riches have been sought in every corner of the New World. But for some, the golden valley has always lain in the land of the Muisca, high in the Colombian Andes near Bogotá.

For centuries, the search has focused on Lake Guatavita, a circle of water filling an ancient volcanic crater. It is one of a string of lakes held sacred by local Indians. The first systematic effort to plumb Guatavita was made in the 1560s by Antonio de Sepulveda, a wealthy wine merchant from Bogotá. Drafting an army of 8,000 Indian workers, Sepulveda sought to drain the lake by cutting a great notch in its rim. The notch is still visible today. A few objects surfaced as the water ran out: a golden staff, breastplates, an emerald the size of a hen's egg. Encouraged, Sepulveda dug deeper. Then the cut collapsed, killing many of the laborers. The project was abandoned, and Sepulveda died poor and disillusioned.

Interest in El Dorado's treasure revived when Alexander von Humboldt, the leading natural scientist of his day, visited the lake in 1801. Caught up in the grand scale of the Andes, Humboldt estimated that the lake might hold some $300 million in riches. In 1823, a British naval captain named Charles Stuart Cochrane explored Lake Guatavita with Don "Pepe" Paris, a well-known citizen of Bogotá. Their collaboration turned up only pottery and bones.

Nevertheless, the legend of El Dorado had a vigorous life of its own. The story seemed to be confirmed in 1856, when Lake Seicha, one of Guatavita's neighbors, yielded an exquisitely crafted object: a small sculpture of a king and his court on a raft of gold (below).

At the turn of the century, an outfit calling itself Contractors Ltd. raised thousands of pounds from the British public and managed to drain Guatavita completely. But before the diggers could probe the center of the lake bed, the sun baked the slime to the consistency of concrete. Drilling equipment was hastily ordered, but by the time it arrived, the water had returned to its original level and swamped Contractors Ltd. under a sea of debt.

In 1965, the Colombian government declared Lake Guatavita off limits to treasure-hunting expeditions. □

Lasseter's Reef of Gold

In 1930, a dark, squat man calling himself Lewis Harold Bell Lasseter walked into the offices of Australia's largest labor union with a story about a huge lode of gold—a reef, he called it—that he had discovered thirty-three years earlier in the remote center of the continent. It was an unlikely tale, but people struggling through an economic depression were eager to believe it. And so the Australian Workers Union funded an expedition, led by Lasseter, to find his eleven-mile-long reef—a gold-laden spine of rock jutting from the desolate land of the Outback.

Lasseter proved to be a difficult guide. Sullen and uncooperative, he seemed to be unfamiliar with central Australia or with bushcraft. After about three months, when no trace of a reef had been found, the group disbanded.

Lasseter then joined up with a German-born prospector named Paul Johns. Transporting their supplies aboard a string of camels, the pair searched unsuccessfully. They argued and parted company. Lasseter's camels ran off, and he camped with an Aborigine band until the nomadic tribesmen moved on. Alone, Lasseter soon died of thirst and starvation. When his desiccated body was found in March 1931, it was identified by a diary in which he reaf-

Posing for a final photograph before his death, Lewis Harold Bell Lasseter *(left)* leads a camel train laden with supplies on his last, fatal search for a reef of gold. Prospector Paul Johns is at right.

firmed his belief in the reef of gold. "To think I have a reef worth millions," said his last entry, "and I'd give it all for a loaf of bread and a drink of water."

Such is the stuff of folklore and legend—an appropriate place for the story, skeptics say. Lasseter and the truth were strangers throughout his life. He was born Lewis Lasseter and only added the names "Harold Bell" in 1924. His model was apparently the author of a popular contemporary novel about fabulous gold finds in the Australian desert. At various times, Lasseter described himself as a "bridge engineer" and "a qualified ship's captain." In reality, he was a drifter, an itinerant handyman.

Lasseter's gold reef first emerged in 1929 when, as a "surveyor and prospector," he asked an Australian mining official to have the government fund an expedition to claim it. At that time, Lasseter said he had found the reef in

1911. The government declined his offer, and it was then that he approached John Bailey of the Australian Workers Union. For reasons known only to Lasseter, he told the union he had discovered the reef in the 1890s. The only unquestionable fact was Lasseter's admission that he was broke, or in his words, "expecting the bailiff."

Despite its suspect origins, Lasseter's reef still lures seekers into the Outback. By one account, between thirty and fifty men have died in the search. However, skeptics say that Lasseter's story did find its proper place—in fiction. In 1931, it was turned into a novel, *Lasseter's Last Ride,* which went through seventeen printings. □

The Greatest Treasure Island

It is the quintessential treasure island—a tiny speck of green in the Pacific, crowned by three volcanic peaks and trimmed in the coconut trees that give the place its name: Cocos Island.

Cocos probably was the model for Robert Louis Stevenson's novel *Treasure Island,* and with reason: Legend has it that pirates and others have been burying treasure on this remote rock for more than 300 years. The reputed depositors include Henry Morgan, the buccaneer who sacked Panama City in 1671; William Dampier, who looted the treasure coast of Spanish America in the early 1800s; and Benito Bonito, the scourge of Central America in the 1820s. Cocos has been an object of fascination—and exploration—for thousands of treasure hunters.

Of all the treasures allegedly buried on the island, the most notorious involves the British schooner *Mary Dear,* which in 1820 carried the wealth of Peru's Spanish oligarchs away from Simon Bolívar's revolutionaries. Loaded with plate, jewels, and such priceless items as a life-size, jewel-encrusted, gold statue of the Virgin from Lima Cathedral, the *Mary Dear* set sail for safety. Just where that haven lay, the ship's crew neither knew nor cared.

It is not known whether the schooner's Scottish captain, William Thompson, planned from the first to steal the treasure or was persuaded to the deed by his crew. But steal it he did. Nor is it known what happened to the wealthy Spanish owners. They never again appear in the story. In any event, Cocos was the *Mary Dear's* safe harbor, and there Thompson hid the riches. He and his men were soon captured by a Spanish vessel, however, and Thompson and his first mate saved their necks by promising to lead their captors to the treasure. According to some accounts, the two seafarers managed to escape into the jungles of Cocos without disclosing their secret.

The infamous story of the *Mary Dear* enhanced Cocos's reputation among treasure seekers of the world. The island's fame lured a British admiral, Henry St. Leger Palliser, to anchor his flagship there for a private treasure hunt in 1897. He was reprimanded for diverting Queen Victoria's property to private use. Palliser retired from the navy and returned to Cocos in 1904 with Earl Fitzwilliam, a wealthy British peer, in the largest private yacht in England. Unfortunately, Fitzwilliam's principal exploration tool was dynamite. One blast killed a score of workers and injured Fitzwilliam himself, and the party left the island.

Cocos has been described as a green jewel by those viewing it from a distance. Up close, it is as inhospitable a place as any pirate might wish. In summer, it is insect infested, hot, and humid. In winter, the rain is heavy and incessant. The interior is a no man's land of dense vegetation and unscalable rock. Wild pigs roam the island, descendants of domestic hogs left there by early mariners.

Nevertheless, one group, led by a German-American adventurer named August Giessler, attempted to colonize the island in 1895. Giessler had promised financial backers that he would recover for them a chest of gems that he claimed to have found and reburied on an earlier visit. But neither colonization nor treasure hunting proved out, and the band abandoned Cocos in about 1900.

Cocos grew in popularity with a treasure-hunting boom in the twentieth century. Sir Malcolm Campbell, a wealthy Scotsman, famous for record speeds in boats and motorcars, returned to Cocos time and again. Franklin D. Roosevelt visited once and maintained a lifelong interest in the island. Both left empty-handed.

The forested cliffs of Cocos Island drop steeply into Wafer Bay, one of the island's few safe harbors.

During the 1930s, the island's alleged riches were sought by one S. MacFarlane Arthur, who raised cash from British investors with pledges of wealth. His company, Treasure Recovery, Ltd., promised to use only the most scientific search methods. "Clues form no part of the Company's programme," the prospectus stated. But Arthur neglected to obtain the necessary permits from Costa Rica, which owns the island. Within a few days of landing, eighteen members of his party were arrested and their equipment was confiscated. Tried and convicted of smuggling and illegal invasion, they were deported to England. Arthur, who was in Panama at the time of the arrest, was already raising funds for a second expedition.

Another foray was led by a mysterious Belgian named Peter Bergmans, who claimed to have found a two-foot gold Madonna, chests of gold, and a human skeleton on Cocos in 1931. When Bergmans arrived, he encountered four Americans, who claimed they had been shipwrecked there for two months. In fact, they had burned their ship in the hope of forcing authorities to let them stay. Before long, both groups were evicted.

In the wake of such highly publicized shenanigans, Costa Rica declared the island a national park and prohibited treasure digging. If some pirate bounty does exist on this remote Pacific rock, it is likely to remain there for many years to come, under joint protection of the government and the sea. □

A Cause's Last Cash

In the closing days of the Civil War, the Union put out a story that Jefferson Davis, the president of the Confederacy, was carrying around $13 million in gold—a fortune that would go to the men who captured him. The story was a gross fabrication, invented to encourage someone in the virtually bankrupt South to turn Davis in. Davis's treasure never materialized, of course, but a more modest sum of Confederate gold may still be waiting to reward some lucky treasure hunter.

On April 2, 1865, when Richmond fell and Davis and his government fled the city, he took with him the Confederate treasury—coins, silver bricks, and gold ingots. Five weeks later, when Davis and his entourage were finally captured at Irwinville, Georgia, they possessed less than $3,000.

Some accounts say that during his flight, Davis arranged to distribute the bulk of the dwindling treasury to pay loyal soldiers and finance his own escape from Union forces. Estimates of the amounts and purposes of the distribution vary widely. However, it is certain that five days before his capture,

$10,000 in gold bullion was transferred between two Confederate officers in Washington, Georgia. The transfer is accounted for in the Last Order of the Confederacy (below). The gold, packed in three boxes, was never seen again.

The times were desperate, and raiders could well have seized it. Some say that loyal soldiers carried the bullion until they heard of Davis's arrest and the fall of the Confederacy, then divided their burden among themselves. Yet another theory—a very popular one, judging from the scores of gold seekers who have poked around the area for more than a century—is that the booty was buried near the site of its last transfer and was never reclaimed. □

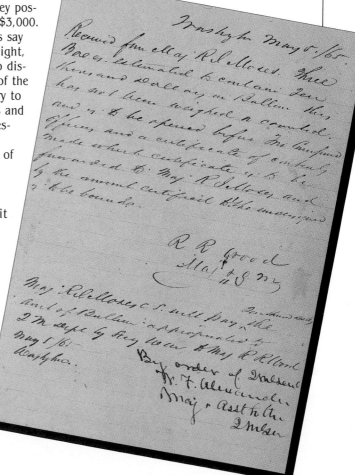

Surrounded by machinery and cables, workmen drill into a natural chimney within California's Kokoweef Mountain in search of an underground river of gold.

No Entrance

In the torchlight flickering within a cavern hundreds of feet beneath the Mojave Desert, two prospectors stuffed their packs and pockets with portions of a fantastic find. Surrounded by acres of black sand flecked with gold, they worked feverishly until one of them suddenly fell ill. His companion, a veteran miner named Earl Dorr, lifted the sick man onto his shoulders and headed out. When he emerged from the cave, Dorr found two prospectors camping outside. They helped carry the sick man to Dorr's car for transport to a Las Vegas hospital some 100 miles away. In the process, the prospectors glimpsed gold trickling out of the sick man's pockets.

There are many versions of the events that followed. Dorr said he blew up the cave entrance before leaving for Las Vegas. He intended to keep the prospectors out. Dorr assumed that he himself could find a second entrance. Other accounts say Dorr returned to find the pros-

pectors in the cave, whereupon he sealed the entrance, entombing them. The sick man, an engineer brought by Dorr to survey the cave, never reenters the narrative.

One fact is sure. Neither Dorr nor any gold diggers to follow have found a way to the gold-bearing sands that they believe lie under California's Kokoweef Mountain.

Dorr first heard about the gold as a boy on his father's ranch in Colorado. There two Indian brothers told him about a fabulous hollow mountain. In its great cavern, they said, they had mined placer gold—gold mingled with sand. They drew maps of the place for the youngster. It could make one rich, the Indians said, but they could never return: A third brother had fallen to his death in the cave, and tribal law forbade their reentry. Dorr kept the maps and, in 1931, made his way to the site.

Dorr claimed to have found a fantastic underworld. According to a lengthy account that he signed before a notary in 1934, the mountain hid an underground canyon rivaling the Grand Canyon in depth. One stalactite, he said, was twenty-seven feet across and hung 1,510 feet from the cave's ceiling. Dorr walked 5,400 feet from the cave's entrance to the canyon floor, where he found a river whose banks glinted with placer gold.

Try as he might, Dorr never could find a second entrance to the sealed cavern. Nor has anyone else. Dorr spent the rest of his life trying to tunnel his way to the river of gold. Countless prospectors have joined in the search, and two died in 1959 when they tried to blast open the cave.

More recently, a group called Exploration, Inc., has leased mineral rights from Dorr's descendants, raised money to buy digging equipment, and tried to bore through to Kokoweef's riches.

Thus far, however, the mountain retains its hoard of gold. □

A Trio of Golden Losers

In the living lottery of greed and opportunity that was played by adventurers in the Old West, gold was the prize most cherished. Some built fortunes out of the metal they wrested from the earth. Others claimed to hold the winning ticket only to lose it before they could cash in. They felt the buttery, smooth caress of gold in their calloused hands, only to have it snatched away. Tales of the nineteenth-century West tell of

three such men: Charles Breyfogle, Pegleg Smith, and a teamster known only as Adams.

Breyfogle's search was so consuming and frustrating that his name entered the English language. For a time, "breyfogling" was synonymous with fruitless prospecting. Breyfogle was searching for gold in California's Death Valley in the 1860s when Indians attacked his party and killed his two companions. After his escape,

Breyfogle wandered for days in the desert until, mad with thirst, he glimpsed a patch of green that he hoped signified water. It proved to be only a mesquite bush. However, nearby he ran across a vein of pink feldspar that was rich in gold. He finally made his way to safety—after thoughtfully tucking samples of the ore into his bandana.

Until his death, Breyfogle repeatedly braved sunstroke, thirst, and the threat of Indian attack to find the vein of gold once more. He never did. But every time in the past century that someone has struck gold in Death Valley, people have speculated that the find was Breyfogle's lost mine.

Thomas Smith got the nickname Pegleg from the wooden leg he earned as a fur trapper in Colorado. There, the story goes, an Indian arrow shattered Smith's left leg. Surviving the attack, he amputated his own limb with a butcher knife, then fashioned a wooden substitute from an ash tree.

By 1829, Pegleg was a mule skinner, driving a wagon train laden with pelts to Los Angeles across the great Salton Sink desert. Making camp one night at the base of the Chocolate Mountains, near three small black buttes, Smith pocketed some distinctively heavy black pebbles. When he arrived in Los Angeles, he examined his find more closely—and discovered that the stones were solid gold, turned black by a coating of minerals that desert dwellers know as "desert varnish." Pegleg made only desultory attempts to find more gold. But the tale he told for years was so intriguing that many who heard it spent their lives looking for what became known as the Lost Pegleg Mine.

Adams's improbable saga began in 1864, when Apaches attacked his freight wagons in Arizona, took his cargo, and burned his wagons. Adams and his horses escaped unharmed. Soon, the stranded teamster joined a group of prospectors, among them a Mexican who claimed to know a place where gold nuggets littered the sands like acorns. He offered to lead the party there in exchange for one of Adams's horses.

The Mexican kept his part of the bargain, taking the men to a place he called Zigzag Canyon, where the sand itself glittered. Adams soon possessed a nugget the size of a hen's egg. But Apaches attacked the party, killing all but Adams, who escaped with his nugget.

Eventually, Adams made his way to civilization, where he used the lump of gold to persuade others to finance forays of rediscovery. With the backing of a retired sea captain named C. A. Shaw, Adams led two unsuccessful expeditions to the New Mexico-Arizona border.

In 1886, Adams died peacefully, if penniless, in Los Angeles. He never found his way back to the golden sands of Zigzag Canyon, but the old prospector and storyteller left behind promises of wealth that lured countless gold diggers. None has found the glittering lode, however, possibly because the directions that Adams gave encompass an area of 4,800 square miles. One local rancher searched for Zigzag Canyon every summer for forty-three years—far longer than Adams himself—without success. ◻

The Dutchman's Deadly Secret

The Superstition Mountains are an ominous presence rising abruptly from the desert floor forty miles east of Phoenix, Arizona. The dry washes and jagged rocks of the range are hostile to those who venture there—as menacing as the Superstitions' reputation. The Apache name for one part of the range translates roughly as "mountain that should not be disturbed."

The Apaches revere the Superstitions as a mystical place. Nevertheless, thousands of hardheaded adventurers have entered the range's hills seeking wealth. Many have found death instead. Few, if any, have ever come close to the object of their quest, the fabulous Lost Dutchman gold mine.

The story of the Lost Dutchman mixes truth and legend, hopes and lies. It appears that the mine was first worked by the Peralta family of Mexico in the 1840s. The Peraltas' activity reportedly ended with an ambush by Apaches, who were seeking to protect their sacred lands. The Peralta burros were laden with gold, the story goes; the Apaches took the animals and left the gold-filled saddlebags—providing a fortune for any who might stumble across them.

For years, maps allegedly passed down through the Peralta family circulated among prospectors. Still, the mine lay undisturbed until a hard-drinking, reclusive German named Jacob Walz—known as the Dutchman—came to the area in the mid-1860s. Prompted by Walz's own boasts, word soon

spread that he had found the Peralta lode. Many tried to trail him to the mine but none succeeded. Some of those who got close to him, including his own partner, died under suspicious circumstances. Skeptics argue that Walz was protecting not the lost mine but a hoard of ore stolen from another mine he had once worked.

Nonetheless, after Walz's death in 1891, the legend of the lost mine grew. A woman named Julia or Helena Thomas, a neighbor who nursed the dying miner, claimed that Walz told her of a mine with two veins of quartz bearing nuggets of nearly pure gold. Moreover, she said, Walz revealed to her the location of the mine—a spot near an isolated peak called Weaver's Needle (above). Other directions that he supposedly gave were as poetic as they were vague: The mine lay where the tip of the needle's shadow rested at four o'clock, and sometimes the setting sun illuminated the gold so that it could be seen glittering through a mountain pass.

Whatever she might have known about the mine, Thomas died without finding it. But thousands of other would-be miners have tried to follow her directions. One was Adolph Ruth, a retired government worker who chanced upon one of the Peralta maps. In 1931, Ruth turned up at a ranch near the edge of the Superstitions asking for di-

rections to Weaver's Needle. The rancher and two prospectors showed him the way and helped him set up camp. Ruth was never heard from again. Searchers found his skull in some thick brush, pierced by two bullet holes. A later search turned up Ruth's body several hundred yards from the place where his skull had been found. The map had disappeared.

Perhaps Ruth was murdered by someone who wanted his map. Or perhaps he actually found the Lost Dutchman mine, and his killer or killers wrested the secret from him. The latter theory rests largely on a notebook found among Ruth's bones. It contained jottings of a few directions and the Latin words once spoken by a triumphant Julius Caesar "*Veni, vidi, vici*"—"I came, I saw, I conquered."

Ruth's cryptic notebook and his grisly death only enhanced the range's lure. In the 1960s, Erle Stanley Gardner, author of the Perry Mason mystery novels, surveyed the rugged terrain by helicopter. He found no mine. But the brush teemed with men who scurried for cover as the chopper flew overhead—proof to Gardner of the Lost Dutchman's enduring appeal.

His exploration resulted only in this advice to future fortune seekers: "Don't go poking about the Superstitions alone," Gardner said, "and it is advisable to be armed and to keep a sharp eye out." □

Secrets of the Tower

Unjust imprisonment, extortion, torture, and murder have all figured in the bloody history of the Tower of London. But no one suspected that buried treasure might also have its place in Tower lore—until the early 1900s, when historians reexamined the diaries of Samuel Pepys, the tireless busybody of seventeenth-century England. Pepys himself had once sought riches in the Tower.

Pepys was a Royal Navy factotum in October of 1662, when he was approached to help find the riches of John Barkestead, a former governor of the Tower who had been hanged for treason that April.

Barkestead had been appointed to the Tower post by Oliver Cromwell in 1652 after Cromwell overthrew the English monarchy. By reason of his position, Barkestead was one of those who signed the death warrant of King Charles I—an action that marked him for revenge when the Royalists unseated Cromwell. Barkestead fled to Holland but was arrested there, returned to England, imprisoned, and executed in the Tower he once ran.

Within six months of his death, a woman Pepys described as "Barkestead's great confidant" told Pepys that the fugitive warden had hidden £50,000 in firkins—small tubs used to store butter—in the Tower's cellars. The money, she said, had been extorted from prisoners. Pepys undertook three digs beneath the Bell Tower, but no treasure was unearthed and he abandoned the quest.

The search was resumed in 1958 by one Charles Quarrell, who tried to find the trove using Pepys's diary and divining rods. Neither led to treasure. Some experts think that both Pepys and later diggers were probing the wrong cellar. If treasure is buried anywhere, they say, it is probably beneath the King's House, where Barkestead lived.

A more popular view is that there is no treasure at all. Pepys himself reached this conclusion—after he had finished digging. Either Barkestead had another hiding place, Pepys wrote, "or else he did delude this woman in hopes to oblige her to further serving him, which I am apt to believe." □

THE TOWER OF LONDON.

The many-turreted Tower of London sprawls across a seventeenth-century painting *(above)*. A 1958 dig in the Tower's bell tower unearthed only old bottles and broken glass in the cellar *(right)*.

Mexican Standoff

The four men who met at a hotel in Cuernavaca one April evening in 1933 were among Mexico's leading citizens. No swashbucklers these, just four gentlemen discussing a plan to swell their fortunes. The plan was sound, allowing them to amass seventeen tons of gold in less than a year. But because they failed to read the law more carefully, the businessmen lost their wealth as quickly as they gained it, and the gold became the sort of buried treasure of which legends are made. Now worth two billion dollars, the cache may still lie in a dusty corner of New Mexico.

The meeting in Mexico took place in a climate of worldwide economic depression. Franklin D. Roosevelt, who had recently taken office as president of the United States, was expected to take drastic measures to cure his nation's fiscal ills. A noted economist had just predicted that the United States would soon devalue the dollar, causing the price of gold to rise. Thus one of the prominent Mexicans, a mine operator named Leon Trabuco, urged his associates to buy up all the gold they could, smuggle it into the United States, and wait for the price to soar.

Over the next few months, the men bought gold in every form they could and melted it down into ingots. They weighed several possibilities for hiding places, ranging from bank vaults to frozen-food lockers. They finally settled on a hole in the ground in northwestern New Mexico between a mesa and Shiprock Peak *(below)*, a spire of rock that dominates the area for

hundreds of miles around. Trabuco smuggled the seventeen tons of ingots into the United States by plane and buried them.

On January 31, 1934, the Gold Reserve Act took effect, immediately raising the metal's price from twenty dollars to thirty-five dollars per ounce and giving the Mexican partners a tidy eight million dollar profit. Most speculators would have sold out right away, but the Mexicans did not. Instead, they waited for a further increase. It was a serious mistake, for the same law that raised the price of gold also made it illegal for individuals to own it in any great quantity. For a brief period, gold owners were able to exchange their holdings for paper dollars. Then the window slammed shut. By waiting to reap an even greater windfall, the four gentlemen of Cuernavaca guaranteed that they would make nothing without breaking the law.

One by one, the speculators died, leaving only Trabuco. He tried to sell the gold to one or another of the foreign agents and émigrés roaming Mexico City during World War II. He offered it to a Gestapo agent, then to the exiled king of Romania. There were no takers. Through a middleman, Trabuco then offered to sell the gold to the United States, but again he could not make the sale. All the offer did was trigger a grand jury investigation in Los Angeles in 1952—and that, in turn, launched a gold rush to Shiprock Peak.

The Treasury Department says that the ingots have never left their hiding place. □

An Unbreakable Code

Thomas Jefferson Beale had the kind of looks that turned heads. He was tall and trim, and his jet black hair, longer than the fashion of the day decreed, gave him a romantic air. Heads spun, therefore, when he arrived one January day in 1820 at the Lynchburg, Virginia, inn run by Robert Morriss.

Beale was as gregarious as he was handsome. He proved a ready conversationalist—the only subject he never broached was himself—and when he slipped from sight two months later, Morriss and his patrons were sorry to see him go. The engaging stranger returned two years later, darker and trimmer than ever. This time he left a locked iron box in Morriss's safekeeping. In a letter mailed shortly after from St. Louis, Beale told Morriss to open the box if he did not return in ten years. It contained papers "which will be unintelligible without the aid of a key," Beale wrote, adding that the key would be furnished later.

Twenty-three years passed, and nothing was heard from the mysterious Beale. Morriss finally opened the box and found a long letter that recounted a tale of treasure. On a trip out West in 1817, Beale's letter said, he and some companions amassed a fortune in silver and gold. They brought the hoard back East and buried it, together with some jewels, in the foothills of Virginia's Blue Ridge Mountains. Beale's box also contained three documents written in code. When deciphered, the letter said, the messages would reveal where the cache was located, its contents, and who should receive it.

Thus was born one of the most mind-teasing treasure hunts in U.S. history—or possibly one of the longest-running hoaxes. The Beale ciphers have stumped some of the finest minds and computers in cryptanalysis. The papers have spawned a society, the Beale Cipher Association, devoted to cracking the code. Its members "have played games with these numbers that would take a million men a billion years to duplicate with paper and pencil," says Carl Hammer, a prominent member of the group and a former director of computer sciences at Sperry Univac.

Ciphers replace each letter in a message with a number or another letter according to a scheme called a key. In the simplest example, the number 1 would replace the letter A, 2 would replace B, and so on. Computers allow cryptographers to create such complex substitution keys that ciphers can be virtually unbreakable. Before the advent of computers, complex keys were based on the sequence of words and letters in commonly available documents or books.

Such was the case, it seems, with the Beale papers. More than a century ago, one man nearly cracked the code. A year before his death, Morriss handed Beale's box and its contents to a friend named James Ward. Toiling day and night over one of the messages, Ward finally chose the Declaration of Independence as the probable key and decoded the document telling the contents of the Beale hoard.

According to Ward, the treasure consisted of 3,000 pounds of gold, 5,000 pounds of silver, and a fortune in jewels. But Ward never deciphered the other two documents, so the cache's location and intended distribution remained a mystery. In 1885, Ward gave up trying to break the code and published a pamphlet containing Morriss's account of Beale's story, Ward's translation of the one document, and all three encoded messages.

The original box and its contents have long since disappeared—a fact that leads skeptics to believe that the entire business of the Beale treasure was the work of a trickster. Some, pointing to similarities in the writing styles of

Ward and Beale, suspect that Ward created the entire scheme, and that Beale may never have existed. Still, the search for the key to the Beale treasure continues. Code breakers estimate that Beale could have had access to more than 2,000 texts as diverse as Shakespeare's plays, the Bible, the Magna Carta, and the Molasses Act of 1733. The Beale Cipher Association is gradually examining them all.

Not all the digging has been deskbound. To the dismay of local farmers, treasure hunters have tried to bring bulldozers onto their land whenever metal detectors have produced promising signals. Even dynamite has been used to blast a way to wealth. The rewards have been less spectacular than the efforts. One man unearthed a car. A woman dug up part of a cemetery and was charged with desecrating graves. Treasure hunter Mel Fisher *(pages 90-92)* claims to have found three empty vaults in the hills, evidence that convinced him that someone had beaten him to the treasure.

Although James Ward offered scant information about the Beale Treasure, he supplied ample advice that future fortune hunters might do well to heed: "Devote only such time as can be spared from your legitimate business to the task," he wrote, "and if you can spare no time, let the matter alone." □

The Search for the Holy Grail

The Holy Grail is considered the quintessential elusive treasure, the most precious and one of the oldest. The saga of the grail far predates the birth of Christ. It is rooted in an ancient Celtic myth about a magic cauldron of life that provides food and drink that can revive the dead. For the last two millennia, however, the grail has been part of Christian legend, where it figures as the chalice that Christ drank from at the Last Supper.

In medieval pious lore, the grail fell into the hands of Joseph of Arimathea, a wealthy merchant who provided the tomb for Jesus' burial. After the Crucifixion, Joseph is said to have made his way to the shores of Britain and thence inland to Glastonbury. There he supposedly established Britain's first Christian community. There too, tradition has it, he concealed the Holy Grail in an ancient well. Chalice Well, as it is now known, is re-puted never to have run dry.

The grail played a role in the chivalric romances of the Middle Ages. It was held to be a great treasure, but one to be sought for its spiritual significance rather than its material value. Only pilgrims of the purest heart had any chance of finding it. The most famous grail legend is that of King Arthur, the sixth-century folkloric monarch of Britain whose court at Camelot was not far from Glastonbury. The best-known version of Arthur's quest is Thomas Malory's *Le Morte d'Arthur.*

In that account, a vision of the Holy Grail, draped in silken cloth, appeared before Arthur's Knights of the Round Table. As the apparition passed through the hall, the nobles were miraculously provided with their best-loved food and drink. When the specter passed, the knights vowed to find the grail and return it to Camelot—a pursuit marked by mystical events, trances, and visions. Since only the purest could possess the grail, the knight Lancelot was banished from the Round Table because of his illicit love for Queen Guinevere.

In other versions of the Arthurian legend, the grail was claimed by Lancelot's son, the virtuous knight Galahad; in others, by a pure young knight named Perceval. In either case, when the knight died, a hand descended from Heaven to take the grail away.

The quest for the grail goes on today. Each year more than 150,000 pilgrims make their way to Glastonbury to view Chalice Well and the ruins of the ancient abbey. If none leaves with the cup in hand, many are infused with the enchantment of its legend. □

Borne by angels, the Holy Grail hovers above King Arthur and his knights at their Round Table in an illustration from a fifteenth-century French manuscript.

ACKNOWLEDGMENTS

The editors wish to thank these individuals and institutions for their valuable assistance:

Camillo Albertini, Milan; Stephen Allee, Department of Chinese Art, Freer Gallery of Art, Arthur M. Sackler Gallery, Washington, D.C.; Vincenzo Astorino, Rossana, Italy; Jörg Biel, Landesdenkmalamt Baden-Württemberg, Stuttgart; Natalino Bosco, Mendicino, Italy; Robert Burgess, Chattahoochee, Florida; Amanda Claridge, British School at Rome; Gregory Cuthbertson, Department of History, University of South Africa, Pretoria; Ray Dorr, Colorado Springs; Moira Farrow, *The Vancouver Sun,* Vancouver; Karolina Franc, Far-Eastern Art Department, Ante Topic Mimara Museum, Yugoslavia; Nathalie Garnot, Charroux, France; Fergus Gillespie, Genealogical Museum, Dublin; Joseph J. Goebel, Jr., Spanish Department, Temple University, Phila-delphia; Klaus Goldmann, Museum für Vor- und rpt und Frühgeschichte, Berlin; Joseph Greene, The Semitic Museum, Harvard University, Cambridge; Prinz Heinrich von Hessen, Hessische Hausstiftung, Kronberg; Landgraf Moritz von Hessen, Hessische Hausstiftung, Kronberg; Nancy Heywood, Essex Institute, Salem, Massachusetts; Lowell S. Hilpert, U.S. Geological Survey, Salt Lake City; Elena Lattanzi, Soprintendenza Archeologica della Calabria, Reggio Calabria, Italy; Patrick Lizé, Dreux, France; Robert Luce, U.S. Geological Survey, Reston, Virginia; Nicolette Luthmer, Hessische Hausstiftung, Archiv und Bibliothek, Eichenzell, Germany; Gordon McEwan, Dumbarton Oaks, Washington, D.C.; Anita Mancia, Istituto Storico della Compagnia di Gesù, Rome; Lindsey Vance Maness, Jr., Petrolmage Corporation, Golden, Colorado; Robert Marx, Indialantic, Florida; Betsy Moye, *The News and Courier,* Charleston, South Carolina; John Oliphant, Vancouver; John S. Potter, Hong Kong; Mirjana Radosevic, Belgrade; Christopher Rawlings, British Library, London; Vincenzo Rizzo, Cosenza, Italy; Ralph J. Roberts, U.S. Geological Survey, Battle Mountain, Nevada; Jim Romano, Brooklyn Museum, New York; Susan Russell-Robinson, U.S. Geological Survey, Reston, Virginia; Shaanxi Archeological Institute, Xian, Shaanxi Province; Shi Shuqing, Museum of Chinese History, Beijing; Imelde Sivero, Florence; Jenny So, Freer Gallery of Art, Arthur M. Sackler Gallery, Washington, D.C.; Annegret Stein-Karnbach, Kulturstiftung der Länder, Berlin; Jan Stuart, Freer Gallery of Art, Arthur M. Sackler Gallery, Washington, D.C.; Gustavo Valente, Cosenza, Italy; Ron Worl, U.S. Geological Survey, Reston, Virginia; Zhao Jin Min, Museum of Chinese History, Beijing.

PICTURE CREDITS

The sources for the illustrations that appear in this book are listed below. Credits from left to right are separated by semicolons, from top to bottom by dashes.

Cover: G. Dagli Orti, Paris, background, © Martin Rogers/Uniphoto, Washington, D.C. **3:** G. Dagli Orti, Paris. **7:** Lee Boltin, background, H. D. Thoreau/Westlight, Los Angeles. **8, 9:** Lee Boltin. **10:** The Hulton Picture Company, London. **11:** Courtesy the Leon Levy Expedition to Askelon, Carl Andrews, photographer. **12:** Photography by Egyptian Expedition, The Metropolitan Museum of Art, New York; Lee Boltin. **13:** Photography by Egyptian Expedition, The Metropolitan Museum of Art, New York; Lee Boltin. **14, 15:** V. Sarianidi, L. Bogdanov, V. Terebenin, Moscow (2); Lee Boltin. **17:** Barry Iverson/*TIME* magazine. **18:** Ron Worl. **19:** Spyros Tsavdaroglou. **20:** William MacWhitty, London. **21:** The Percival David Foundation of Chinese Art, London. **22:** Shaanxi Archaeological Institute—courtesy the Trustees of the British Museum, London. **23:** Jörg Biel, *Der Keltenfürst von Hochdorf,* Konrad Theiss Verlag, Stuttgart, 1985. **24-26:** Courtesy the Trustees of The British Museum, London. **27:** Lee Boltin. **28:** Photo Reunion des Musées Nationaux, Paris. **29:** National Museum of History, Sofia, Bulgaria. **30:** Mary Evans Picture Library, London—G. Dagli Orti, Paris. **31:** National Museum of Ireland, Dublin. **32:** Alejandro Balaguer, courtesy Enrico Poli Collection. **33:** Salvat, Mexico. **35:** Lloyd's of London, London, background, M. Freeman/ANA. **36:** National Maritime Museum, London. **37:** Library of Congress. **38, 39:** Larry Sherer, courtesy The George C. Marshall Foundation, Lexington, Virginia. **40:** The Metropolitan Museum of Art, The Elisha Whittelsey Collection, The Elisha Whittelsey Fund, 1951; Rare Book Division, The New York Public Library, Astor, Lenox and Tilden Foundations. **41:** From *Navires et Marins de la Rame a L'Helice,* by Guilleux La Roerie et commandant J. Vivielle, Paris, Duchartre et Van Buggenhoudt, 1930. **42, 43:** Library of Congress; M. Freeman/ANA; Syndication International, London. **44:** UPI/Bettmann, New York. **45:** Public Record Office, London. **46:** Musée de la Marine, Paris; Giraudon, Paris. **47:** Library of Congress USZ62-70501. **48:** Larry Sherer, from *The Scourge of the Indies: Buccaneers, Corsairs and Filibusters,* by Maurice Besson, Random House, 1929. **49, 50:** David Bristow, Cape Town, South Africa. **51:** Lloyd's of London, London. **52:** From *The Russo-Japanese War Fully Illustrated,* Vol. 3, no. 9, Kankado Publishing Co., Tokyo, 1905. **53:** Official U.S. Navy Photograph. **55:** Brian Payne/Black Star, New York, background, H. D. Thoreau/Westlight, Los Angeles. **56, 57:** Courtesy the Trustees of the British Library, London. **58, 59:** Peter Newark's Historical Pictures, Bath. **60:** Courtesy the Trustees of the British Library, London. **61:** E.T. Archive, London; Public Record Office, London. **63:** Photo Loft, Concord, New Hampshire. **64:** Peter Newark's Historical Pictures, Bath; courtesy the Trustees of the British Library, London. **65:** Courtesy Essex Institute, Salem, Massachusetts. **66, 67:** Peter Newark's Historical Pictures, Bath; The Historic New Orleans Collection, Museum/Research Center, New Orleans. **68:** Peter Newark's Historical Pictures, Bath. **69:** PDI, Dublin/courtesy The Genealogical Museum, Dublin (2); Bord Failte, Dublin, photo: Brian Lynch. **71:** John Oliphant. **72, 73:** Courtesy Ova Noss Family Partnership Archives, Santa Ana, California. **74, 75:** Brian Payne/Black Star, New York—Toni Ott, Landshut—Brian Payne/Black Star, New York. **76:** Ullstein Bilderdienst, Berlin. **77:** Hessische Hausstiftung—Associated Press (2). **78:** Walter Frentz, Überlingen. **79:** The Bridgeman Art Library, London/courtesy Narodni Gallery, Prague. **80:** From *The Rape of Art,* by David Roxan and Ken Wanstall, Coward-McCann, Inc., New York, 1964, copied by Larry Sherer. **81:** National Archives 11-SC-203869. **82:** Rizzoli, Milan; Farabola, Milan. **83, 84:** UPI/Bettmann, New York. **85:** *Sunday Times,* London/Ian Yeomans, background, Don Kincaid. **87:** Rick Friedman/Black Star, New York—Brent Peterson. **88:** Flip Schulke. **89:** Bob Brooks (2)—Robert Marx. **90:** Karen Kasmauski Wheeler Pictures/Woodfin Camp, Washington, D.C. **91:** Courtesy Robert F. Burgess. **93:** Kenneth McLeish. **94:** Courtesy Robert F. Burgess. **95:** Robert Marx. **96, 97:** Courtesy Robert F. Burgess; Robert Marx. **98:** Robert Hunt Library, London; *Sunday Times,* London/Ian Yeomans. **99:** Doug Ayers (2)—Joseph C. Amaral. **100:** Wide World Photos, Inc., New York. **101:** Robert Marx; Peter Stackpole. **102:** Robert Marx. **103:** Bob McMillan. **104:** Larry Sherer, from *The Treasure of the Great Reef,* by Arthur C. Clarke and Mike Wilson, Harper Collins, New York, 1964—Wide World Photos,

BIBLIOGRAPHY

Books

Andrews, Ernest M.:
Dowsing Made Easy: You Can Do It. East Point, Ga.: Ernest M. Andrews, Sr., 1987.
Georgia's Fabulous Treasure Hoards. Hapeville, Ga.: Ernest M. Andrews, 1966.
Astorino, Vincenzo. *... Nel Busento, la Valle dei Re.* Cosenza, Italy: Editrice MIT, 1967.
Atlas of the Greek World. New York: Facts On File, 1980.
Australian Dictionary of Biography (Vol. 9). London: Melbourne University Press, 1983.
Bailey, Philip A. *Golden Mirages.* New York: Macmillan, 1940.
Bamford, Francis, and Viola Bankes. *Vicious Circle: The Case of the Missing Irish Crown Jewels.* New York: Horizon Press, 1967.
Berton, Pierre. *My Country: The Remarkable Past.* Toronto: McClelland & Stewart, 1976.
Besson, Maurice. *The Scourge of the Indies: Buccaneers, Corsairs, & Filibusters.* New York: Random House, 1929.
Biel, Jörg. *Der Keltenfürst von Hochdorf.* Stuttgart: Konrad Theiss Verlag, 1985.
Birch, Walter De Gray. *The Commentaries of the Great Afonso Dalboquerque, Second Viceroy of India* (Vol. 3). New York: Burt Franklin, 1970 (reprint of 1884 edition).
Bray, Warwick. *The Gold of El Dorado.* London: Times Newspapers, 1978.
Brion, Marcel. *Alaric: The Goth.* Translated by Frederick H. Martens. New York: Robert M. McBride, 1930.
British, Allied and Neutral Merchant Vessels Sunk or Destroyed by War Causes (Vol. 1 of *Lloyd's War Losses: The Second World War*). London: Lloyd's of London Press, 1989.
Burgess, Robert F.:
Sunken Treasure: Six Who Found Fortunes. New York: Dodd, Mead, 1988.
They Found Treasure. New York: Dodd, Mead, 1977.
Cahill, Robert Ellis. *New England Collectible Classics No. XIV: New England's Pirates and Lost Treasures.* Salem, Mass.: Chandler-Smith, 1987.
Caygill, Marjorie L. *Treasures of the British Museum.* London: British Museum Publications, 1987.
Ceram, C. W. *Gods, Graves, and Scholars* (2d rev. ed.). Translated by E. B. Garside and Sophie Wilkins. Toronto: Bantam Books, 1972.
Ceram, C. W. (Ed.). *Hands on the Past: Pioneer Archaeologists Tell Their Own Story.* New York: Alfred A. Knopf, 1966.
Chadwick, John. *The Mycenaean World.* Cambridge: Cambridge University Press, 1976.
Chamberlin, Russell. *Loot! The Heritage of Plunder.* New York: Facts On File, 1983.
Chandler, David Leon. *One Hundred Tons of Gold.* Garden City, N.Y.: Doubleday, 1978.
Charroux, Robert. *Treasures of the World.* Translated by Gloria Cantù. New York: Paul S. Eriksson, 1962.
Clark, James C. *Last Train South: The Flight of the Confederate Government from Richmond.* Jefferson, N.C.: McFarland, 1984.
Clarke, Arthur C., and Mike Wilson. *The Treasure of the Great Reef.* New York: Harper & Row, 1964.
Coffman, F. L. *1001 Lost, Buried or Sunken Treasures: Facts for Treasure Hunters.* New York: Thomas Nelson, 1957.
Cohen, Joan Lebold. *China Today* (2d ed.). New York: Harry N. Abrams, 1980.
Cooper, Gordon. *Treasure-Trove, Pirates' Gold.* London: Lutterworth Press, 1951.
Dalton, O. M. *The Treasure of the Oxus: With Other Examples of Early Oriental Metal-Work* (3d ed.). London: Trustees of the British Museum, 1964.
Defoe, Daniel. *A General History of the Pyrates.* Edited by Manuel Schonhorn. Columbia: University of South Carolina Press, 1972.
de Jaeger, Charles. *The Linz File: Hitler's Plunder of Europe's Art.* Exeter, England: Webb & Bower, 1981.
Desroches-Noblecourt, Christiane. *Tutankhamen.* Boston: New York Graphic Society, 1978.
Doak, Wade. *The Elingamite and Its Treasure.* London: Hodder & Stoughton, 1969.
Dobie, J. Frank. *Coronado's Children: Tales of Lost Mines and Buried Treasures of the Southwest.* New York: Grosset & Dunlap, 1930.
Dombrowski, Roman. *Mussolini: Twilight and Fall.* Translated by H. G. Stevens. London: William Heinemann, 1956.
Dos Passos, John. *The Portugal Story: Three Centuries of Exploration and Discovery.* Garden City, N.Y.: Doubleday, 1969.
Dow, George Francis, and John Henry Edmonds. *The Pirates of the New England Coast, 1630-1730.* New York: Argosy-Antiquarian, 1968.
Drago, Harry Sinclair. *Lost Bonanzas: Tales of the Legendary Lost Mines of the American West.* New York: Dodd, Mead, 1966.
Dunbar, Gary S. *Historical Geography of the North Carolina Outer Banks.* Edited by Fred Kniffen. Baton Rouge: Louisiana State University Press, 1958.
Earle, Peter. *The Wreck of the Almiranta: Sir William Phips and the Search for the Hispaniola Treasure.* London: Macmillan, 1979.
Elisseeff, Danielle, and Vadime Elisseeff. *New Discoveries in China.* Translated by Larry Lockwood. Secaucus, N.J.: Chartwell Books, 1983.
Ely, Sims. *The Lost Dutchman Mine: The Fabulous Story of the Seven-Decade Search for the Hidden Treasure in the Superstition Mountains of Arizona.* New York: William Morrow, 1953.
Esquemeling, John. *The Buccaneers of America.* New York: Barnes & Noble, 1951 (reprint of 1684-85 edition).
Fox, Robin Lane. *The Search for Alexander.* Lon-

don: Allen Lane, 1980.

Furneaux, Rupert. *The Great Treasure Hunts.* New York: Taplinger, 1969.

Garcilaso de la Vega. *Royal Commentaries of the Incas: And General History of Peru.* Translated by Harold V. Livermore. Austin: University of Texas Press, 1966.

Gardner, Erle Stanley. *Hunting Lost Mines by Helicopter.* New York: William Morrow, 1965.

Garlake, Peter. *The Kingdoms of Africa.* Oxford: Elsevier/Phaidon, 1978.

Gosse, Philip. *The History of Piracy.* New York: Tudor, 1932.

Gougaud, Henri, and Colette Gouvion. *Egypt Observed.* Translated by Stephen Hardman. London: Kaye & Ward, 1979.

Grant, Neil. *Buccaneers.* London: Angus & Robertson, 1976.

Grissim, John. *The Lost Treasure of the Concepción.* New York: William Morrow, 1980.

Grohskopf, Bernice. *The Treasure of Sutton Hoo: Ship-Burial for an Anglo-Saxon King.* New York: Atheneum, 1970.

Groushko, Michael:
Lost Treasures of the World. Secaucus, N.J.: Chartwell Books, 1986.
Treasure. Philadelphia: Running Press, Courage Books, 1990.

Grousset, René. *Conqueror of the World: The Life of Chingis-Khan.* Translated by Marian McKellar and Denis Sinor. New York: Viking Press, 1966.

Hamilton, George. *The Treasure of the Tuamotus.* London: Stanley Paul, 1939.

Hancock, Ralph, and Julian A. Weston. *The Lost Treasure of Cocos Island.* New York: Thomas Nelson, 1960.

Hartog, Leo de. *Genghis Khan: Conqueror of the World.* New York: St. Martin's Press, 1989.

Haydock, Tim. *Treasure Trove: Where to Find the Great Lost Treasures of the World.* London: Fourth Estate, 1986.

Heller, Julek, and Deirdre Headon. *Knights.* New York: Schocken Books, 1982.

Helm, Thomas. *Treasure Hunting around the World.* New York: Dodd, Mead, 1960.

Hemming, John. *The Search for El Dorado.* New York: E. P. Dutton, 1979.

Hendrix, Bobbie Lou. *Crater of Diamonds: Jewel of Arkansas.* Antoine, Ark.: Bobbie Lou Hendrix, 1989.

Hibbert, Christopher:
Benito Mussolini. London: Longmans, 1962.
The Emperors of China (Treasures of the World series). Chicago: Stonehenge Press, 1981.

Hoffman, Paul. *Archimedes' Revenge: The Joys and Perils of Mathematics.* New York: W. W. Norton, 1988.

Hudson, Kenneth, and Ann Nicholls. *Tragedy on the High Seas.* New York: A & W Publishers, 1979.

Johns, Catherine, and Timothy Potter. *The Thetford Treasure: Roman Jewellery and Silver.* London: British Museum Publications, 1983.

Kemp, P. K., and Christopher Lloyd. *Brethren of the Coast: Buccaneers of the South Seas.* New York: St Martin's Press, 1960.

King, Charles. *The Story of Genghis Khan.* London: J. M. Dent, 1971.

Lamb, Harold:
Genghis Khan and the Mongol Horde. New York: Random House, 1954.
The March of the Barbarians. New York: Doubleday, Doran, 1941.

Latil, Pierre de, and Jean Rivoire. *Sunken Treasure.* New York: Hill & Wang, 1962.

Lister, R. P. *The Secret History of Genghis Khan.* London: Peter Davies, 1969.

Lloyd, Alan. *King John.* Newton Abbot, Devon: David & Charles, 1973.

Lloyd, Christopher. *Sir Francis Drake.* London: Faber & Faber, 1957.

Longworth, Ian, and John Cherry (Eds.). *Archaeology in Britain Since 1945.* London: British Museum Publications, 1986.

Martin, Edward J. *The Trial of the Templars.* London: George Allen & Unwin, 1978.

Marx, Robert F.:
The Lure of Sunken Treasure. New York: David McKay, 1973.
Robert Marx: Quest for Treasure. Dallas, Tex.: Ram Books, 1982.
Sea Fever. Garden City, N.Y.: Doubleday, 1972.
Shipwrecks in the Americas. New York: Bonanza Books, 1983.

Matthews, John, and Marian Green. *The Grail Seeker's Companion.* San Bernardino: Borgo Press, 1987.

Meylach, Martin. *Diving to a Flash of Gold.* Garden City, N.Y.: Doubleday, 1971.

Mihan, George. *Looted Treasure: Germany's Raid on Art.* Translated by Harry C. Schnur. London: Alliance Press, 1944.

Milne, A. A. *Now We Are Six.* New York: E. P. Dutton, 1927.

Mitchell, John D. *Lost Mines & Buried Treasures along the Old Frontier.* Glorieta, N.Mex.: Rio Grande Press, 1970.

O'Connor, D'Arcy. *The Big Dig: The $10 Million Search for Oak Island's Legendary Treasure.* New York: Ballantine Books, 1988.

Paine, Ralph D. *The Book of Buried Treasure.* New York: Arno Press, 1981.

Penfield, Thomas. *Dig Here!* (rev. ed.). San Antonio, Tex.: Naylor, 1966.

Penrose, Barrie. *Stalin's Gold: The Story of HMS Edinburgh and Its Treasure.* Boston: Little, Brown, 1982.

Perrin, Rosemarie D. *Explores Ltd. Guide to Lost Treasure in the United States and Canada.* Harrisburg, Pa.: Cameron House, 1977.

Peterson, Mendel. *The Funnel of Gold.* Boston: Little, Brown, 1975.

Potter, John S., Jr.:
The Treasure Diver's Guide. Garden City, N.Y.: Doubleday, 1960.
The Treasure Diver's Guide (rev. ed.). Port Salerno, Fla.: Florida Classics Library, 1988.
The Treasure Divers of Vigo Bay. Garden City, N.Y.: Doubleday, 1958.

Prescott, William H. *The History of the Conquest of Mexico.* New York: Van Allen Bradley, 1843.

Sanceau, Elaine. *The Reign of the Fortunate King, 1495-1521.* Hamden, Conn.: Archon Books, 1969.

Sarna, Nahum M. *Exploring Exodus: The Heritage of Biblical Israel.* New York: Schocken Books, 1986.

Sawyer, L. A., and W. H. Mitchell. *The Liberty Ships.* Newton Abbot, Devon: David & Charles, 1973.

Sayer, Ian, Douglas Botting, and the London *Sunday Times. Nazi Gold.* New York: Congdon & Weed, 1984.

Schurz, William Lytle. *The Manila Galleon.* New York: E. P. Dutton, 1939.

Seagrave, Sterling. *The Marcos Dynasty.* New York: Harper & Row, 1988.

The Search for Alexander. Boston: New York Graphic Society, 1980.

Sebring, Thomas H. *Treasure Tales: Shipwrecks and Salvage.* Devon, Pa.: Cooke, 1986.

Slack, Jack. *Finders Losers.* London: Hutchinson, 1968.

Snow, Edward Rowe:
Pirates and Buccaneers of the Atlantic Coast. Boston: Yankee, 1944.
True Tales of Buried Treasure. New York: Dodd, Mead, 1960.

Stick, David. *Graveyard of the Atlantic.* Chapel Hill: University of North Carolina Press, 1952.

Stirling, N. B. *Treasure under the Sea.* Garden City, N.Y.: Doubleday, 1957.

Storm, Alex. *Canada's Treasure Hunt.* Winnipeg, Canada: Greywood, 1967.

Strange Stories, Amazing Facts. Pleasantville, N.Y.: Reader's Digest Association, 1976.

Stuart, Gene S. *The Mighty Aztecs.* Washington, D.C.: National Geographic Society, 1981.

Thorndike, Joseph J., Jr. (Ed.). *Discovery of Lost Worlds.* New York: American Heritage, 1979.

Titler, Dale M. *Unnatural Resources: True Stories of American Treasure.* Englewood Cliffs, N.J.: Prentice-Hall, 1973.

Tompkins, B. A. (Ed.). *Treasure: Man's 25 Greatest Quests for El Dorado.* New York: *Times*

Books, 1979.

Trupp, Philip Z. *Tracking Treasure.* Washington, D.C.: Acropolis Books, 1986.

Turner, Malcolm. *Shipwrecks & Salvage.* Cape Town: C. Struik, 1988.

Vanderbilt, Arthur T., II. *Treasure Wreck.* Boston: Houghton Mifflin, 1986.

Verrill, A. Hyatt. *They Found Gold: The Story of Successful Treasure Hunts.* Glorifta, N.Mex.: Rio Grande Press, 1972 (reprint of 1936 edition).

Viemeister, Peter. *The Beale Treasure: A History of a Mystery.* Bedford, Va.: Hamilton's, 1987.

Voynick, Stephen M. *The Mid-Atlantic Treasure Coast.* Wallingford, Pa.: Middle Atlantic Press, 1984.

Wagner, Kip. *Pieces of Eight: Recovering the Riches of a Lost Spanish Treasure Fleet.* New York: E. P. Dutton, 1966.

Warren, W. L. *King John.* London: Eyre & Spottiswoode, 1961.

Webb, Robert N. *Genghis Khan: Conqueror of the Medieval World.* New York: Franklin Watts, 1967.

Weight, Harold O. *Lost Mines of Death Valley.* Twentynine Palms, Calif.: Calico Press, 1970.

Westwood, Jennifer (Ed.). *The Atlas of Mysterious Places.* New York: Weidenfeld & Nicolson, 1987.

Whedbee, Charles Harry. *Blackbeard's Cup and Stories of the Outer Banks.* Winston-Salem, N.C.: John F. Blair, 1989.

Wheeler, Margaret. *History Was Buried: A Source Book of Archaeology.* New York: Galahad Books, 1967.

Wilson, Colin, and Damon Wilson. *The Encyclopedia of Unsolved Mysteries.* Chicago: Contemporary Books, 1987.

Wilson, Derek. *The World Atlas of Treasure.* London: Collins, 1981.

Wood, Michael. *In Search of the Trojan War.* New York: Facts On File, 1985.

Wycherley, George. *Buccaneers of the Pacific.* Indianapolis: Bobbs-Merrill, 1928.

Youngs, Susan (Ed.). *'The Work of Angels': Masterpieces of Celtic Metalwork, 6th-9th Centuries AD.* London: British Museum Publications, 1989.

Periodicals

"About That Gold in the East River." *The New York Times,* August 9, 1987.

Alva, Walter. "Discovering the New World's Richest Unlooted Tomb." *National Geographic,* October 1988.

"Ancient Gold Unearthed." *Reno Gazette,* August 6, 1989.

Andrews, Ernest M. "I Hunt Buried Treasure in Georgia." *Atlanta Journal and Constitution Magazine,* April 8, 1956.

Antrobus, Edmund. "The Treasure of Tobermory Bay." *American Forests,* June 1977.

The Archaeological Team of Famen Temple. "Excavation of the Tang Dynasty Underground Palace at Famen Temple." *Wenwu* (Beijing), 1988, no. 10.

"Arkansas Allowing 4 Companies to Explore Public Diamond Mine." *New York Times,* November 20, 1989.

Arnold, David. "Life Aboard a Pirate Ship Is Being Slowly Revealed." *Boston Globe,* October 13, 1986.

"Art McKee Dies." *Skin Diver,* October 1980.

Bailey, Sarah. "Mr. Pepys the Treasure Hunter." *Strange Stories from the Tower of London,* 1978.

Baker, James N., Patrick Rogers, and Peter Annin. "Holding Art for Ransom: The Germans Buy Back a Stolen Masterpiece." *Newsweek,* May 14, 1990.

Barada, Bill. "Treasure of Montezuma." *Skin Diver,* 1988, Vol. 37, no. 9.

Benchley, Peter. "Bermuda: Balmy, British, and Beautiful." *National Geographic,* July 1971.

Berkowitz, Lois. "Has the U.S. Geological Survey Found King Solomon's Gold Mines?" *Biblical Archaeology Review,* September 1977.

Biel, Jörg. "Treasure from a Celtic Tomb." *National Geographic,* March 1980.

"The Big Find: Ancient Spanish Mint Ship Yields Richest Treasure to Date." *Look,* March 9, 1965.

Brinkley, Joel. "Archeologists Unearth 'Golden Calf' in Israel." *New York Times International,* July 25, 1990.

"Briny Bonanza: Divers Salvage Soviet Gold." *Time,* October 5, 1981.

Brodeur, Paul. "The Treasure of the *Debraak.*" *New Yorker,* August 15, 1988.

Cardone, Bonnie J. "Maravillas Treasure: A Fortune in Historical Artifacts Just Found!" *Skin Diver,* January 1989.

Carpenter, Betsy. "Is a Treasure Hunter's Gain History's Loss?" *U.S. News & World Report,* August 21, 1989.

Caso, Alfonso. "Monte Albán: Richest Archeological Find in America." *National Geographic,* October 1932.

Castro, Janice. "Davy Jones Meets the Computer." *Time,* October 1, 1984.

Clark, Howard D. "The Cavern of Kokoweef Mountain." *True Treasure,* Winter 1967.

Clifford, Barry. "An Under-Water Odyssey." *Art & Antiques,* November 1986.

Connolly, Lucia Greene. "A Treasure Island Dream Comes True." *New England Living,* Late Summer 1988.

Cooper, Nancy, and Melinda Livin. "The Quest for Marco's Gold." *Newsweek,* August 3, 1987.

Cross, E. R. "Deep Gold." *Skin Diver,* January 1990.

Daniloff, Ruth. "Cryptanalysts and Fortune Hunters Lead a Merry Chase in the Virginia Countryside in Search of Beale's Treasure." *Smithsonian,* April 1981.

Davidson, Mark, and Nirmali Ponnamperuma. "A Look Forward to Encountering New Neighbors." *Science Digest,* February 1978.

"The Debate on Shipwrecks." *Science Digest,* February 1986.

Diesenhouse, Susan. "Treasure Hunter Has Rights to Pirate Ship, Court Rules." *New York Times,* December 13, 1988.

Dornberg, John. "The Mounting Embarrassment of Germany's Nazi Treasures." *ARTnews,* September 1988.

Dorr, Ray. "Hollow Mountain—Filled with Gold?" *Argosy,* September 1967.

Douglas, Hal. "New Light on 17 Tons of Gold." *Treasure,* October 1989.

Duffy, Howard M., "The Famous Tayopas Still Baffle the Best." *Treasure Search,* November-December 1986.

Elmer-DeWitt, Philip. "The Golden Treasures of Nimrud." *Time,* October 30, 1989.

"'£5m' for Gold-Find Farmer." *London Daily Express,* July 30, 1986.

Foran, W. Robert. "Tristan Da Cunha: Isles of Contentment." *National Geographic,* November 1938.

Ford, Richard. "A Little Irish Luck for £8m Treasure Hunters." *London Daily Express,* December 11, 1986.

Frazier, Herb, and Jim Parker. "Treasure from 8,000 Feet Deep." *News and Courier,* September 15, 1989.

Gauger, Marcia. "Arthur Clarke Spins Tales of Outer Space, But He's at Home in a Sri Lanka Sarong." *People,* December 10, 1982.

"'Golden Calf' Discovered in Israel." *Harvard Gazette,* July 27, 1990.

"Gold-Filled Tomb Yields 2,700-Year-Old Secrets." *Reno Gazette,* May 28, 1989.

Goodman, Susan. "Mining a Watery Pirate's Lair." *Friends,* March 1987.

Harrington, Spencer P. M. "Royal Treasures of Nimrud." *Archaeology,* July-August 1990.

"High Tech Hunts Sunken Treasure." *U.S. News & World Report,* August 27, 1984.

Hind, Cynthia. "The Treasure of Lobengula." *True Treasure,* Fall 1967.

Honan, William H.:

"Bank in Texas Admits It Has Missing German Art Treasures." *New York Times,* June 19, 1990.

"A Trove of Medieval Art Turns Up in Texas." *New York Times,* June 14, 1990.

Hope, W. H. St. John. "The Loss of King John's Baggage Train in the Wellstream in October,

1216." *Society of Antiquities in Archaeologia,* 1907, Vol. 60.

Kendall, Ena. "In Search of the Golden Hare." *Observer,* September 16, 1979.

"A 'King Tut' for the New World." *U.S. News & World Report,* September 26, 1988.

Lawren, Bill. "The Truth about Pirates." *Omni,* June 1987.

Lemonick, Michael D. "The Return of the Golden Calf." *Time,* August 6, 1990.

Leviero, Anthony. "Hesse Gems Found in Station Locker." *New York Times,* June 9, 1946.

Lewis, Jo Ann. "WWII German Art Hoard to Be Returned by Soviet: 360 Master Drawings Taken for Safekeeping." *Washington Post,* August 16, 1990.

Lyon, Eugene. "The Trouble with Treasure." *National Geographic,* June 1976.

"A Man's Obsession and Its Rewards." *Life,* March 10, 1967.

Marcus, Amy Dockser. "Judge Gives Lost Gold to Salvagers." *Wall Street Journal,* August 15, 1990.

Marks, William E. "The Wreck of the Pirate Ship *Whydah.*" *Martha's Vineyard Magazine,* Fall 1988.

Martin, Steve:
"Brother XII's Fabulous $400,000 Treasure Boxes." *Treasure Search,* April 1980.
"Montcalm's Missing Millions." *Treasure Search,* March-April 1989.

Marx, Robert F. "Treasure Hunting: It's Become Big Business." *Skin Diver,* April 1982.

Mingis, Ken. "Pirates! The *Whydah* and Her Crew of Bloodthirsty Democrats." *Providence Sunday Journal,* March 22, 1987.

Mydans, Seth. "In Wilds of Manila, a Hunt for Lost Treasure." *New York Times,* March 5, 1988.

Oliphant, John. "Brother Twelve." *West Magazine,* August 1990.

Palmieri, Edmund L., and John Kobler. "What Happened to Mussolini's Millions." *Life,* January 17, 1949.

Paterson, T. W. "Brother XII's Missing Gold." *Canadian West,* November 1988.

Paul, Anthony. "Quest for Yamashita's Hoard Still Haunts Manila." *Far Eastern Economic Review,* June 25, 1987.

Peters, Adrian. "Ocracoke." *Cruising World,* March 1989.

Plenge, Heinz. "The Robber's Tale." *Connoisseur,* February 1990.

Preston, Douglas. "The Mysterious Money Pit." *Smithsonian,* June 1988.

Prideaux, Tom. "Now It's Our Turn to Be Fascinated by Tut's Treasure." *Smithsonian,* November 1976.

Raven, Susan. "The Future of the Past." *Sunday Times,* March 29, 1981.

Remnick, David. "The Guardian of the Lost Art: Russian Viktor Baldin, Waiting 45 Years to Return a Cache of Drawings to Germany." *Washington Post,* August 17, 1990.

Riding, Alan. "Gold Bar Found in Mexico Thought to Be Cortés's." *New York Times,* April 19, 1981.

Rieker, Jane. "Treasure Hunter Jack Haskins Finds an Undersea Fortune in the Depths of the Library." *People,* March 5, 1979.

"The Rillaton Gold Cup" (Notes and News section). *Antiquity,* July 1983.

Ringle, Ken. " 'Storybook Treasure' Found off South Carolina." *Washington Post,* September 14, 1989.

Rogal, Kim. "Treasure of the Edinburgh." *Newsweek,* October 5, 1981.

Ryan, Michael. "Barry Clifford's Zany Crew— Including JFK Jr.—Prove that Way Down Deep, They're Golddiggers." *People,* August 22, 1983.

Sarianidi, Viktor Ivanovich. "The Golden Hoard of Bactria." *National Geographic,* March 1990.

"Seeking a Legend in the Steps of the Hopeful Dead." *The Herald,* July 24, 1990.

"1717 Wreck of Galleon off Cape Yields Treasure and Hints at Pirates' Lives." *New York Times,* October 26, 1986.

Shalett, Sidney. "Colonel, Wac Captain Held in German Royal Gem Theft." *New York Times,* June 8, 1946.

Shenker, Israel:
"A Hound-and-Hare Sequence Broke the *Masquerade* Code." *Smithsonian,* May 1982.
"A Treasure Awaits Anyone Who Solves *Masquerade* Riddle." *Smithsonian,* December 1980.

"The Skull of Lobengula." *Time,* January 10, 1944.

Smirke, Edward. "Some Account of the Discovery of a Gold Cup in a Barrow in Cornwall, A.D. 1837." *The Archaeological Journal,* September 1867.

"Solomon's Mines: End of the Search?" *Science News,* May 29, 1976.

Stackpole, Peter. "Treasure-Diving Teddy Tucker Still Builds a Legend." *Smithsonian,* May 1975.

"Thetford." *Current Anthropology,* March 1981.

Thompson, Dick. "The Secrets of a Moche Lord." *Time,* September 26, 1988.

Todorchev, Anne. "Working the Fields." *Art & Antiques,* November 1988.

"The Treasure of Silver Shoals." *Time,* January 15, 1979.

"Le Trésor de Famensi." *Arts Asiatiques,* 1989, Vol. 44.

Trupp, Philip. "Ancient Shipwrecks Yield Both Prizes and Bitter Conflict." *Smithsonian,* October 1983.

Tucker, Teddy:
"Adventure Is My Life" (Part 1). *Saturday Evening Post,* February 24, 1962.
"Adventure Is My Life" (Part 2). *Saturday Evening Post,* March 3, 1962.
"Adventure Is My Life" (Conclusion). *Saturday Evening Post,* March 10, 1962.

Wagner, Kip. "Drowned Galleons Yield Spanish Gold." *National Geographic,* January 1965.

Wald, Matthew L. "Bell Confirms that Salvors Found Pirate Ship of Legend." *New York Times,* November 1, 1985.

Walker, Bryce S. "Tales of Sunken Gold and Hunters of the Depths." *Smithsonian,* January 1987.

Wang Zhaolin. "Another Cultural Pearl on the Silk Road: Increasing Research on Famen Temple." *Outlook* (Beijing), October 29, 1990.

Welchman, John. "All the Gold in Bulgaria." *Connoisseur,* January 1987.

White, David Fairbank. "A $400 Million Pirate Treasure." *Parade,* January 27, 1985.

Woolf, Jenny. "Kit Williams." *Express Newspaper* (London), November 16, 1986.

"Worth Its 'Wait' in Gold." *Mankind,* November 1981.

"Yes, Virginia, There Was a Golden Calf." *Newsweek,* August 6, 1990.

Other Sources

Conrad, Judy (Ed.). "Story of an American Tragedy: Survivors' Accounts of the Sinking of the Steamship *Central America.*" Booklet. Columbus, Ohio: Columbus-America Discovery Group, 1988.

"Harvard Archaeologists Find Ancient Calf Figure." Press release. Cambridge, Mass.: Harvard University, July 25, 1990.

Hilpert, Lowell S., Ralph J. Roberts, and Gavin A. Dirom. "Geology of Mine Hill and the Underground Workings, Mahd Adh Dhahab Mine, Kingdom of Saudi Arabia." Technical report USGS TR-03-2 (IR 592). Reston, Va.: USGS, 1976.

"King Solomon's 'Lost Mine' Found." Press release. Reston, Va.: USGS, May 24, 1976.

"Un Mistero Da Scoprire." Transcript of film. Rome: Telestars, June 1989.

Panizza, Mario, and Vincenzo Rizzo. "An Example of Geomorphology Applied to Archeology: 'Gryfon Hill' in Bisignano (Cosenza, Italy)." Paper presented at the Second International Conference on Geomorphology. Frankfurt: Geooko Verlag, September 3, 1989.

"Plunder!" "Frontline" transcript, program 812. New York: WGBH Educational Foundation, May 8, 1990.

Index

Time-Life Books is a division of Time Life Inc.,
a wholly owned subsidiary of
THE TIME INC. BOOK COMPANY

TIME-LIFE BOOKS

Managing Editor: Thomas H. Flaherty
Director of Editorial Resources:
Elise D. Ritter-Clough
Director of Photography and Research:
John Conrad Weiser
Editorial Board: Dale M. Brown, Roberta Conlan,
Laura Foreman, Lee Hassig, Jim Hicks,
Blaine Marshall, Rita Thievon Mullin, Henry
Woodhead

PUBLISHER: Joseph J. Ward

Associate Publisher: Ann Mirabito
Editorial Director: Russell B. Adams, Jr.
Marketing Director: Anne C. Everhart
Director of Design: Louis Klein
Production Manager: Prudence G. Harris
Supervisor of Quality Control: James King

Editorial Operations
Production: Celia Beattie
Library: Louise D. Forstall
Computer Composition: Deborah G. Tait (Manager),
Monika D. Thayer, Janet Barnes Syring,
Lillian Daniels

**Library of Congress
Cataloging-in-Publication Data**
Lost treasure / by the editors of Time-Life Books.
p.   cm.   (Library of curious and unusual facts).
Includes bibliographical references.
ISBN 0-8094-7703-3 (trade)
ISBN 0-8094-7704-1 (lsb)
1. Treasure-trove.
I. Time-Life Books. II. Series.
G525.L83 1991
909—dc20   90-20110 CIP

LIBRARY OF CURIOUS AND UNUSUAL FACTS

SERIES EDITOR: Laura Foreman
Series Administrator: Roxie France-Nuriddin
Art Director: Susan K. White
Picture Editor: Sally Collins

Editorial Staff for *Lost Treasure*
Text Editor: John R. Sullivan
Associate Editor/Research: Catherine M. Chase, Jane
Martin
Assistant Editor/Research: Andra H. Armstrong, Ruth
Goldberg
Assistant Art Director: Alan Pitts
Copy Coordinators: Jarelle S. Stein (principal),
Anthony K. Pordes
Picture Coordinator: Jennifer Iker
Editorial Assistant: Terry Ann Paredes

Special Contributors: Sarah Brash, Margery A. du-
Mond, Lydia Preston Hicks, Gina Maranto, Sandra
Salmans (text); Adele Conover, Flora Garcia, Cather-
ine B. Hackett, Edward O. Marshall, Vivian Noble,
Beth Winters (research); Hazel Blumberg-McKee
(index)

Correspondents: Elisabeth Kraemer-Singh (Bonn),
Christine Hinze (London), Christina Lieberman (New
York), Maria Vincenza Aloisi (Paris), Ann Natanson
(Rome).
Valuable assistance was also provided by Mirka
Gondicas (Athens); Mia Turner, Li Yan (Beijing);
Pavle Svabic (Belgrade); Angelika Lemmer (Bonn);
Judy Aspinall, Linda Marshall (London); Trini Ban-
drés (Madrid); John Dunn (Melbourne); Patricia Ali-
sau, Andrea Dabrowski (Mexico City); Sasha
Isachenko (Moscow); Elizabeth Brown, Katheryn
White (New York); Ann Wise (Rome); Dick Berry,
Mieko Ikeda (Tokyo).

The Consultants:
William R. Corliss, the general consultant for the
series, is a physicist-turned-writer who has spent the
last twenty-five years compiling collections of
anomalies in the fields of geophysics, geology, archaeology, astronomy, biology, and psychology. He
has written about science and technology for NASA,
the National Science Foundation, and the Energy
Research and Development Administration (among
others). Mr. Corliss is also the author of more than
thirty books on scientific mysteries, including *Mysterious Universe, The Unfathomed Mind,* and *Hand-
book of Unusual Natural Phenomena.*

Kenneth J. Kinkor is a historical research consultant and author who has worked on the salvage of
the pirate shipwreck *Whydah.* He has also done research for other treasure-hunting ventures, as well
as genealogical research. He lectures frequently on
the topic of pirates and is president of Haysifter's
Research and Development Company in Chatham,
Massachusetts.

Daniel Arthur Koski-Karell is Executive Director of
the National Institute of Archaeology in Washington,
D.C. and CEO of Karell Archeological Services, a
consulting firm. His professional experience
includes the archaeology of both historic and pre-
historic periods.

John Reed is an author, researcher, and consultant
on treasures and treasure hunting worldwide. He
travels widely and maintains a large collection of
books, files, and research materials on this subject.

Marcello Truzzi, a professor of sociology at Eastern
Michigan University, is director of the Center for
Scientific Anomalies Research (CSAR) and editor of
its journal, *Zetetic Scholar.*

Other Publications:

AMERICAN COUNTRY
VOYAGE THROUGH THE UNIVERSE
THE THIRD REICH
THE TIME-LIFE GARDENER'S GUIDE
MYSTERIES OF THE UNKNOWN
TIME FRAME
FIX IT YOURSELF
FITNESS, HEALTH & NUTRITION
SUCCESSFUL PARENTING
HEALTHY HOME COOKING
UNDERSTANDING COMPUTERS
LIBRARY OF NATIONS
THE ENCHANTED WORLD
THE KODAK LIBRARY OF CREATIVE PHOTOGRAPHY
GREAT MEALS IN MINUTES
THE CIVIL WAR
PLANET EARTH
COLLECTOR'S LIBRARY OF THE CIVIL WAR
THE EPIC OF FLIGHT
THE GOOD COOK
WORLD WAR II
HOME REPAIR AND IMPROVEMENT
THE OLD WEST

*For information on and a full description of any of
the Time-Life Books series listed above, please call
1-800-621-7026 or write:*
Reader Information
Time-Life Customer Service
P.O. Box C-32068
Richmond, Virginia 23261-2068

This volume is one in a series that explores
astounding but surprisingly true events in history,
science, nature, and human conduct. Other books in
the series include:

Feats and Wisdom of the Ancients
Mysteries of the Human Body
Forces of Nature
Vanishings
Amazing Animals
Inventive Genius

Time Life Inc. offers a wide range of fine recordings,
including a *Rock 'n' Roll Era* series. For subscrip-
tion information, call 1-800-621-7026 or write
Time-Life Music, P.O. Box C-32068, Richmond, Virginia 23261-2068.